The Global Struggle for More

Books by Bernard D. Nossiter

The Mythmakers: An Essay on Power and Wealth
Soft State: A Newspaperman's Chronicle of India
Britain—A Future That Works

The Global Struggle for More

Third World Conflicts with Rich Nations

Bernard D. Nossiter

A Twentieth Century Fund Essay

1817
Harper & Row, Publishers, New York
Cambridge, Philadelphia, San Francisco, Washington
London, Mexico City, São Paulo, Singapore, Sydney

 For information address Harper & Row, Publishers, Inc., 10 East 53rd Street, New York, N.Y. 10022. Published simultaneously in Canada by Fitzhenry & Whiteside Limited, Toronto.

FIRST EDITION

Copy editor: Ann Finlayson
Designer: Erich Hobbing
Indexer: Auralie Logan

Library of Congress Cataloging-in-Publication Data

Nossiter, Bernard D. The global struggle for more.
(Icon editions)
"A Twentieth Century Fund essay."
Bibliography: p.
Includes index.
1. Developing countries—Economic policy.
2. Developing countries—Economic conditions.
3. Debts, External—Developing countries. 4. Developing
countries—Foreign economic relations. I. Title.
HC59.7.N676 1987 337'.09172'4 86-45762
ISBN 0-06-435851-8 87 88 89 90 91 HC 10 9 8 7 6 5 4 3 2 1
ISBN 0-06-430168-0 (pbk.) 87 88 89 90 91 HC 10 9 8 7 6 5 4 3 2 1

The Twentieth Century Fund is an independent research foundation which undertakes policy studies of economic, political, and social institutions and issues. The Fund was founded in 1919 and endowed by Edward A. Filene.

For Jason

Contents

Foreword

The so-called third world of developing countries has traveled a rocky road in the postwar era. Involved in a seemingly endless marathon, they have managed to somewhat narrow the gap when going downhill between themselves and the front runners, only to fall behind at the next upward slope. Actually, for all the talk of the third world or the South (vs. the North), the developing countries are not as monolithic as the advanced industrial countries picture them or as they sometimes picture themselves. Some developing countries, especially those in Asia, have actually succeeded in closing a good part of the gap. Others, such as the oil-producing countries, struck it rich following the first big rise in the price of oil in 1973, and then suffered sharp checks to their growth with the slowdown in consumption and the subsequent fall in the price of oil and other commodities and in the value of the dollar. And many developing countries, including some that have benefited from the fall in the price of oil, have been caught in the vise of the debt crisis, which has proved so burdensome over the past few years.

It would be nice if the developing countries turned out to be like the tortoise of Aesop's fable. In reality, though, it takes sustained growth by the advanced countries to improve the lot of the developing countries, which, because they start from a much lower base, can grow much faster. That is something made clear by more than one study sponsored by the Twentieth Century Fund over the past thirty years. We at the Fund have had a continuing interest in the process of economic development. Some of our studies have been critical of various fads and fashions in development; others have called for more help from the advanced countries, or different forms of help from that which has been given in the past. And many of our studies have also examined the political aspect of development, especially the demands of the developing countries for a new economic order.

Despite all the work that the Fund has sponsored, we were pleased that Bernard D. Nossiter, a veteran journalist, agreed to take a fresh and forward look at the North-South conflict. As a former United Nations bureau chief for the *New York Times,* he writes with the special insight of an economist who has observed at firsthand the political maneuvering of the developed and developing countries. His account, which provides the informed layman with a balanced assessment of the critical problems in this critical area, contains some useful recommendations for alleviating, if not always resolving, them.

I want to express the appreciation of the Fund for Nossiter's Fund Essay. It is, I think, a useful guide and a trenchant one. We can be sure that the marathon will be going on well into the next century, but he offers hope that it will not always be as uneven and as tortuous a contest as it has been over the past two decades.

M. J. Rossant, Director
The Twentieth Century Fund
October 1986

Preface

If carefully examined, official documents dealing with North-South conflicts and the government behavior they rationalize reflect some peculiar ideas. Washington tends to consider third world nations almost exclusively as instruments in the Cold War. With the rest of the industrial West, the United States views the Latin Americans, Asians, and Africans suspiciously as heretics from free market orthodoxy, threats to the banking system, convenient for exports but invaders of domestic markets. Many third world nations, in turn, regard the wealthier industrial countries as a rich but selfish uncle, meanly refusing to distribute goods and services due in return for past and present misdeeds, blindly adhering to an obsolete capitalism that borders on exploitation, hypocritically professing an open trade that is denied in practice. Neither view is particularly useful or realistic except for home consumption and the tedious requirements of formal debate in international forums.

The argument here is that something more serviceable can be found to answer some of the large questions dividing North from South. To be useful, these prescriptions obviously must rest on something approaching political and economic reality. Just as clearly, they must serve the vital interests of both camps or suffer the rejection that has marked so much of each side's agenda. The running dispute need not be staged in an arena for zero-sum games although it is usually treated that way. This is convenient for rulers who privately prefer things as they are.

Nomenclature in this field is notoriously imprecise but convention has firmly established usage. The South is also known as the third world, the poor countries, the underdeveloped, the less developed or developing nations. The rubric embraces 120 flags flown in Asia, Africa, and Latin America. Some, like India, are well north of the equator, but India is nevertheless a leader of the South. Several like Brazil, Mexico, South Korea, and Hong Kong are substantial manufacturers unlike most of their brethren whose economic life depends on raising food and fiber or extracting a few minerals. A handful of Persian Gulf oil producers—Saudi Arabia, Kuwait, and the United Arab Emirates—are anything but poor and enjoy incomes per head larger than the $13,160 reported for the United States in 1982, or did so until oil prices collapsed. Some are not developing in any sense; they become poorer year by year even though they may be well-endowed with natural resources. Zaire is one. But all, developing or regressing, present at least in public a common set of demands on the North. These are the rich nations of North America, Western Europe, Japan, Australia, and New Zealand. They are also known as the industrial nations or market economies. This too is a misnomer since most now produce a decreasing share of manufactured goods and a growing proportion of services. Their mixed economies, moreover, include a large measure of state-controlled output, from medical services to weapons, that lies outside the play of markets.

Finally, the Soviet Union and its Eastern European allies might be but are not known as the second world. At the United Nations, this group is politely if inaccurately called socialist. Here it will be described simply as the Soviet bloc.

There is a vast literature devoted to the great questions—third world debt, gyrating prices of raw materials, trade and above all aid, that peculiar distribution of grants from one government to another. A certain professional deformation, however, marks much of this work. The economists tend to ignore the political setting. The political commentators scant the economic problems. More often than not, both implicitly assume an identity of interests among rulers and ruled in Africa, Asia, and Latin America; this way error lies.

I have been looking at North-South conflict since 1964 when *The Washington Post* sent me to cover the first UNCTAD (United Nations Conference on Trade and Development) meeting at Geneva. There, the third world and the industrial nations began what has largely become an endless dialogue of the deaf. As the *Post*'s South Asia correspondent in Delhi, I watched the equally futile UNCTAD II. At the United Nations for *The New York Times,* I reported the rude end of third world dreams for a single package that would neatly tie up all the issues. The lesson was clear: these matters—aid, trade and the rest—must be treated separately or not at all. A global approach only made it easier for both sides to do nothing.

When the Twentieth Century Fund invited me to look at these issues systematically, I had a rare chance to pull together what I had seen and the leisure to further explore what others had written. The Fund financed a substantial share of the research and writing of this book. I am grateful to Beverly Goldberg and Gary Nickerson of the Fund for some useful suggestions.

Several score economists, bankers, and officials in New York, Washington, Geneva, London, Bonn, and Frankfurt generously gave me their time and tried to lead me down the path of right thinking. If they didn't always succeed, they may have saved me from gross mistake. Above all, I owe a large debt to Azizali Mohammed and the external relations department of the International Monetary Fund and Peter Vogel, his opposite number at the World Bank, for putting me in touch with helpful officials and patiently replying to repeated queries.

William Gilmartin, Robert Lekachman, Harvey Segal, and John Temple Swing read portions of the manuscript. Inevitably, it expresses my views and not theirs and they must be held blameless. Gerald Mildner prepared the endnotes and checked the text. The network of United Nations libraries, particularly the special units devoted to international law, the Law of the Sea, statistics, and UN documents provided invaluable aid. Librarians in the special units took great pains to search out recondite materials. Nothing, however, can match the hospitality and collection of the New York Public Library. Its Allen Room is a writer's dream, permitting a leisurely examination of books, a typewriter for notes and, not least of its amenities, freedom to puff on a pipe.

My wife, Jackie, typed several versions of the manuscript, the fate of a writer's mate. My debt to her is much larger than that. Her encouragement at times when the work seemed all burden and little joy helped me to persevere.

New York
June 1986

The Global Struggle for More

Chapter 1

The Great Debt Trauma

On a Friday, Jesus Silva Herzog, Mexico's Finance Minister, examined the nation's treasury and found only $100 million in foreign exchange. On Monday, Mexico was due to pay $280 million on its vast foreign debt, and more was owed in the days, months, and years to follow. Mexico was in default, and the repercussions threatened the financial system of the entire Western world. Silva Herzog placed hurried calls to Donald T. Regan, the stockbroker turned secretary of the U.S. Treasury, Paul Volcker, chairman of the Federal Reserve, and Jacques de Larosière, managing director of the International Monetary Fund, the three guardians of Western finance. Regan, with the help of Volcker, quickly arranged a bridging or temporary loan of $1.5 billion from the Bank for International Settlements, the discreet institution in Basel that serves the central banks of the rich. Washington also agreed to buy $1 billion of Mexico's oil for burial in the United States strategic reserve. A Band-Aid had been put in place. Time had been gained for financiers to find a sturdier crutch, a crutch not only for Mexico but other imperiled debtors, and for the banks that had by then poured more than $400 billion into the developing world.[1]

Silva Herzog's distress calls on August 12, 1982, launched a crisis that inflamed every sensitive issue dividing the developing nations of the South from the wealthier nations of the North.

The debt drama turned on wild swings in commodity prices, the source of much of the foreign earnings of the South, the shrinking of Northern markets and the closing of outlets for the new Southern manufacturers, and on a flow of funds from the North uncertain in volume and often governed by international institutions in which the South has only a minority voice. The crisis even offered a test of the South's frequently proclaimed unity: Would Mexico and other debtors unite to force concessions from a financially vulnerable North or would each debtor seek salvation on its own? This web of interlocked issues, extending far beyond the immediate concern with debt, will be explored at length, to distinguish the real from the imaginary, the plausible from the fanciful.

The clash of South and North, conducted at long diplomatic gatherings rather than on any battlefield, is a by-product of World War II. With the peace, the South began pressing a wide range of demands or, more accurately, pleas for a reordering of the world economy. How the South has organized or failed to organize for this struggle is a major theme of this book. So too is the South's view of its plight, its belief that poverty is no fault of its own but inherent in a global system it cannot shape. Is the third world entitled to deny responsibility for its condition? Can it legitimately reject the link between development failures and domestic impediments: traditional cultures that fix class and caste; pervasive bureaucracies that frustrate farmers and entrepreneurs; systems of land ownership, pricing, and taxation that discourage output; wide disparities in income that diminish savings or drive them abroad? At least in public, the South will hear none of this. It holds that its material well-being is thwarted by a skewed global economic order.

The South sees itself depending largely on exports of raw materials whose prices in world markets are foredoomed to buy fewer and fewer of the manufactured goods the South needs to grow. New arrangements must be put in place to protect and raise commodity prices; the North should collaborate in these agreements. Moreover, there are heavy barriers protecting Northern markets, not only against competing raw materials but also against the manufactured goods that some third world nations now produce. These barriers must come down if the South is to realize its potential. Even more, Northern markets should offer privileged entry for Southern products, an advantage against developed competitors. All this the South seeks.

Above all, the South wants Northern capital, bank loans on

easier terms, more loans at subsidized rates, and outright grants or gifts of money like the great sums that rebuilt war-torn Europe. Ever-growing volumes of aid will compensate for past damage the system has done to the South and make up for its lack of savings.

There is still more in the third world catalogue: cries for easier and cheaper access to the North's technical know-how; an equal Southern voice in the international institutions making development and other loans; power to insure that Northern investment in Southern plants will serve third world goals.

The North has treated much but not all of this with the skepticism of bankers asked to forgive Southern debt. Some concessions have been made, however, just as Northern creditors have eased the terms of their loans when they concluded this was in their interest.

The strengths and weaknesses of third world demands, particularly the South's insistence that global peace and prosperity depend on their satisfaction, require close attention. Is the South really proposing, as it claims, a New International Economic Order or is it simply multiplying devices to extract resources from the North? Are agreements to fix raw materials prices practical and, if so, why are there so few? Can the South's goal of a more even flow of export earnings be realized in some other way? The barriers to Southern goods are incontestable fact, and it is clear that they are rising higher everywhere in the West. Whose interests are served and who is hurt by the swelling tide of protectionism? Is this a politically irreversible trend or are there measures that could allay Northern anxieties over Southern competition and shrink the obstacles to trade? Aid is a critical issue, but who gains from it? Should a distinction be made between third world leadership groups and the masses of poverty-ridden people? Does aid spur growth or impede it? Is aid designed for development or to support the political and strategic objectives of donors?

In the early 1980s, the sheer weight of the debt crisis and the need for emergency measures thrust these questions aside. The very nature of the drama forced Northern banks and financial authorities to collaborate with Southern debtors in a manner markedly unlike the quarrels over the traditional third world agenda. But any lasting solution to the debt problem, the avoidance of widespread default, will depend in great measure on answering some of the questions raised by the South, on what prospects are offered for expanded third world foreign earnings through growth in the industrial North. This study will conclude with an examination of the tie between well-being in the third world and Northern expansion, and the conditions necessary to achieve the sustained prosperity of the earlier postwar years.

The North's shaky loans climaxed a dozen years of stress in an industrial world that once seemed to have all but banished the business cycle. For almost twenty-five years after the War, the West enjoyed nearly uninterrupted increases in material output and incomes, high levels of employment, and modest inflation containing only hints of future trouble. This comfortable state of affairs was first jolted in 1971 with the breakup of the global monetary system, an arrangement in which Western currencies were exchanged at more or less fixed rates. The system was frequently punctuated by abrupt devaluations of the British pound or the French franc, but all this was regarded, in the convention of the day, as conforming to the rule of fixed exchange rates. But in the new post-1971 order, currency rates changed daily, determined by supply, demand, and occasional nudges from finance ministries and central banks. This novelty, intended to be temporary, was still in vogue in 1986, although it has come under increasing criticism in the West. Nevertheless, flexible exchange rates probably saved the West from horrendous monetary upheavals that dizzying oil price increases would otherwise have caused.

The price of oil, not currency rates, is central to explain the decline of the prosperous era and the great rise in third world debt.* The first oil shock, a series of quakes in the last three

*Edward F. Denison, in his bold attempts to measure the elements of American growth and stagnation, disagrees. According to Denison, oil accounted for less than 1 percent of the drop in potential national income in the 1973–79 period and only about 2.6 percent in the next three years. (Edward F. Denison, *Trends in American Economic Growth, 1929–1982*, Washington, D.C.: Brookings Institute, 1985, pp. xvi and xvii. On his method, see p. 54.)

The key word here is "potential," the income if high employment had pre-

months of 1973, lifted a barrel of crude from $3 to $11.65. This jump of nearly 300 percent acted like a mammoth sales tax, simultaneously inflating prices and depressing demand and income for consumers. Oil is a ubiquitous cost in the modern world, so the increase pushed up prices everywhere. Householders paid more for heating, motorists for gas; industries fueled by oil charged more for their products. The shock reached the impoverished villages of the third world, where transistor radios, bicycles, and fertilizer all rose in price. At the same time the oil tax reduced incomes everywhere, forcing consumers to spend more of their pay for costlier oil and the products it hit, leaving less for other goods and services. According to one estimate, the higher prices cost the third world—excluding oil producers, of course—$16.1 billion in 1974. By 1979, the bill had reached $39 billion, or nearly $9 billion more than all the foreign aid the poor received.[2]

In the West, most governments, regardless of party label or proclaimed theology, turned smartly right and then left. They first decided to combat inflation, but a deep recession and its damaging effect on jobs and output produced a drastic change in policy. Governments now stimulated their economies to strengthen demand and incomes. Their policies worked. In the industrialized nations, output tumbled 4 percent in the first half of 1975, as central banks tightened the supply of credit and governments held down spending. The reverse course—easier money, tax cuts, and enlarged government outlays—produced a brisk 5.5 percent rise in total output from mid-1975 to mid-1976.

The United States followed the path of its partners: initial restraint, then stimulus. Jobs and output enjoyed a higher priority than prices. Most of the early restraint came from the Federal Reserve. "The unwillingness of the monetary authorities to underwrite a continued acceleration of inflation drove interest rates

vailed instead of growing joblessness. Thanks to oil and the policies it triggered, actual income slumped sharply, 6.5 percent below Denison's potential in 1974–79 and a devastating 9.8 percent in the next four years. Moreover, Denison's method, relying on oil's cost in the economy and its reduced use, minimizes oil's consequence even for the potential economy. Denison can't capture the reduced productivity of labor flowing from prolonged unemployment and premature retirement, both consequences of the government's response to the oil shock. Nor does he report the reduced efficiency of capital caused by the forced conversion of plants to avoid the use of oil.

upward," the President's Economic Report noted dryly in 1975. But "the most pressing concern of policy is to halt the decline in production and employment."[3] So taxes were cut, the Federal Reserve relaxed its grip on the money supply and the United States rapidly emerged from its sharpest postwar slump in early 1975.

But inflation, the other half of this Hobson's choice, was rising at painful rates. In the United States, the consumer price index rose 47 percent from 1973 through 1978; in the West generally, the figure was 60.7 percent.[4] The lesson was clear. The West could, if it chose, cope with oil's destruction of jobs and production, but how to deal with oil's price inflation was still unsolved.

The distortion of oil led to an unexpected gusher for the West's commercial banks, particularly those in the United States. Newly rich oil nations, notably those with small populations like Saudi Arabia, Kuwait, and the United Arab Emirates, were suddenly flush with billions of dollars they could not spend at home. Limited if highly publicized amounts were invested in Western real estate and Western industry. Most of the Arab money, however, sought havens to insure some return, safety, and liquidity or assurance that cash could be pulled out on short notice. The Arabs turned to the Western banks, and the banks accepted their deposits eagerly.

As nature abhors a vacuum, bankers detest an idle deposit. Banks pay interest on deposits, a cost and a liability in their bookkeeping; a loan brings in interest, income, and this is an asset. Flooded with new funds, the banks looked for new places to lend and discovered the third world, particularly third world governments. At the time of the oil shock in 1973, third world debt to Western banks was $45 billion. Over the next six years, these loans grew briskly, 21.5 percent a year, to reach $190 billion.[5]

For the banks, the business was splendid. The loans, everyone agreed, were perfectly safe. "A country does not go bankrupt," said Walter Wriston, chairman of Citicorp, the leader of the nine United States banks that took the lion's share.[6] He meant that a sovereign state, unlike a troubled corporation, could not go under when its liabilities exceeded its assets. This was true but irrelevant. Many Latin American nations and some American states not only could but did postpone or default on payments to British bondholders in the nineteenth century, and Latin American loans had to be written off again in the Great Depression.[7] No special magic now existed to preserve a sovereign from owing more than it could earn.

The business, however, was enormously profitable for the banks. In the depths of the debt crisis, Citicorp earned 19.5 percent of its profits, $168 million, from Brazil alone. Chase's earnings in Brazil were not far behind, more than $70 million or about one sixth of total profits. To reach these handsome levels, the banks fixed an elaborate schedule of interest rates and fees: third world borrowers were charged either several percentage points more than the United States prime rate or Libor, the London Interbank Offer Rate, whichever was higher. (Libor is the interest that banks in London pay to attract deposits from other banks for six months.) The loans, moreover, were tailored to protect the banks against inflation. Every six months, the rate was reset to reflect the change in the prime or Libor level. It was a floating rate, and it usually floated upward. The foreign business was so good that "Lenders hunted borrowers," a study reported for the Organization of Economic Cooperation and Development or OECD, the economic voice of rich governments. By 1981, Chase was earning an estimated 27 percent of its profits from Argentina, Brazil, and Mexico alone.[8]

In fact, a relatively small part of the third world engaged in these transactions. Banks always prefer lending to those least in need and most likely to repay. The foreign loans fueled by oil dollars were no exception. An overwhelming share went to the wealthiest third world nations. By December 1983, eight third world borrowers alone accounted for $300 billion, or 46 percent of the debt governments owed the commercial banks. The richest five debtor nations owed $210 billion: Brazil, $72 billion; Mexico $72 billion; South Korea $27 billion; Argentina $26 billion, and Venezuela $13 billion.[9] Some of the biggest debtors were themselves oil exporters: Venezuela, Mexico, Indonesia, and Algeria. But they are heavily populated and eager for still more funds to invest or consume. Their oil income fell short of their desires, and so they turned to the banks.

Other third world nations would have welcomed a chance to share in this cornucopia, but in the language of banking, they were not "creditworthy." Countries like Bangladesh, Mali, Chad, and many more were simply too poor to be regarded as good customers. For foreign exchange, for dollars and other hard currencies, apart from what they earned in trade, these nations had to rely on the aid programs of Western governments or loans from the International Bank for Reconstruction and Development, or World Bank, and the International Monetary Fund.

Strictly speaking, the global debt problem embraces all the loans, private and official, that the nations of the South have accumulated. By the end of 1984, this had reached $920 billion. The crisis, however, centers on the debt owed to the commercial banks: $630 billion, or 68 percent of the total.[10] This is largely because lending governments in the West offer easier terms than the banks, and governments will not collapse if repayments are postponed indefinitely or even forgiven. Much of the official lending is foreign aid, offered for a mix of political, strategic, and economic reasons. Government leaders, unlike banks, do not suffer profit losses when interest payments are postponed, and do not suffer a drop in the price of shares. They don't charge fees for their services, and almost automatically reschedule or postpone overdue payments, as long as they think politico-strategic dividends are forthcoming. A Zaire, Liberia, or Togo that can't pay up sends its ministers off to Paris, meets its Western government creditors, promises to reform its budgetary manners, and wins a fresh delay. The process can be and is repeated frequently. If a third world nation is naïve enough to repudiate its debt to a Western government, this would not affect the ability of Washington or Paris to tax and spend. The IMF and the World Bank take a different view. They demand payment when their loans are due. But the major share of official debt is owed to governments.

Polonius to the contrary, there is nothing inherently unsound in borrowing or lending. A developing country should tap the capital of rich nations to advance from a poor, largely agricultural society into a wealthier, industrial economy. Without loans or foreign investments, a developing nation is limited to its own resources, its own savings; it must pay for imports of fertilizer (or the foreign-made machines for a fertilizer plant) exclusively from the coffee, rubber, tin, or other commodities it can sell abroad. The extra inflow of hard currency serves another vital function. It can add to the stock of local savings that pay for investment in roads, power, port improvements, and other vast projects that may yield faster growth. To escape from dependence on raw materials, to become an exporter of steel, textiles, electronic products, and more, a nation must accumulate more hard currency, more dollars or marks, than its exports will earn. Aid from governments, credits from foreign suppliers, loans from international institutions can all help, provided these are not misdirected by suppliers or misused by recipients. So can private investments, a French-built machine tool plant in the Ivory Coast, a British-backed food-processing factory in Kenya. And so too can loans, particularly those used for investments that yield a return in hard currencies to pay off the debt.

This last is one key to what went wrong. If bankers are specialists, their skill lies in assessing commercial risk, the prospect that an enterprise will use its loan for a specific purpose and earn enough to repay its debt. There is no reason to think that bankers are particularly skilled in assessing sovereign risks, the chances that a nation will earn enough from its exports of goods and services to pay back the foreign exchange it borrows. In the third world, Citicorp, Manufacturers Hanover, Morgan Guaranty, Continental Illinois, and the others largely ignored their customary way of doing business. Borrowers gave only cursory explanations of how their debt might finance profitable projects, one earning dollars to meet the bills coming due. In effect, the banks simply financed deficits in each client's balance of payments, the gap between its earnings and spending abroad. Banks assumed that flags pay debts, that the outpouring of currency would somehow yield enough to meet the interest and fees the lenders charged. The banks demonstrated they are no more capable of judging sovereign risk than selecting lottery winners.

Their recklessness, moreover, had been sanctioned by the most important international authorities. Only three months before the crisis became common knowledge, the World Bank's president, A. W. Clausen, hailed the banks for contributing to third world "dynamism," and claimed that the "dramatic" increase in loans had "helped to cushion" developing countries' "adjustment to the vicissitudes of the global economy." A recent president of the Bank of America, Clausen told his audience of bankers, with evident satisfaction, that it "knows what the commercial banks have done in the developing countries better than anyone. After all, you are the ones who did it."[11]

The borrowers, flush with funds, were equally imprudent. A useful rule of thumb holds that a borrowing nation should limit its debt so that the payments due in any one year are one fifth of its earnings from the export of goods and services. This is the debt-service ratio. Thailand, for example, has enacted this 20 percent rule into law, limiting the foreign debt it can amass. The ratio is modern Micawberism. It tells a country that there is a day of reckoning, that earnings from trade should cover its debt repayment costs five times.

In 1973, Mexico's debt service ratio was 25 percent, Argentina's 21 percent, and Brazil's 36 percent. Argentina and Mexico, at least, were not far from the golden rule. Brazil was within reach of it. But by 1982, the rule had been junked. Mexico's ratio had climbed to 58 percent, Brazil's to 87 percent, and Argentina's to 103 percent.[12] In other words, everything Argentina earned abroad would be eaten up by debt payments and still fall short of its bill. Mexico and Brazil were rapidly falling into the same pit. There was less and less to pay for imports to spur growth or support the lives of affluent, privileged Latins working abroad in Paris and New York.

The uncontrolled borrowing, moreover, inspired debtors to misuse funds recklessly. Projects were begun on a Pharaonic scale and often left unfinished. Venezuela alone started twenty-seven schemes, each costing $100 million or more, which ate up $27.4 billion or nearly 80 percent of all its output in 1979. A World Bank study counted 1,600 projects of $100 million or more begun in the 1970s. Of those involving $1 billion or more, nearly half were plagued by large, unforeseen increases in expense and delays. Argentina threw up bridges where no traffic ran, built nuclear reactors when the capacity to generate electricity exceeded demand. Like others, including Peru, Buenos Aires used easily borrowed dollars to buy jet fighters and other expensive arms on a lavish scale.[13]

The Latin Americans, the biggest debtors, took the easy money from New York, Frankfurt, Paris, London, and Tokyo to finance ever-enlarging domestic budget deficits. A study by the Brookings Institution estimated that in the 1970s the Latins borrowed about 25 percent more than they needed to pay for the total deficit in their balance of trade, the foreign account. This, the study said, "reflects the lack of supply constraints."[14]

To be sure, when the lending banks tried to channel their funds to specific projects or agencies, the sovereigns easily defeated them. Some $4.5 billion was lent to Argentina's state petroleum company, but little of it increased investment. The oil company was allowed to keep only $300 million; the other $4.2 billion was siphoned off for arms, subsidized cut-rate gasoline prices, the foreign exchange bills of Argentinian tourists, and the purchase of luxury apartments in the Uruguayan resort of Punta del Este.[15]

No one is ever likely to know how many billions in loans enriched officials or enabled businessmen to build up bank accounts and other investments in the rich North. The mayor of Mexico City, Hank Gonzalez, achieved some notoriety with his $1 million mock Tudor mansion in New Canaan, Connecticut, embellished with swimming pool, stables, and gold-plated bathroom faucets. One Argentine developer was erecting a $1 billion luxury apartment complex in Manhattan even as his country struggled with creditors to ease the nation's debt burden. Mexicans were estimated to have bought $25 billion in United States real estate and salted away another $20 billion in United States banks. But nobody could match President Mobutu Sese Seko of Zaire, whose personal Swiss bank accounts were said to contain $5 billion, a bit more than his nation's unpayable debt. The Brookings study concluded that the "massive capital flight from Mexico, Venezuela, and Argentina account[s] for the larger part of the crisis," a leakage put at $42.5 billion for the three years from 1980 through 1982 alone.[16] The crisis changed nothing. Most of the new loans to Latin America between 1982 and 1985 were dissipated in flight capital, Morgan Guaranty Trust Company regretfully disclosed.[17] The strange trip that sent bank dollars to well-placed Latins for return to New York undoubtedly played a significant part in weakening third world economies. But even those dollars that stayed behind were so misused, so often found their way into unproductive outlets, that it is hard to single out one cause.

This recital does not mean that all of the $285 billion borrowed from commercial banks by 1980 simply vanished in foreign bank accounts or lies buried in worthless monuments. Goods and services were produced, and the third world as a whole grew at a brisk yearly pace of 6 percent in the 1970s.* Roads were built that did link towns, land was irrigated, and power supplied from completed dams. Schools, hospitals, and housing were constructed. The bank money, wittingly or otherwise, helped pay for this. Nevertheless, it is hard to argue from the fragmentary and anecdotal evidence available that lenders and their sovereign borrowers were either prudent or vigilant. Many third world borrowers are run by one-party, one-man, or one-general governments. There could not be nor was there much public scrutiny of how they used their largess. For the banks, it was simply a profitable business with sovereign borrowers, who would somehow find a way to pay.

In public at least, the banks and their friends in the international institutions are understandably defensive about the crisis. The Bank for International Settlements in Basel, the semiprivate and almost impenetrable instrument of the central banks, has said that to describe third world loans as "misdirected and irresponsible" would be "too sweeping," although it conceded that the banks "have made some serious mistakes."[18] Paul Watson, an official at Continental Illinois, writing just before the second oil shock that was to help destroy his bank, declared that the deals were mostly sound; they had been made between "well-capital-

*Between 1973 and 1982, total domestic output for the ten biggest debtors expanded each year as follows: Mexico, 6.2 percent; Brazil, 5.2; Venezuela, 3.5; Argentina, 0.2; South Korea, 7.2; Philippines, 5.8; Chile, 3.0; Indonesia, 7.0; Yugoslavia, 5.2, and Egypt, 9.4. Chile and Argentina, both ruled by military juntas, had the slowest growth. *World Bank Atlas 1985*, pp. 6–9.

ized, sophisticated lenders and borrowers who have the organization and management to utilize the resources productively."[19] Watson was secretary of the bank's "country exposure committee," which determined risks abroad. Arthur Burns, former chairman of the Federal Reserve, praised the banks for their helpful role in recycling money from oil countries to developing nations.[20] Outside the fraternity, however, John R. Williamson of the Institute for International Economics described the third world lending as "frenzied." It had risen a remarkable 32.5 percent a year from 1972 to 1981.[21]

The second oil quake, starting in 1979, ended the lending spree, although few foresaw this at the time. The oil states had left the price of crude mostly untouched between 1974 and 1978. (It rose about 10 percent to $12.82 a barrel, but this was well under the rise in other prices, so the purchasing power or real price of oil actually fell about 10 percent.) But now the producers embarked on a second round of rapidly spiraling increases, lifting oil by early 1981 to $34.70 a barrel, a leap of more than 170 percent.[22]

This time, the Western response was sharply different from the cycle of brief restraint and prolonged stimulus that followed the first oil shock. Now the assault, led by the United States and the Federal Reserve, was directed with single-minded intensity against inflation. Since consumer prices in the West were rising by 15 percent a year in 1980, this concern was understandable. The lame duck administration of Jimmy Carter warned that a "draconian level of demand restraint" would be needed to bring inflation down to acceptable levels.[23] Nevertheless, Draco's economics prevailed at the Federal Reserve.

Governments tried to wipe out budget deficits by raising taxes, curbing expenditures, or both. Even the Reagan administration, dedicated to lower taxes in upper brackets and increased defense spending, ran a deflationary budget in 1981. In effect, governments tried and often succeeded in withdrawing more funds from their economies than they were putting in, shrinking total demand. But the major blow against oil-induced inflation was struck by the central banks. The Federal Reserve sharply curbed the growth of the money supply, making loans more expensive and harder to find. This forced businesses and individuals to cut their demand for everything from raw materials to automobiles, from housing to machinery. Less demand should mean a slower rate of price increases, and it did.

On the one front where the Fed fought, a notable victory was scored: The rate of U.S. inflation fell from 13.5 percent in 1980 to 6.1 percent in 1982. Elsewhere in the West, the results were equally gratifying. Inflation among the OECD nations dropped from 12.8 percent to 7.8 percent.[24]

Monetarism, the economic doctrine that holds that prices are largely determined by the supply of money, seemed vindicated. This time, there would be no easy, antideflationary escape from oil.

Apart from prices, however, the effects were brutal. Less money for would-be borrowers drove interest rates to levels not seen since the eighteenth century. Libor, the London price on which third world debt is largely based, almost doubled—from 9.2 percent to 16.6 percent. One sensitive indicator of Federal Reserve policy is the price banks pay to borrow reserves from each other, the Federal Funds rate. This more than doubled between 1978 and 1981 from 7.93 percent to 16.38 percent, falling back slowly in 1982. As late as 1983, however, it averaged 9.09 percent.[25]

The United States and other Western economies stagnated for three years, the longest slump since the Great Depression. "The present experience of high real interest rates persisting during a long period of low capacity utilization is unprecedented since 1929–1933," wrote the OECD.[26] This was no accident but policy. President Reagan's economic report for 1982 said, "The decision to end inflation over a period of several years will be sustained by the Administration, even though short-run costs will be suffered before long-term benefits begin to accrue."[27] Unemployment grew to levels unseen since the 1930s. For the OECD countries as a whole, one worker in fifteen was jobless in 1981, and the figure was heading higher.[28] For the United States, unemployment reached one in ten in 1982.[29]

At the end of 1982, the ordeal was brought to a halt. The Federal Reserve relented, and the Reagan administration began pumping funds into the economy with arms spending and a tax cut. The record deficits that helped the economy recover revived interest in the fiscal theories of John Maynard Keynes. They also raised troubling questions about the wisdom of what the OECD called "an uncharacteristically important role" that "monetary policy has been assigned."[30]

For the third world, and especially the big borrowers from commercial banks, the slump's impact was horrific. The floating rates on their loans soared upward. Mexico, Brazil, and the others were confronted with ever-rising bills for their old debt as well as for any new loans they could find. Each of the two big Latin borrowers, in debt to the commercial banks by $75 billion and $84 billion in 1982, had to find another $500 million every time rates rose 1 percent. (For all debtors by 1985, each one percentage point altered costs by $6 billion.)[31] At the same time, the Western slump shut down the third world's biggest markets. Falling Western output meant less demand for the copper, cocoa, coffee, steel, manufactured goods, and everything else sold by the developing countries. Prices as well as volume tumbled. Sugar prices fell 71 percent between 1980 and 1982.[32] Even oil cracked, crumbling 15 percent to $28 a barrel early in 1983 and below $27 the next year.

There was more. The clamor in the West to preserve shrinking jobs led to the closing of markets by fiat. The rich nations threw up new barriers or increased old ones against foreign steel, electronic goods, textiles, footwear, and other goods. Third world exporters faced a mandated as well as an economic shrinkage in markets. The new barriers, moreover, were far more impenetrable than traditional tariffs or import taxes. An enterprising producer can get under a tariff by cutting his price enough, but the new wave of protectionism typically limited the physical volume of imported goods, setting quotas that no amount of economic ingenuity could overcome. Increased foreign aid might have eased the pain, but the Reagan administration was cool to such an approach unless it served what were thought to be national strategic interests. An older brand of conservatism had urged the third world to rely on trade, not aid. In practice, the new regime was ambivalent about both.

As a final twist, the high interest rates in the United States attracted tens of billions of dollars from Western Europe, from the American banks who had invested there as well as Europeans. As they moved their funds from francs and marks to higher-yielding dollars, the value of the dollar rose against other currencies. This was an added blow to third world borrowers. Most of its debt is denominated in dollars, so interest and other payments must be made in dollars. A Mexican machinery maker's chief clients may be in France, but he buys his spare parts in the United States. Because it now takes more francs to buy a dollar, he must somehow increase his French sales—in the face of Europe's slump—to continue to earn the same amount of currency for his spare American parts.

If debt-ridden oil producers like Mexico and Venezuela endured unexpected pain from the discovery that oil prices move down as well as up, the drop provided some relief for most of the third world, who must import crude. Their joy, however, was dampened by the climbing dollar. Oil, like the loans of commercial banks, is sold for dollars. As the dollar rose, it shrank the dividend from the falling price of crude.

In all, the Western response to the second oil shock, the decision to deflate, cost third world nations, according to one estimate, more than $140 billion in goods and services: $41 billion in extra interest, $79 billion in lower commodity prices and $21 billion in reduced export volume. This loss came on top of increased oil charges of $260 billion between 1974 and 1982.[33] Loans from Western banks had helped pay the bills in the 1970s, but now the banks had had enough. The retreat of the banks and the steep fall in Southern incomes, moreover, deepened the slump in the North. Mexican, Brazilian, Venezuelan, and other customers for Northern goods vanished. As credit dried up and deflation gripped the South, exporters in the industrial world lost orders.

Silva Herzog's phone call did yield one useful by-product. The banks were compelled for the first time to disclose just how lavishly they had loaned to the third world. Citicorp, reflecting Chairman Wriston's breezy assurance, was the most "exposed." In 1983, its third world paper was $9.8 billion, or twice its capital, the sum invested by stockholders. For the Bank of America, the total was $6.8 billion or 148 percent of its capital; Chase Manhattan, $6.1 billion or 220 percent; Manufacturers Hanover, $6.8

billion or 245 percent; Morgan Guaranty, $4.1 billion or 150 percent; and Chemical Bank, $3.5 billion or 182 percent. These six, moreover, had each loaned Mexico and Brazil alone sums equal to or exceeding their stockholders' stake.[34] If these loans were defaulted, the banks would collapse, and the chain reaction would destroy the West's financial system. This, of course, did not and could not happen. The banks relied on the hint of a promise that, in the event of distress, they would be rescued by the Federal Reserve and other central banks. The commercial banks expected their central banks either to take sour loans to foreign governments off their hands or to inject enough new capital to keep them afloat.

This belief was not entirely fanciful. Only a half-century earlier, the collapse of one large Austrian bank, the Kreditanstalt, transmitted the United States slump to Europe, creating a worldwide depression that helped bring Hitler to power and led to the Second World War. It was clear that no leading Western bank would be allowed to go under again. At Basel in 1974, the central bankers issued a Delphic communiqué announcing their readiness to act as "lenders of last resort."[35] No details were offered; none were needed. All understood that a big enough bank could count on salvation.

(The point was proved by the Continental Bank of Illinois, the nation's eighth largest. Bad loans to Southwest oil speculators as well as third world debt had wrecked Continental, but it was prevented from failing by billions in daily loans from the Federal Reserve. The Reagan administration then created the country's first nationalized bank, at least briefly, handing Continental over to the Federal Deposit Insurance Corporation until new, private managers were found.)

From the banks' standpoint, the problem posed by Mexico and other troubled third world debtors was relatively simple: Insure that borrowers could get enough money to pay the interest they owed. The day of reckoning for outstanding principal must simply be postponed. Interest matters because this is income for a bank, the income that determines salaries, bonuses, profits, and share prices. As long as a debtor pays interest, his loan, no matter when the principal is due, is a "performing asset."

The simple solution, then, was to lend Mexico and the others enough to meet their interest payments. But this caused a dilemma. The banks must keep large third world borrowers alive, "performing," but the banks were and are distressed about lending more money to dubious debtors.

The International Monetary Fund, with strong support from the Federal Reserve, solved the problem. The IMF loaned Mexico and the others $19.8 billion in Special Drawing Rights, Fund currency, in 1982 and 1983 (equal to about $22 billion at the end of 1985). But in return, the Fund insisted that the commercial banks put in fresh billions of their own. Some smaller banks resisted, but the large ones saw where interest lay. The Southern debtors would not get their money for nothing. Quite the contrary. Not only would they pay handsomely in new interest charges and fees, they would also have to accept the tutelage of the IMF and agree on austere domestic programs that might make them creditworthy again. The Southern debtors disliked the size of their fresh interest burden and objected to the severity of the measures demanded by the Fund. But they feared the alternative, declaring an indefinite moratorium on any payment of debt. That would surely cost them new loans for at least a generation, cut off their foreign aid, and dry up the short-term credits desperately needed for imports.

The package arranged for Brazil was typical. The IMF loaned Brazil the equivalent of $5.25 billion for ten years; in return Brazil's commercial bank creditors put up $9.1 billion. For thirty months, Brazil would pay the banks only interest and fees; then it would have eight years to pay off the new loan.[36] To be sure, almost all this "new" money would be swallowed up by interest charges on old loans. The banks and the IMF, then, were lending chiefly to maintain Brazil's standing as a dutiful borrower, writing checks to receive checks for past debt. On its part, Brazil was compelled to squeeze its economy so hard that a central bank governor resigned, and the Brazilian Congress refused to accept the Fund's anti-inflation curb on wages. But a new central bank head was found, a compromise was reached on pay, and Brazil took its medicine.

At the end of 1982 and throughout 1983, Mexico and twenty-nine other nations went through this ritual, receiving IMF and bank money for interest and pushing off the repayment of principal for a few years. By 1984, however, it was clear that the new schedules for amortizing principal were unreal. Mexico then broke new ground, winning from its creditors a postponement until the end of the century. Brazil sought the same treatment, but agreement with the banks was slow because Rio resisted another dose of the IMF's austerity cure. As long as the interest payments and fees kept rolling in, the banks were satisfied. Bankers want income, and a paid-up loan yields none. So Band-Aids became crutches, and crutches stiffened into braces.

The striking feature of all this was the pivotal role of the IMF. As a broker-lender, the Fund was playing a role that cannot be found in its charter. The Fund, with the World Bank, is one of the two great financial institutions created after the War. It was designed as the guardian of the international currency exchange system, serving as a barrier against another 1930s when nations sank into autarchy, each seeking self-sufficiency at its neighbor's expense. At its simplest, the Fund is a pool of currencies, contributed by its 148 members, lending to nations suffering a shortage of foreign exchange. In practice, the Fund has assumed far weightier responsibilities. It makes its loans under conditions supposed to preserve the global monetary system and promote open and unimpeded trade. To achieve these ends, Fund officials subject borrowers to prolonged scrutiny. They insist that borrowers adopt domestic policies that are supposed to reverse the foreign exchange losses that led them to the Fund. In the best of all possible worlds, the Fund will steer borrowers on a course to stimulate exports, shrink imports, and check inflation, thereby putting the borrower's balance of payments aright.

These policies enjoy the bloodless name of "conditionality," and they are a source of deep anger in the South whose nations are the Fund's principal clients. Third world countries complain that Fund "remedies" impose a harsh austerity on fragile societies, interfere with a nation's internal affairs, and are insensitive to the political facts of third world life. But the West and its executive directors, typically from conservative finance ministries, control the Fund's board, and generally support stringent conditionality. After all, third world borrowers should not simply receive money without doing what is needful to cure the problems that gave rise to their loan requests.

Industrial nations direct the Fund through weighted votes. Each member contributes to the currency pool a sum more or less reflecting its economic strength, and the amount of this contribution determines the size of its vote. In 1985, the IMF's pool was worth 89.3 billion of Special Drawing Rights or SDRs.* The U.S. share was 17.9 billion, or 19.29 percent of the vote. For France, it was 4.5 billion, or 4.85 percent of the vote; West Germany, 5.4 billion, or 6.05 percent; Japan, 4.2 billion, or 4.57 percent; and Britain, 6.2 billion, or 6.69 percent.[37] Since no loan can be approved if 51 percent oppose it, the United States and eight industrial nations enjoy a collective veto. This concentration of power in Western hands is another source of third world distress.

The debtors may not have been grateful for the Fund's austerity prescriptions, but they welcomed the renewed stream of dollars from the banks. Unforced credit from the once-eager banks dried up rapidly when the alarm bells clanged. Bank loans had risen by $71 billion in 1981 but slumped to $36 billion in 1982 and fell to only $20 billion in 1983.[38] Pressure from the Fund and the Federal Reserve—as well as the large banks' profit statements—kept the flow from evaporating entirely.

In public, bankers and financial authorities issued reassuring statements. The problem of the unpayable principal went largely unmentioned. There were, however, some exceptions. Brazilian Finance Minister Ernane Galveas said: "People keep asking, 'When is Brazil going to pay off its debt?' We're not going to pay off our debt. The bankers know it . . . and the governments know it. We're going to pay our interest to the extent of our possibilities, and when we cannot, the bankers will lend us the money and then we will."

A Citicorp vice-president, Jack Guenther, was equally blunt.

*A Special Drawing Right is a composite unit of the leading currencies, worth about $1.10 at the end of 1985. SDRs are created from time to time by the IMF's industrial nations to overcome shortages of global liquidity, the lack of international payments. Thus, an SDR is an international reserve asset, fiat money for central banks to promote trade. New issues are shared among IMF members according to their quota or contribution to the Fund.

"Let's be clear," he said. "Nobody's debts are going to be repaid." One authority, Robert A. Roosa, former Treasury undersecretary for international monetary affairs, described the web of loans for interest and remote rescheduling of principal as "accounting legerdemain."[39]

The sleight of hand reached a new level of dexterity over Argentina's payments in 1984. Buenos Aires strenuously resisted the deflation demanded by the IMF, with President Raul Alfonsin contending that a recession would undermine his newly installed democracy. So Argentina held up the $500 million of interest it owed the banks at the end of the first quarter of 1984. This was a default, although nobody dared call it by its name. In the end, the banks collected $100 million of their own money; $300 million more came from four large debtors (Brazil, Mexico, Venezuela, and Colombia), with Secretary Regan pledging that the United States would reimburse them after Argentina struck a deal with the IMF; and Argentina scraped up another $100 million from its own reserves. In other words, the United States government and the banks provided a transfusion to preserve the notional earnings of banks. Three months later, when the farce threatened to repeat itself, the banks ended the artifice. They began slicing the overdue interest from their profits—a truth-in-accounting measure that cost Manufacturers Hanover alone $21 million.[40]

Bankers, however, count their blessings in the short run and the head of the Deutsche Bank, West Germany's biggest, spoke for the majority in the industrial world. Wilfred Guth hailed the "unprecedented cooperative effort of the debtor countries, the International Monetary Fund, governments and central banks of creditor countries and commercial banks."[41]

There had been no Kreditanstalt, nor had any third world debtor formally repudiated its obligations. The banks, moreover, were earning handsome profits from the new charges for the restructured debts.

The advantages for the borrowers were less clear. In theory, they had preserved their creditworthiness and so saved their foreign assets—airliners, plants, and bank deposits—from seizure. In fact, lending countries own far more assets in the borrowing nations than the reverse. Any seizure by creditors would have led to the takeover of their Latin oil, machinery, mining, and other interests. Most importantly, and despite credit worthiness, the debtors won only a trickle of loans, apart from those induced by the IMF. Moreover, they had paid an enormous price.

The West's slump and the IMF's austerity drastically cut imports, slashed government spending and credit, sharply reduced incomes, and made tens of millions jobless. How many millions is unknown, partly because such statistics are often guesswork in the third world, but mainly because of the great surge in the underemployed. This is the army that enlists the dismissed factory worker, who is forced back to his family village, or the once-employed man sitting on a street corner, selling shoelaces, pencils, and souvenirs.

One group of economists estimated that unemployment rose above 30 percent in some third world countries, the buying power of wages was cut by a third, and half the population suffered a drop in income.[42] The damage varied widely. Asia was largely spared. Nations like India and Pakistan had been too poor to entice large commercial bank loans, and others like Thailand and South Korea ran economies sober enough to continue receiving funds. The heavily indebted African countries simply stagnated, or so the statistics recorded. Latin America, however, had been the biggest and most incautious borrower, and here income per person plunged 12.5 percent between 1980 and 1983, slicing one eighth from living standards, reducing them to levels reached seven years earlier. There was little prospect that they would recover for the rest of the decade. Total output in the major Latin nations—Mexico, Brazil, Argentina, Chile, Colombia, Peru, and Venezuela—tumbled nearly 4 percent in 1983 alone. This meant a fall in income per person of about 6 percent in a single year.[43] There was still another income drop for fourteen of the twenty Latin nations in 1985.[44] The Brookings study concluded, "it is easy to imagine resentment and frustration exploding and turning against governments when they fail to persuade the United States and other industrial countries of the need for more generous terms."[45]

It was precisely to avert such an explosion and a return of the military dictatorship that made President Alfonsin of Argentina so difficult a customer. He repeatedly delayed any agreement with the IMF, insisting he must raise the real wages of his workers despite roaring inflation. He would not, he said, impose recession as the price of the Fund's seal of approval. After prolonged bargaining, however, Alfonsin and the Fund struck a deal that encouraged the banks to lend more money—for Argentina's interest payments.

Elsewhere, there were more dramatic outbursts against the Fund's austerity demands. Peru suffered a general strike in 1984 over the IMF's insistence on increases in the price of subsidized rice, curbs on pay for the military, doctors, and teachers, a cutback in public works and heavier taxes. In the tiny Dominican Republic, the Fund's program led to three days of rioting that left sixty dead and hundreds injured. The outburst was touched off by higher prices for imported wheat, gasoline, medicine, and more—the consequence of a Fund-ordered devaluation that brought the peso closer to its market rate. In the Sudan, the Fund's demands for increases in the price of bread, gasoline, soap, and oil contributed to riots that brought down President Gaafar al-Nimeiry.[46] Nimeiry had been a close and heavily aided friend of the Reagan administration; he was toppled after a week's visit to Washington.

The borrowers, of course, had been guilty of contributory negligence, piling up debt at a reckless rate, pursuing domestic policies that drove inflation in 1982 to 59 percent in Mexico, 98 percent in Brazil, and 165 percent in Argentina (over 1000 percent by 1985),[47] fostering inefficient industries and encouraging lavish consumption, largely by the privileged, at home and abroad. But the striking differences between the penalties for the borrowers and the rewards for the lenders raised some disturbing questions.

Nevertheless, the great financial institutions pronounced their work was good. The commercial banks, said the BIS, had "kept their nerve" and did not push any borrower into default.[48] But why would they? A default would have wiped out the flow of interest and the banks' capital, threatening failure. The BIS was concerned about the arm-twisting employed by the IMF to compel new loans, "unthinkable" under normal circumstances. But this was a special case and, the BIS might have added, in the banks' own interest.

The IMF acknowledged that it had broken new ground but pointed to the happy result. Just a year after the Mexican cry for help, "there does not exist a global debt crisis," and "the current liquidity problems can be solved."[49] Not everyone, however, was so sanguine. One skeptical banker said, "Somehow the conventional wisdom of 200 million sullen South Americans sweating away in the hot sun for the next decade to earn the interest on their debt so Citicorp can raise its dividend twice a year does not square with my image of political reality."[50]

The debtor nations pleaded for easier terms, and the commercial banks, evidently fearful of pushing them too far, made some concessions to those who had more or less faithfully followed the IMF's austere path. In one round, Mexico and Brazil were rewarded with fractional reductions in fees and interest charges. This small step was advertised as a reward for good behavior; both countries had sharply reduced their import bills. In a second round, Mexico was relieved of a fee of $500 million, and its interest charges were tied to Libor alone rather than the prime rate or Libor, whichever was higher.[51] But Brazil had had enough and defied the IMF's belt tightening. This rewarded Rio twice over. Its economy grew a handsome 7.4 percent in 1985.[52] The banks, fearful of losing their best third world customer, finally came to an agreement with Brazil, despite its refusal to accept the Fund's tutelage. The deal would save Brazil an estimated $320 million in interest charges in 1986 alone.[53]

The IMF played no part in persuading the banks to relax fees and rates, and its stance toward debtors provoked some strong criticism in the North as well as in the South. The Fund's conditions, its deep immersion in the details of a debtor's economy, constitute an astonishing measure of control. Is it necessary for the IMF to insist on the price of rice, the level of wages, or utility profits when its objective is to reduce a deficit in a balance of payments? Should a debtor country not choose its own policies to reach the single goal that is the basic condition for its loan?

Beyond this, the Fund is wedded to a standard solution for all who seek its credits. Deflation, the compression of credit and spending, is the remedy the IMF invariably demands. In a time of world slump, the Fund then adds its weight to the fall in incomes and output.

The great debt trauma then is the result of several forces. The South's voracious appetite for and misuse of Northern loans is one. The commercial banks, pouring oil deposits into developing countries with scant regard for the prudence that is supposed to govern their dealings, is another. Like the South Sea Bubble and the Tulip Craze, lending to sovereigns, particularly in Latin America, became a raging fashion, and every major bank joined the stampede.

There were few restraints. Rules limiting loans to any one client were evaded. Reserves immobilize money that might earn interest, and so are unwelcome to banks. At home, banks must keep a percentage of their deposits at the Federal Reserve; abroad, in the Eurocurrency market, no such rule applies. It was this market that scooped up the bulk of the OPEC funds that eventually found their way to the third world.

In the end, the recklessness of borrowers and lenders laid the foundation for the debt crisis, but the bubble burst as a direct result of deliberate Western policies. The decision of the Federal Reserve and other Western central banks to combat OPEC's second oil shock by persistent disinflation, squeezing credit and compressing demand, made inevitable the failure of Southern borrowers to meet their payments. If a different choice had been made, if the West had decided to expand to resist the oil threat to jobs and output, interest rates would have been held down, trade could have increased enough to sustain raw materials prices and markets for third world goods, and Southern debtors might not have run short of foreign exchange.

But the peculiar circumstances of the 1970s insured that inflation would become the first priority, that jobs and output would suffer. Prices had been rising rapidly throughout the decade, and the second oil shock gave them a fresh impetus. This unchecked rise could not be dismissed; it threatened to unravel the fabric of industrial society, undo all calculations, destroy savings, and undermine the basis of order and the property system. Clearly, inflation had to be treated and treated drastically, but there is no commandment asserting that the Federal Reserve, a money squeeze, and deflation were the best remedies. A different prescription might have produced far less harrowing results for borrowers and lenders, a much less painful life for the tens of millions made jobless or impoverished in both the North and South, and increases instead of losses for the wealth of nations.

There is reason to believe that the wrong medicine was administered, that the deflation imposed on the world was an avoidable, self-inflicted wound, much like that of the early 1930s. The damage resulted because the Federal Reserve and other western central banks struggled against an inflation of costs with instruments designed to subdue an inflation of demand.

The second oil shock, like the first, caused no pervasive increase in demand, no rush of new paper incomes seeking a slower-growing supply of goods. To the contrary, skyrocketing crude prices deflated demand and reduced the buying power of the money incomes people received. Increased oil prices were an added cost burden. But the central banks' response, shrinking the growth in the supply of money, strikes at demand, not cost. Less credit means that all must choke off their purchases of goods and services (unless prices fall, an unlikely event for all goods but raw materials in a world of large corporations and trade unions). The upward shove in costs from increased oil prices was much like the upward push from union-set wages or product prices fixed by the monopolistic competition of corporations.

Cost push, or administered price inflation, is the characteristic form of inflation in the modern industrial world. Central banks, with their control of the money supply, lack an appropriate tool for it. Their technique, driving up interest rates and holding down credit, is too sweeping, too crude for modern inflation. In the language of economists, the central banks are applying macroeconomic remedies to microeconomic problems, employing measures that strike at an entire economy instead of dealing with particular firms or industries.

To be sure, the central bank measures did reduce inflation, in the United States and elsewhere in the West. An elephant gun can destroy a rodent. But the costs were disproportionate. In the

United States the Federal Reserve could argue that it had no choice, that on top of oil's cost push, the Reagan administration added macroeconomic inflationary pressures of its own, spending more than it was collecting to enlarge defense and diminish the tax burden of the better-off. But these deficits came at a time when men and plants were idle, when there was spare capacity to produce a stream of goods and services offsetting any increase in money to fund the debt. Moreover, the central bank began its assault on inflation in 1979, well before the large Reagan deficits appeared. Unemployment and idle factories signal a lack of demand. But it was demand inflation that the Federal Reserve persisted in fighting. The Western slump, the resulting debt crisis, the spiraling interest rates, the fall in commodity prices, the closing of industrial markets, and the appreciating dollar can all be traced to the moves of the central bank, actions better suited to a different economic climate.

Was there an alternative? The BIS, although an instrument of central banks, thought so, at least briefly. On the eve of the Mexican appeal, the BIS urged governments to consider "incomes policy," a bland term for an innovative approach, a microeconomic attack on microeconomic problems. An incomes policy tries to influence wages and prices directly, acting on the particular institutions that set them, large corporations and unions. The technique ranges from simple exhortation to direct controls. It has been tried, with mixed success, in every industrial country, including the United States. Although there is no assurance that an incomes policy would have worked in the late seventies and early eighties, the BIS said it is "undeniable . . . [that] incomes policy can contribute to the maintenance of real income growth."[54] More simply, the demand deflation of central banks will surely shrink incomes and wipe out growth.

The crisis, and its attendant misery, threw into high relief several features of the enduring quarrel between North and South, the level of commodity prices, obstacles to trade, the volume of aid. It also disclosed a damaging gap between third world pretensions and performance. At every global gathering, the South proclaims its unshakable unity but it was conspicuously absent this time, at least through 1986. The debtor countries made only token efforts to establish a common front; had they succeeded, they might have terrified their creditors with threats of a massive default and forced far easier terms. But Mexico and Brazil, the biggest debtors, feared contamination from the others. Believing they could one day turn on the tap in New York again, they evaded all but the most generalized common statements. Indeed, the only joint action debtors took was to serve as a conduit for U.S. Treasury funds to assure banks of Argentina's overdue interest. So each debtor government dealt separately with the combined forces of the banks, the IMF, and the Federal Reserve.

The crisis had one other remarkable effect. It buried, at least for the duration, the third world's unending and unanswered plea for a new world economic system, a reordering of the world economy that would transfer to the South a larger share of the world's wealth. All developing nations were threatened, one way or another, by the debt emergency and the Western slump. So radical chants gave way to the cooler tones of third world finance ministers. The new theme was "immediate measures," and it was echoed in the declarations even of the nonaligned. At a 1983 gathering in New Delhi, the nonaligned deplored "the prevailing world economic crisis," appealed to the IMF and the World Bank, and called for a global conference on money and finance "as a matter of urgency."[55] All this reflected the preoccupation with the shrinkage in world demand. There was little prospect that the rich would sit down with the poor to discuss these matters. But the nonaligned did make clear they understood that their New International Economic Order must now await the resolution of the debt trauma and its consequences.

Chapter 2

The Rising South

Since the birth of the United Nations, the South has used its chambers and rostrums to demand a more favorable distribution of the world's goods. Although the third world has sought a wide network of channels to shift resources from North to South, the U.N. is the South's most appealing arena. If the postwar world had organized itself to assure universal peace, why could it not assure universal prosperity? Moreover, Article 1 of the U.N.'s charter enjoins "international cooperation in solving international problems of an economic, social, cultural or humanitarian character. . . ."[1] Finally, the U.N. has practical political uses. Outmatched by East and West in the U.N.'s early years, the growing number of newly independent states assured the third world by the 1960s of an overwhelming majority of votes on any issue on which it could unite. Economic demands on the North were surely something on which the South could unite easily.

Trygve Lie, the U.N.'s first secretary general, heard the rising clamor and chose an expert committee to prescribe for the third world's ills. An unusually distinguished group, it included W. Arthur Lewis, then of Manchester and later a Nobel laureate, Theodore W. Schultz of Chicago, and D. R. Gadgil of the Gokhale Institute of Politics and Economics in Poona. Insisting on the primacy of measures that poor nations must take themselves, these experts first urged third world nations to reform their own societies, something the South was uneager to hear. "Economic progress will not occur," the U.N. experts said, "unless the atmosphere is favorable to it."[2] So poor countries should end barriers to free and equal opportunity, redistribute land and reform systems of tenure to give farmers incentives to increase output, end privilege based on caste or race, provide mass education, carefully survey physical and mineral resources, and train farmers, laborers, scientists, and administrators, investing in human resources to increase their productivity. Wealthy industrial nations can help, the experts wrote, by ending subsidies for exports that compete with the products of poor nations, providing supplier credits like those of the Export-Import Bank, thus enabling the poor to acquire needed imports more easily, and encouraging private firms to invest in the underdeveloped world.

Inevitably, the experts called for a new aid agency, something the South did want to hear. Writing in 1951, the economists were impressed by the striking success of the $13 billion Marshall Plan in reviving war-wracked Western Europe. So they urged an international development agency to give poor nations $3 billion a year.[3] The money should not be granted automatically, however, the report said. It should go to governments that are efficient and honest, although the experts acknowledged that few might qualify. Most remarkable of all, the U.N. panel urged a political test for aid recipients:

> Some countries are ruled by corrupt or reactionary cliques whose regimes might be overthrown by the people if there were no foreign aid, and who may be settled in their rule because foreign grants have become available. Members of the United Nations will not wish to have any hand in fastening such governments on peoples. They might therefore wish to lay down certain minimum conditions before an underdeveloped country was admitted to the list of those eligible to receive grants.[4]

There is a simple, almost archaic ring to such language. It was rarely heard in the U.N. again. As the organization was transformed from a club of the rich to a congress of the poor, the doctrine spread that all third world nations—corrupt, repressive, democratic, exploitive—all are equal and all are entitled.

The terms of the debate, at least as it is conducted by the South, have changed drastically. Proposals for internal economic and social reform have vanished. All that is left is the IMF's austere conditionality, a narrow monetarist version. Instead, the argument has focused almost exclusively on what the rich should do, without any demands on the poor. By the 1980s, when the U.N. was a sea of third world flags, what the rich should do was made plain. As one third world document phrased it, "massive transfers" of resources from the North were required.[5]

If the debt crisis of the 1980s temporarily muted these demands, there was every reason to believe that they would be dusted off again if and when borrowers and lenders reached a stable accommodation. For one thing, demands on the North conveniently obscured domestic failures in the South. For another, the North has frequently yielded to third world proposals, although never in the precise form sought by the developing world.

At its earliest sessions, the U.N.'s General Assembly rang with complaints from Mexico, India, Pakistan, and others that nothing comparable to the Marshall Plan had been arranged for developing countries. The gap between rich and poor was cited as a danger to world peace. Syria warned against "a full scale war" that "might be precipitated" by global inequality.[6] Chile called for a U.N. agency that would dispense $2 billion a year. It would be hard to achieve democracy, Chile contended, if living standards are not lifted.[7]

The third world got down to cases in 1947 and 1948 at the long U.N. meetings in Havana and Geneva to create an International Trade Organization, the ITO. There, much of what was to become the standard Southern agenda turned up in the talks. India, Ceylon, the Latin Americans, and the Middle East countries demanded protection for their new and future industries. Rich countries could afford to surrender quotas or physical limits on competing imports; the poor could not. Rich countries could trade equivalent tariff cuts with each other; the poor should have the right to award themselves cut-rate or preferential tariffs. Chile complained that its raw materials exports bought less and less of the North's manufactured goods.[8] Commodity agreements must be put in place to prop up the prices of the raw materials sold by the South. Foreign investors often exploited their hosts, Southern delegates complained; poor countries must control them.

So many of these demands found their way into the ITO's charter that it was never ratified by the U.S. Senate and became a dead letter. Nearly two years of talks, however, did produce one surviving mechanism, the General Agreement on Tariffs and Trade (GATT), the third great postwar economic institution. But the South dismissed GATT and its rules of even-handed treatment for trade as an instrument of the rich. The ITO experience only intensified third world pleas for a different order, one assuring privilege for the South.

The struggle to protect commodities prices has particular force because so many third world nations depend on one or two raw materials for their foreign earnings. In the late 1970s, Colombia and El Salvador still relied on coffee for half of their export earnings; for Burundi, coffee provided almost nine of every ten foreign dollars earned. Cocoa brought in more than half of Ghana's export receipts, copper more than 90 percent of Zambia's earnings and half of Chile's, tin nearly half of Bolivia's foreign exchange.

Unquestionably, commodities prices fluctuate. In the 1980s slump, coffee fell from $1.70 a pound to $1.16, copper from 99 cents a pound to 58 cents; jute bounced back and forth between $385 and $283 a ton, at one point shooting up to $807.[9] This is not simply a boom and bust phenomenon; one report concluded that primary commodity prices fluctuated nearly twice as much as those for manufactured goods between 1950 and 1970, and more than three times between 1969 and 1979.[10]

The South, of course, is far more upset with downswings than upswings. But the mere existence of these fluctuations poses genuine obstacles to development, making investment uncertain and timid, sometimes wrecking national plans. But just how the prices of sisal, tin, cocoa, and the rest should move is unclear. All third world nations insist on stability, but stability means different things at different times.

There was nothing ambiguous, however, in the South's cry for foreign aid, and it became the focus of concern after ITO's collapse. All in the South could agree that ever-increasing grants from the North, free of any conditions, would be an undiluted blessing. So, the South pressed throughout the 1950s for a Marshall Plan of its own. Unlike the European version, however, this program would be run exclusively by the United Nations and under General Assembly rules: one flag, one vote. The rich would provide the funds; the poor would do the spending. The existing programs, aid from separate sovereign nations, raise political problems, Marshall Tito told the General Assembly.[11] He meant that donors demand a political price, support for their foreign or economic policies. A U.N. fund would save the poor from embarrassing strings.

There was in fact an international finance agency already in existence, the World Bank, but it fell short of third world aspirations. The Bank makes loans, not gifts or grants. It charges interest and insists on repayment with no delays. Above all, it is firmly controlled by the West, not the third world majority in the U.N. The Bank is the sister agency to the Fund, and its quotas and voting structure are almost identical. Member nations provide its capital in amounts roughly equal to their economic strength, and their votes are proportional to this capital. By 1984, the United States share was 19.2 percent. Together, the eight larger industrial states—the United States, Britain, West Germany, France, Italy, Japan, Canada, and the Netherlands—held 52.6 percent of the votes, enough to block any loan.[12] Inevitably, politics, not economics, have sometimes governed decisions. The leftist Allende regime in Chile, for instance, was cut off; its successor, a right wing military dictatorship, quickly won Bank loans.[13]

Unlike the Fund, which depends exclusively on government contributions, the Bank raises virtually all the money it lends in private capital markets, through the sale of well-rated bonds. The Bank's managers, jealous of these ratings, are careful to make loans that will not upset the confidence of Western financiers.

At first, the institution made only bankable loans to the third world, loans for projects that would yield a predictable return. Money for a dam in Pakistan was bankable; hospitals or schools were not. Nigeria could get funds to build roads carrying goods to ports; a loan to train farm extension workers was not bankable. Borrowers repay these loans in hard currencies earned by their exports. They are charged an interest rate close to that paid by the Bank for its bonds.

In theory, both Bank and Fund are agencies of the U.N. But their agreements with the U.N. guarantee them independence. Private lenders would settle for nothing less.

Delegates had barely settled in at the U.N. before third world countries began complaining about the Bank. Too much money was going to Europe. (The Bank's first task was the reconstruction of Europe, and its formal title, the International Bank for Reconstruction and Development, reflects this priority.) Loans for the third world were too limited; they failed to support all the elements of development, notably health and education. The terms were too stiff. Colombia complained that it couldn't get loans for schools and hospitals although both were vital for development. Pakistan grumbled that loans to poor countries were "inadequate." Brazil deplored the Bank's refusal to lend for the local currency costs of a project and its failure to deliver more than $1 billion to the third world in its first ten years.[14]

The South's remedy was Sunfed, a Special United Nations Fund for Economic Development, controlled by the U.N. and free from narrow Western banking rules. With its growing majority, the third world repeatedly pushed through the Assembly resolutions to establish Sunfed.

Led by the United States, the West strenuously opposed an institution in which its sole role was to give and the South's to get. But in the 1950s, at least formal respect was paid to U.N. resolutions, and in public, the West moved softly. The United States suggested a U.N. fund derived from any savings in disarmament; unfortunately there were none. The United States then proposed the establishment of a $100 million fund for technical aid, to survey investment prospects that the Bank or some other Western agency would finance.[15] This fund was approved—"We must be thankful for small mercies," said Ceylon—but this was a pale shadow of Sunfed.[16]

Having failed to dampen Southern demands with delay, diversion, and the disarmament gambit, the West now tried a new tactic, substitution. Instead of Sunfed, the industrial states created a new and more liberal wing of the World Bank. The International Development Association, IDA, would offer money to the South on far easier terms—soft loans—but control would remain exclusively in the hands of the North. Nevertheless, the agency would be a striking departure, the postwar world's last major economic institution, a genuine international aid agency.

Much of the impetus for IDA came from the Bank itself, increasingly worried over Southern demands for a competing U.N. fund. Eugene R. Black, the Bank's shrewd president, said bluntly that "the International Development Association was really an idea to offset the urge for Sunfed."[17] Black, like any other banker, had little use for soft loans. But if anybody would make them, he reasoned, it had better be the Bank. If new business was to be done, Black wanted to do it.

"Whenever men despair of being able to meet their needs through peaceful means, there will be found the seeds of tyranny and conflict," Christian Herter, the U.S. Secretary of State, told the General Assembly in 1959. Reflecting the prevalent belief that money equaled development and development preserved stability, Herter said, "If peaceful change is to be accomplished . . . it must go forward at an increasing pace in the economic field."[18] With this, he announced that the West had agreed on IDA, and the agency opened for business a year later.

Although the industrial nations—the sole contributors to IDA's funds—kept a strong grip on the agency, it was designed to satisfy many of the Southern complaints about the Bank. It is a lending institution, but sets such easy terms its loans resemble grants. In time, IDA made loans the Bank had long refused—for secondary schools, housing, programs to improve health—as well as the profitable projects dear to the Bank.[19] IDA's liberal policies infected the Bank, which relaxed its notions of what was appropriate. The Bank began lending in hitherto forbidden sectors like education, housing, and clean water supply. The Bank even agreed to an easier payment schedule for India, its chief client, limiting repayments to 20 percent of India's export earnings rather than fixed amounts on fixed dates.[20] This was a stunning departure from conventional banking practice. In effect, the Bank linked repayments to India's ability to pay, a reform that some Latin nations were to suggest for their commercial debts in the 1980s.

As welcome as IDA has been to the South, it lacks the crucial feature the third world sought: control, U.N. or third world control over the funds. If anything, IDA is even more closely tied to Western governments than the Bank. Governments supply all of IDA's funds, while the Bank enjoys some measure of independence by raising money in London or Wall Street. Every three years, Western donors supply IDA with new money. Washington's influence is especially strong, because the contribution from the United States, the largest donor, typically determines how much others will give.

The Bank's new offspring began life endowed with $686 million, and systematically expanded its resources until 1982. Then Western weariness with aid and the Reagan administration's hostility toward international organizations reversed the trend. Washington slashed its promised contribution by $300 million, and IDA ended up with $1 billion less than it had been promised.[21]

Still, IDA is a political phenomenon. It is a substantial aid agency created largely in response to third world cries at the U.N. It is not the unfettered money machine the South sought and remains a subtle instrument of Western policy. Since IDA is financed by the West, only political fantasists could expect otherwise.

IDA's birth, of course, depended on more than U.N. speeches and third world complaints. It was closely linked to the Cold War. Both West and East believed that the third world would heavily influence the outcome of their struggle for supremacy, and each strove to win the allegiance of Latin, Asian, and African nations, or at least to offset the influence of the other.

In the United States, leaders frequently asserted that the battle could be decided by enlightened American self-interest, an American willingness to finance the development of newly independent states. Unless the new nations could overcome the mass poverty of their people, they would be racked by internal disorder, become breeding grounds for Communism, fall to the Soviet side. This argument was repeated on public platforms, in the liberal press, in Congress. It was a major theme of public discussion and the principal rationale for foreign aid.

The United States drive to create IDA was rich in conventional Cold War rhetoric. It was employed by the most sophisticated public leaders of the day. Testifying for IDA, John J. McCloy, chairman of the Chase Manhattan Bank and a leader of the nation's foreign policy establishment, argued that the West and the United States could not survive without the markets and raw materials of the developing world. The Soviet Union, he told a House Banking and Currency Subcommittee, had made the developing countries "their principal battleground."[22] The United States now faced a North-South as well as an East-West conflict, he said, an early use of what was to become a fashionable geopolitical division.

Another persuasive voice was that of Paul G. Hoffman, an auto executive and the successful administrator of the Marshall Plan. He warned that if third world countries are

> forced to rely on the Soviet Union for aid and are gradually sucked into the role of satellites, we face all the dangers inherent in a shrinking free world. . . . Russia has become the principal backer of Sunfed, about which many questions could be raised. However, we can't fight something with nothing.[23]

Today, that debate has a period flavor. The West has seen Ethiopia, Mozambique, Egypt, Indonesia, Somalia, and others switch sides too often to believe in the unalloyed efficacy of aid money. There are serious questions about the utility of aid itself, whether it promotes or retards development. But there is no reason to doubt that eminent Americans believed what they said at the time. Rivalry with the Soviet Union as well as the cries in U.N. chambers built IDA.

The third world's partial success over IDA, together with new additions to Southern ranks in 1960, provoked fresh political ambitions among the developing nations. For the first time, Asians, Africans, and Latin Americans began to discuss a common front on economic affairs to replace the national posturing that marked the earlier debates. The third world began to believe that agreement on common phrases could somehow translate into power and fresh Northern concessions.

In politics the South had already begun to organize. Twenty-nine African and Asian heads of state met at Bandung, Indonesia, in 1955 to pronounce on war, peace, colonialism, and liberation. Six years later, at Belgrade, under the guidance of Marshal Tito, Prime Minister Nehru of India, and President Nasser of Egypt, Asians and Africans joined with Latin Americans to create the nonaligned movement.

This was an attractive model for Southern nations with unfulfilled economic claims. By 1960, the third world could count sixty-seven members in the U.N., far more than the twenty of the West or the nine in the Soviet group.[24] If nothing else, third world countries could organize voting blocs at the U.N., a congenial task for diplomats more at ease with politics than economics.

The impetus for an exclusively economic grouping again came from Tito. He urged Nasser to call a conference in Cairo, and it met in July 1962. Thirty-six nations came from Asia, Africa, and Latin America. After ten days of deliberations, they produced a document that, with minor changes, would appear at successive gatherings for the next twenty years. The basic theme of the Cairo declaration held that poverty is a legacy of European colonizers; no fault attaches to third world rulers. "Developing countries have made progress," the statement said, "in spite of unfavorable factors mainly inherited from a colonial past. . . ."*[25] Written in language that was often opaque, the declaration urged three principal claims: price support agreements for raw materials, opening of Northern markets to goods from the South, and enlarged aid on a yearly level equaling 1 percent of the incomes of industrial countries.

Then, as now, there was an almost mystical belief in the utility of global conferences, a conviction that if the North met with the South, the self-evident reasonableness of the third world position would induce the North to yield. So the Cairo declaration called for a universal meeting, and a reluctant West agreed. (The Soviet Union had first urged an international economic conference as far back as 1956; Moscow wanted to build pressure against West-

*Since the Latin Americans were liberated from Spain a century and a half ago, this is a remarkable testament to the persistence of Madrid's colonial legacy. This problem can be cured by asserting that United States' economic colonialism simply replaced Spain's.

ern curbs on strategic goods to the Soviet bloc and promote East-West trade generally. The North could ignore this, but it was harder to resist the call from the South.)[26] A United Nations Conference on Trade and Development, UNCTAD, was fixed for 1964.

Whatever was said in public, most industrial states opposed the idea. They feared that the third world's overwhelming numbers would lead to resolutions damaging to the economic interests of developed countries. In public, some, like France, professed support for the assembly. France rather liked commodity agreements, at least for the products of its ex-colonies. Moreover, France and some others recognized that third world resolutions agreed upon at a trade conference were at worst an embarrassment; they had no more binding power than U.N. resolutions elsewhere. The United States, however, was sorely troubled even by the prospect of words. Richard N. Gardner, then a deputy assistant secretary of state in charge of these matters, described the forthcoming gathering as "an economic Munich for the West."[27]

Gardner's fears proved to be as exaggerated as third world hopes. But at least the developing nations that labored to prepare papers, resolutions, and speeches for the conference found a common vocabulary and what they claimed were common interests. At the UNCTAD meeting in Geneva, they transformed themselves into a permanent caucus, the Group of 77. Although their numbers have since swollen to 120, the South's economic organization still styles itself the Group of 77.

Does the Group of 77 matter? When so many nations so often agree on the same package of words, it is frequently believed that something important has been said. A commission of notables led by Willy Brandt, West Germany's former chancellor, said the "Group of 77 represents the solidarity of developing countries which is of historic importance, enabling them to present a common stand and bring to bear their combined strength in North-South negotiations."[28] A State Department glossary of international organizations said that the caucus "remains very cohesive" despite differences among its members.[29] This last is the point. The Group of 77 can agree on general statements of intent. But when specific agreements are negotiated over the price of raw materials or the breadth of territorial seas, unity dissolves, and national interest prevails.

The Group's members, moreover, are deeply divided by ideology, culture, and level of development. The Ivory Coast is free market and pro-West; Cuba operates a command economy and is a Soviet bloc member. India, formally democratic, leans toward the Soviet Union; Pakistan, a military dictatorship, is linked to the United States. Sophisticated Mexico has little in common with the tribal politics of Uganda. The economic differences are even more striking, from industrializing Brazil, exporting manufactured goods, to backward, agricultural Mali.

Finally, fellow feeling within the 77 takes second place to connections that directly affect the flow of goods and services. Gamani Corea, UNCTAD's former secretary general (and thus an unofficial secretary general for the 77), has said that the Group's members are far more concerned with their links to industrial nations, East and West, or even with others in their own regions, than they are with global bodies. There are so many international meetings, Corea said, and they work at an abstract level. A trade or aid arrangement with another nation is concrete; it affects the flow of real resources.[30]

Nevertheless, the Group of 77 has become a permanent feature of the political landscape, a caucus that hangs together by blurring differences and posing lofty demands. It is a political fact, and it has had some consequences for the way the world's business is transacted, although far fewer than its founders expected. It has spurred some changes in the three Western institutions, Bank, Fund, and GATT. It has created a new international bureaucracy to serve its ends, turning the UNCTAD conference into an UNCTAD agency. Its texts largely shaped the North-South agenda for nearly twenty years, until the debt crisis forced attention to more pressing concerns. Even then, the problems posed by the third world—although not its answers—help explain some of the major obstacles to development.

The first UNCTAD conference at Geneva in 1964, 2,000 delegates carrying 120 national flags, observers from the Vatican and Switzerland, was a model for those to follow every three or four years. Despite twelve weeks of speeches, earnest caucusing among delegates from North and South, and the laborious working and reworking of resolutions, little of substance was agreed. The reason was simple. The industrial countries that account for most international trade—then about 70 percent[31]—saw no gain in changing anything. The Group of 77 could and did win handsomely all the votes at Geneva. But these ballots bound no one. The third world had to content itself largely with paper victories. That is why the 77 left Geneva claiming that their most important achievement was their own unimpaired unity.

The balance sheet, however, was not entirely barren. Even before the conference began, it had inspired some limited reform, and more was produced after the assemblage broke up. In an effort to defuse a major Southern claim, the IMF took a cautious step in 1963 to aid nations suffering a sudden drop in raw materials prices. The Fund created a Compensatory Finance Facility, enabling a developing nation to borrow an extra 25 percent of its quota when its export earnings fell through no fault of its own.[32] Third world countries could now obtain a small slice of foreign exchange when drought or frost struck their crops. To be sure, 25 percent of a minuscule quota wasn't much, but at least a principle had been established. The West had recognized that commodity price gyrations interfered with development and deserved special treatment.

UNCTAD's promoters had a far greater ambition, a peaceful revolution in the ways nations do business. This, they argued, was a necessary condition for the poor to overcome their backwardness. To a remarkable extent, UNCTAD thinking was the thought of one man, Raul Prebisch, a lively Argentinian economist. His diagnosis and prescription not only animated UNCTAD but continue to inspire much third world reflection. Eloquent, elegant, and imaginative, Prebisch had served as director general of Argentina's central bank and pondered the Depression's disastrous consequences for his country. He elaborated his ideas as chief of the Economic Commission for Latin America, a U.N. agency, and was the inevitable choice for UNCTAD's first secretary general. In that strategic post, Prebisch prepared an influential report that was a rare piece of synthesis. It traced the third world's lack of development to the global system, exonerating third world leaders and their institutions.

Prebisch offered UNCTAD a theory of bloodless but inexorable exploitation. Developing countries were victims, the developed victimizers. Raw materials, the commodities that developing countries export, buy decreasing quantities of the manufactured goods they must import from the North. In economics the third world is doomed to ever-deteriorating terms of trade.[33] This is not because the North is evil; it flows from the law of markets. Exchange, contrary to Adam Smith and the virtues of specialized labor, or David Ricardo's doctrine of comparative advantage, is not mutually beneficial. Trade enriches the North at the expense of the South.

The South, argued Prebisch, faces an ever-decreasing Northern demand for its raw materials. As industry becomes more sophisticated, it requires less and less iron ore, zinc, copper, and other metals. Moreover, synthetics replace natural goods like rubber. The demand for raw materials declines. If the South cuts its prices, it will gain little and may lose much because the extra volume of physical sales will be outweighed by the drop in their value.

Southern foodstuffs fare as badly. Engels' law reflects the fact that there are limits to the food consumption of the richest of men. Therefore, the greater a man's income, the smaller the share he spends on food. So the increasingly rich North spends a decreasing proportion of its income on the cocoa, tea, coffee, bananas, and other foodstuffs exported by the poor.

Consider the other, happier side of the market. As Southern incomes rise, there is a more than proportionate increase in the South's demand for machines, machine tools, looms, autos, refrigerators, and other Northern manufactured goods. Each increment of additional Southern income creates an appetite for a larger increment of Northern goods. While the relative fall in demand for Southern metals, foodstuffs, and fibers depresses the prices of third world products, the growing Southern demand for Northern goods tends to push their prices higher.*[34]

*A variant of this explanation appeals particularly to students of monopolistic competition. They contend that third world producers sell in more or less competitive markets to a handful of large, commercial buyers. These few buyers are oligopsonists, free to some extent of impersonal market forces, able to impose lower prices than they would pay in a freely competitive market. At the same

Labor markets, Prebisch argued, reinforce these trends. In the South, there is a surplus of unemployed or underemployed farm workers, desperate for work at any price. They compete for relatively scarce jobs, driving wages down. But in the North, well-organized unions regulate the labor market. They prop up wages and costs, boosting prices still higher.[35]

In the world that Prebisch mapped for UNCTAD and its successors, markets, technology, and impersonal laws account for exploitation. The South sells for ever-lower prices but must buy at ever-higher prices. One ton of coffee bought one machine yesterday; tomorrow it will take two tons of coffee. To drive home his point, Prebisch calculated that the buying power of the South's commodities in the industrial world had fallen 26 percent between 1950 and 1961.[36] Statesmen, he said, must rectify this.

> There must be . . . a political decision of the first importance, namely a decision to transfer, in one way or another, to the countries exporting primary commodities the extra income accruing to the industrial countries as a result of the deterioration in the terms of trade.[37]

What is to be done? Prop up and increase the prices of commodities, redress the imbalance by replacing the market with controls. Producers and consumers should agree to put a floor under, and perhaps a ceiling over, commodity prices. Prebisch continued the tradition of deliberate ambiguity, whether raw materials prices were to be held steady, match increases in industrial costs, or rise above them. The developing countries clearly prefer the third course, since it would shift resources from rich to poor.

The second and most innovative layer of Prebisch's three-tiered prescription attacked the third world's frustrating attempts to develop its own industry. If the structure of markets condemned raw materials producers to fall further behind industrial nations, then surely they must industrialize themselves,

---

time, exporters of finished goods tend to be large corporations with a measure of monopolistic or oligopolistic power. They can extract more from their third world customers than if they were small competitors, no one of them large enough to influence price.

build their own factories. Unfortunately, domestic markets in most third world nations are too poor to support industry; they need outlets in the North. But Northern markets are frequently blocked by tariffs or taxes on imports, by quotas that limit the physical volume of imports, and other protective devices. Tariff barriers had been falling due to the periodic negotiations in the General Agreement on Tariffs and Trade, but mostly for the goods that the rich traded. Barriers against the textiles, shoes, leather products, and other goods made most cheaply by the South remained in place and were increased.

All these barriers, said Prebisch, echoing the third world nations at the U.N., should be swept away.[38] The South should have a chance to expand its factories by unhindered selling to the North; Northern consumers would enjoy cheaper goods. He went even further, to his most original idea. The South's struggling new factories should enjoy *preferential* tariffs, a tariff advantage over competing Northern producers. If the tariff on a machine tool in Japan was 15 percent, identical products from India or Brazil should enter duty-free. If the rate on smelted copper in the United States was 12 percent, smelted copper from Zaire should enjoy a zero duty. In effect, India, Brazil, Zaire, and others would gain a form of inverted protection. They could compete on an equal basis with domestic producers of manufactured and semimanufactured goods. They would then acquire a competitive advantage over the foreign factories of the North.

The third world saw preferential tariffs as a springboard to launch their own factories and escape from dependence on the exports of raw materials with their built-in tendency to lose purchasing power. Industrialization meant modernization, breaking the chains of impersonal exploitation.

Prebisch's third major remedy was outright aid, foreign assistance, a grant to the poor of claims on the resources of the rich.* He was obviously uneasy over advocating more aid, the single

*At the U.N., the South even fixed a precise target for the volume of aid: Every year, each rich nation should contribute seven-tenths of one percent of its gross national product or total output. Some Western nations have proclaimed allegiance to this goal, but performance has fallen far short. In 1983, the United States gave less than half the target amount, 0.24 percent, and the rich as a whole gave 0.36 percent. Since the target was chosen arbitrarily, it is impossible to say

most popular third world demand. Aid has the stigma of charity. Money would not be given without a demand for something in return. It was needed, but threatened the South's independence. To make aid more respectable, Prebisch described it as compensation, a rebate to the third world for the years of declining commodity purchasing power.[39]

His major themes were warmly embraced by the third world majority at UNCTAD and expressed in countless speeches and resolutions. Prebisch's doctrine became the foundation of the South's agenda, an intellectually coherent attempt to explain third world backwardness and a way out.

As it happens, both the analysis and the solutions are badly flawed. Prices of Southern raw materials do fluctuate much more than those of Northern manufactured goods. But this is more a symptom than a cause of distress. What the third world needs is protection against sharp drops in its export earnings, a drop that forces it to abandon imports of tools and machinery needed to develop. A steady rise in foreign exchange—export receipts, not commodity prices—will enrich the South. Prebisch and the third world assume that prices and earnings are identical. They are not. Higher commodity prices can choke off demand or encourage rival substitutes. This misplaced focus on prices has haunted the South from the start of the debate.

Similarly, Prebisch's innovative demand for preferential tariffs was misguided. Successive rounds of negotiation in GATT were shrinking tariffs and diminishing their importance, devaluing any preference. A zero duty on an Indian machine tool will not help Delhi much if the tariff on the same tool in France has come down from 25 to 5 percent. Prebisch cannot be blamed for failing to foresee the new wave of protection in the 1970s, the "voluntary export restraints" and "orderly marketing arrangements." They would do far more damage to Southern exporters than tariffs, striking particularly at the new industries of the biggest debtors,

---

whether the levels are too high or too low. Targets in General Assembly Resolution 3362, 7th Special Session, United Nations, September 16, 1975, p. 924. For actual figures, *Development Cooperation* (Paris: 1984, p. 210). See also Mossein Askari and John Thomas Cummings, *Oil, OECD and the Third World* (Austin, Texas: University of Texas, 1978).

Mexico and Brazil. Just as with commodity price agreements, Prebisch's tariff proposal missed the heart of the problem. A closer look at alternative approaches is needed.

His uneasiness over aid is justified. Uncertain grants from the North may simply strengthen narrow leadership groups in the South and spare them from necessary domestic reforms. Prebisch himself had something to say on this point:

> Much remains to be done by the developing countries in taking the internal measures which would enable them to make more effective use of the external assistance available to them.[40]

Concentrated land ownership frustrates agricultural output; uneducated masses need schooling to become more productive; incomes in the South flow to a few, encouraging conspicuous consumption instead of widening demand to spur investment; local industry is inefficient, sheltered by high tariffs and other walls. "One's house must be put in order," Prebisch's report said.[41]

There is little in UNCTAD's record to show much attention was paid to this unwelcome warning, an echo of the U.N. experts thirteen years earlier. Instead, the South has seized on Prebisch's principal theme, ever-worsening terms of trade, as the major explanation for underdevelopment. If this argument falls, the South can make claims on humanitarian, political, or military grounds. But its economic rationale disappears.

Unfortunately for Prebisch, empirical evidence does not give much support to his thesis. To demonstrate the decline in terms of trade, Prebisch and his followers frequently choose 1950 as a starting date. It is a most peculiar year, the year the Korean War began. The demand for raw materials by the United States and others was enormous, and commodity prices shot up sharply. Thereafter, they fell throughout the decade, not to recover until the 1960s. If Prebisch had chosen the mid-1950s as his base, when prices of commodities were low, the purchasing power of raw materials would have reflected an increase.

Sometimes, Prebisch resorted to a price table constructed by the old British Trade Board that went back to 1876. It seemed to show that Britain's imported raw materials had been falling for half a century compared to Britain's exported finished goods. But the table omitted the two world wars, when raw materials boomed. Even worse, the commodity prices included freight charges while the finished goods did not. Since freight rates fell swiftly in the modern era, the table reports this fact and says little about relative commodity prices.[42]

As awareness of these defects spread, UNCTAD decided to settle the question. It hired a panel of economists and asked, "Has there been a secular deterioration of the terms of trade of developing countries?" The experts' reply was unequivocal:

> While opinions on this matter differed, there was general agreement that the statistics presented *did not provide any clear evidence of a long-term deterioration in the net barter terms of trade of developing countries,* although they did suggest that these terms of trade were subject to substantial short-term fluctuations. [Emphasis added.][43]

This was a Scotch verdict: unproven.

Apart from the empirical problem, several economists, notably A. S. Friedeberg, have demonstrated theoretical difficulties with Prebisch's attempt to root third world claims in impersonal economic law.[44] Prebisch describes only the deterioration of what is called the barter terms of trade. But what if a new fertilizer sharply decreases the cost of producing 1,000 bushels of wheat? Wheat prices may fall, but the cost of producing the extra bushels needed to buy a tractor could fall even more. Despite the fall in wheat prices, the terms of trade for the wheat producer could rise; he would need fewer inputs of cost to obtain the same or even more output of wheat and the tractor he ultimately seeks. This is called the single factoral terms of trade, or commodity terms of trade corrected for productivity changes.

Again, a fall in wheat prices could stimulate an even bigger increase in demand. A producer might gain larger earnings and receive a bigger volume of imports for his exports at the lower price. So terms of trade can be measured by what is called the export quantity index.

This last proposition is of more abstract than practical interest. Decreases in raw materials prices rarely spur much extra demand. Many commodities confront relatively inelastic demand schedules, at least for a wide range in price. The two cases ignored by Prebisch, the single factoral terms of trade and the export quantity index, however, do show that whether third world producers gain or lose depends on more than Prebisch's simple changes in relative prices.

But none of this has shaken the third world's faith in Prebischian economics, and it lives on at virtually every gathering of the South. In 1983, the nonaligned economic declaration made commodity prices its first topic for discussion, deploring "the steady deterioration in the terms of trade of developing countries."[45] A ministerial meeting of the same group two years earlier gave pride of place to raw materials and urged measures to "improve the purchasing power of the unit value of the export earnings of developing countries."[46] In 1980, the Group of 77 listed as its first concern, "Improvements in and protection of the purchasing power . . . of primary commodities. . . ."[47] To be sure, these statements all came against the background of a Western slump that had driven raw materials prices down. But they were issued in a manner implying that this was the natural and permanent order of things, a pure Prebischian view.

As Prebisch's argument began to dissolve in the academic world (despite its vigor among political leaders in the South), a new theory of exploitation arose. *Dependencia,* or dependency, has enjoyed a vogue, particularly in Latin American universities. Unlike the Prebisch constructs, however, it has had only a marginal effect on the behavior of third world governments. Marxist in tone, *dependencia* is more notable for generalization than supporting fact, and turns on personal or corporate actors rather than on the inexorable workings of impersonal economic law. A dependent economy, Theotonio Dos Santos has written, is one "conditioned by the development and expansion of another economy to which the former is subjected." This pattern marks North-South relations and leads to the "transfer of resources from the most backward and dependent sectors to the most advanced and dominant ones."[48]

In the postcolonial world, dependency theorists contend, multinational corporations, operating through local subsidiaries, are the instruments of dominance. They gain control over third world resources, especially minerals, and compel third world governments to build roads and communications to serve their plants rather than the nation. They control foreign trade and withdraw more in repatriated capital and profits than they invest; they jealously guard decision making and technical knowledge; they encourage consumption by the rich and exploit poor workers; they invest in sectors and technology unsuited for their third world hosts; they squeeze out local entrepreneurs, widen the gap between city and country, and cheat third world nations of taxes by inflating their deductible costs, overpaying for goods bought from their parents. Finally, they interfere in the politics of their host governments and corrupt third world officials.

No doubt this catalog describes the actions of some multinationals in some places sometimes. But dependency theory as an explanation for underdevelopment has been implicitly rejected by Southern governments. They have ignored the obvious solution, outlaw all multinationals, and instead have reached out to attract more of these firms with their capital, technology, and jobs. Even China, a long holdout against foreign investors, now welcomes them.

Concern over multinationals has led many countries to regulate foreign firms: to require that a substantial or even majority share be held by local citizens; to compel the transmission of technical know-how; and to prohibit foreign investment in key industries, from communications to steel. But these rules have also been relaxed or ignored almost everywhere. Argentina, Brazil, Chile, Mexico, India, Indonesia, South Korea, Peru, Venezuela, Pakistan, Bangladesh, Bolivia, Jamaica, and Sri Lanka all eased their controls in the late 1970s and 1980s. They want more, not less foreign investment. The Japanese discovered they could satisfy local ownership requirements in Thailand, Malaysia, and Indonesia with dummy directors, complaisant generals and politicians, or well-connected local businessmen.[49] "Most developing countries have shown increased flexibility and pragmatism in the implementation of their domestic ownership policies," concluded the U.N.'s Center on Transnational Corporations, a spiritual home for some dependency theorists.[50] This is a polite way of suggesting that multinationals can slide past firm rules in the soft states that characterize the third world.

Dependency theory still crops up in third world pronouncements, particularly those from the nonaligned. But as an explanation of backwardness, it is swamped by all the other evils the nonaligned decry: "imperialism, colonialism, neo-colonialism, expansionism, apartheid, racism, Zionism, exploitation . . . force . . . domination and hegemony. . . ."[51] In practice, the same nations who issue such pronouncements urge multinationals to set up plants inside their borders. Dependency theorists might argue that the actions of governments mean little, that the rulers of third world states are merely *compradors,* or foremen for the great exploitive corporations of the North. This seems, however, a less-than-convincing description for governments in China, Yugoslavia, India, or Mexico.

The first UNCTAD meeting, like those to follow, ended in a flurry of overwhelming votes to bring Prebisch's solutions into being. The industrial nations were hostile, but some were more discreet than others. The United States, for example, voted against thirteen of the "general" and "special" principles adopted by the conference and abstained on seven of the remaining fifteen. Other industrial nations used the United States as a shield to register opposition less stridently. Britain cast seven no votes and nine abstentions, Germany four and eleven, and Japan one and thirteen. The France of General de Gaulle, pursuing its role of special friend to the third world, limited itself to thirteen abstentions.[52]

The United States frequently stands alone, or nearly alone, in these matters. It equates rigor with leadership and relishes blunt talk. At the 1974 U.N. conference on the New International Economic Order, the West was persuaded to let resolutions pass without a recorded vote, but the United States delegate declared that his country, "like many others, strongly disapproves of some provisions in the document and has in no sense endorsed them."[53] In contrast, the French hailed the artificial consensus, then quietly listed a long string of reservations. NATO allies often fail to vote with Washington. On what Washington regarded as the ten most important issues in the 1983 General Assembly, one third of the NATO ballots differed from the

United States. Even if Greece, Turkey, and Spain, all with close third world ties, are excluded, the level of dissent was still 25 percent.[54] United States militancy, politically useful in a country increasingly hostile to the U.N., becomes a convenient shelter for other industrial nations. They may be just as opposed to third world propositions, but prefer not to say so nakedly.

In all these dramas, the Soviet Union is barely visible. It invariably votes for third world propositions but explicitly disclaims any responsibility for carrying them out:

> We will never accept . . . the false concept of dividing the world into "poor" and "rich" countries or into the "North" and the "South," which places the Socialist states on the same footing as the developed capitalist states that have extracted so much wealth from countries which have for so long been under their colonial domination.

So ran one typical Soviet statement. It is the capitalist states that "bear direct responsibility for the economic backwardness of the developing countries," Moscow insists.[55]

Although the Soviet Union is rich and industrial by third world standards, Moscow is rarely pressed by the South. Third world governments recognize the futility of, say, assigning an aid share to the Russians or seeking tariff preferences in a command economy. Many third world states, moreover, call themselves socialist and admire the rapid development and power of a once backward nation.

The UNCTAD votes were political symbols, not economic counters. In a few cases, third world ideas would be translated into action, although on a much lower scale and with far less benefit than the South had hoped. But not a single dollar, franc, or mark would move to the third world, no cocoa, iron ore, or sisal would be traded, not one machine would travel between South and North because of words adopted or rejected at Geneva. Nevertheless, Prebisch and the conference had forced world attention onto a set of problems and ideas that to this day form the enduring core of the North-South debate.

Chapter 3

The New Order

UNCTAD had not put the West at bay, but it did stimulate a growing conviction, particularly among the international institutions, that something should be done. To stand pat seemed unworthy and politically unwise. So the IMF doubled the sum it would lend nations suffering an unexpected drop in export earnings. The increase was modest, from 25 percent to 50 percent of a member's quota, but it reflected a slightly altered climate. The IMF created another innovation in 1974, an Extended Fund Facility to make loans up to eight years, well beyond the usual three-to-five-year limit.[1] Purse strings had been prudently loosened.

Perhaps the boldest and possibly the most unsettling reforms were made by GATT's members. Stung by the largely accurate charges that its tariff-cutting exercises chiefly benefited the rich, GATT began altering its rules. Its cardinal principles, first laid down by the United States, held that nations should trade more or less equal reductions in tariffs—reciprocity—and that a tariff cut given to one must extend to all—most-favored-nation treatment.

The Prebisch proposal for preferential tariffs, special advantage for the third world, breached both sacred rules. In fact, the rules had already been violated, although this was rarely acknowledged. A Canadian-American agreement on duty-free entry for autos broke the most-favored-nation clause; France had induced the Common Market to give preferences to the former French colonies in Africa.

In the wake of UNCTAD, GATT agreed that developing nations are entitled to unrequited benefits and could receive tariff reductions denied to the rich. This may have been a pyrrhic victory, however. It threw a cloak of legitimacy over the new and far more restrictive devices that the West would soon employ to choke off Asian and Latin steel, cars, electronic exports, and much more. As a final gesture, GATT decided that agreements to rig commodity prices were proper.

But it was preferential tariffs that consumed official energy, a tribute of sorts to Prebisch. At first, the United States resolutely opposed so blatant a violation of reciprocity and most-favored-nation principles. The threat of low-cost competition for simple manufactures was equally unwelcome. But political considerations won out. An expanded Common Market would soon include Britain. Preferences or tariff-free entry for products from former colonies in Africa and Asia would inevitably spread and with them spheres of influence. Colombia's coffee would confront a tariff in Europe; the Ivory Coast's would enter duty-free. Latin Americans pressed Washington for an American preference sphere, but the administration of Lyndon Johnson had global ambitions. It concluded that the least worse course lay in offering United States preferences to all, weakening the European hold over its ex-colonies.

By 1976, the great industrial traders, the United States, Japan, and the Common Market nations were each offering their own brand of preferences. All wrap their packages in strings, limiting the amount of any item that can enter duty-free and excluding many products outright. The United States denies tariff-free entry to third world textiles, shoes, oil and oil products, watches, some electronics goods, some steel and glass products.

A select group of third world nations, the first to industrialize, have extracted gains from the new rules. Three, Taiwan, Hong Kong, and South Korea, are not in the United Nations. Others are Mexico, Brazil, Yugoslavia, Singapore, India, and Iran before the fall of the Shah. The most exuberant report, by UNCTAD, estimated that preferences had increased third world sales to the North by $4 billion in 1980.[2] Between the tight limits imposed by the rich and the concentration of manufacturing in the South, preferences were never likely to fulfill the UNCTAD dream of spurring industry in the developing world. More importantly, the erosion of tariffs generally and the rise of far more severe barriers to trade have all but made preferences irrelevant. The long struggle for preferences was a prime example of the third world pursuing a reasonable goal—more open markets—with the wrong means.

Apart from preferences and the cautious steps by the Fund, little was done to advance third world demands in the ten years after the first UNCTAD. The agenda was rehearsed repeatedly at third world meetings, at UNCTAD gatherings, and in the U.N., and it inspired a voluminous academic literature. But despite UNCTAD's pleas, aid flows from North to South dropped steadily. The South as a problem had simply lost much of its appeal. Third world economies had grown smartly, nearly 6 percent in the 1960s, more than the 5 percent of the West.[3] To be sure, figures for the growth of gross national product for nations whose statistics are more guess than fact do not bring bread to villages. Some, like India, grew at rates that barely matched the increases in population. Nevertheless, the central notion of increasing misery that lay behind the South's demands could not be sustained.

At the same time, some Western nations were absorbed with their own balance of payments, with a growing gap between their exports, imports, and the capital they sent abroad. This was particularly true of the United States. Foreign aid increases the deficit in a nation's payments balance because it provides recipients with a claim on resources. Aid givers typically staunch much of the outflow by tying their funds, requiring that the money be spent in the donor's country. But there is still leakage. So a nation with a payments deficit is reluctant to expand assistance.

The most important reason for the West's diminished interest in third world utterances, however, was the transformed political climate between East and West. In the 1950s, aid and aid-giving institutions were sold to taxpayers as weapons in the Cold War. Money would help bring prosperity to the South, saving it from the temptations of Communism, winning friends and sometimes allies in the struggle against the Soviet Union. But after the Soviet Union withdrew its missiles from Cuba in 1962, the Cold War cooled off. The competition for third world clients or friends diminished. The need for concessions to Southern states seemed less compelling.

When President Nixon made fresh overtures to the Soviet Union and China in the early 1970s, it appeared that détente had been established. Third world convulsions caused by economic distress were no doubt unfortunate, but it became harder to argue that United States security was affected. The traditional argument for aid was weakened.

Then an accident of history intervened. In 1970, Colonel Muammar Qaddafi, the radical new leader in Libya, decided he wanted a higher price for his oil. He demanded a cut in Libya's oil production and insisted that Occidental Petroleum, his principal producer, pay more tax or royalty based on a higher price. Other states, notably Iran, Saudi Arabia, Iraq, and Nigeria thought this was sensible and insisted on even larger concessions from the great international companies who exploit oil in their lands. Libya returned for another round. There were still more increases, relatively modest. By 1973, the price of a barrel of oil had risen from $2.20 a barrel to $3. It had all been accomplished, moreover, with astonishing ease. The great companies, particularly the Seven Sisters,* appeared to resist the demands. But they knew that their profits rise when prices rise, sag when prices sag, regardless of the legal state of their concessions. The companies have a vested interest in higher prices because they themselves own vast amounts of oil.

The curious feature of this affair was the lack of coordination between the producer countries. They had formed their own would-be cartel, the Organization of Petroleum Exporting Countries or OPEC, in 1960, in hopes of arresting what was then a downward drift in oil prices. But they had never acted in concert on anything that mattered, notably the price of oil and the supply from their wells. In 1970, it was Libya alone, followed by others,

*The Seven Sisters are Exxon (formerly Standard Oil of New Jersey), Mobil (formerly Standard Oil of New York), Chevron (formerly Standard Oil of California), Gulf (later swallowed by Chevron), Texaco, and two European concerns, British Petroleum, and Royal Dutch Shell. They are bound together in consortia or joint enterprises throughout the world. The most important is Aramco, linking Exxon, Mobil, Chevron, and Texaco in a virtual monopoly to exploit Saudi oil.

that set the ratchet in motion. But the ease with which OPEC members suddenly multiplied their wealth had a stunning effect on the oil states and the third world. The South revived its largely dormant agenda.

In September 1973, leaders of the nonaligned states, the third world wearing its political rather than its economic hat, assembled for their triennial gathering, this time in Algiers. Since the host country prepares the documents for these gatherings, Algeria, radical and socialist, was certain to infuse all papers with a militant, bristling tone. Algeria, moreover, is a member of OPEC and was exhilarated with the astonishing success of the oil states.

So the nonaligned produced an Economic Declaration that denounced "imperialists," meaning the West, hailed the triumphs of an OPEC that now began to act in unison, and urged the creation of similar cartels for all the other raw materials the third world exports. The language was, perhaps, the most striking example of dependency theory deployed by the government leaders of the South.

Among other things, it said:

> Imperialism not only hampers the economic and social progress of developing countries but also adopts an aggressive attitude towards those who oppose its plans, trying to impose upon them political, social and economic structures which encourage alien domination, dependence and neo-colonialism. . . . This situation accounts for the considerable disparities between the industrialized countries and the underdeveloped world . . . the developing countries in general are still subject directly or indirectly to imperialist exploitation . . . as is illustrated by the manifold and increasingly pervasive activities of transnational and monopolistic commercial, financial and industrial companies. . . .[4]

The twenty-four page, single-spaced document cited oil as a model:

> The results obtained in the hydrocarbons sector, which was previously exploited for the sole benefit of the transnational oil

> companies, demonstrate the power and effectiveness of organized concerted action by producing and exporting countries.[5]

Go thou and do likewise for sisal, coffee, zinc, cocoa, and the rest.

> The Heads of State or Government recommend the establishment of effective solidarity organizations for the defense of the raw materials producing countries such as the Organization of Petroleum Exporting Countries . . . to recover natural resources and ensure increasingly substantial export earnings.[6]

The declaration renewed the familiar demands for aid, trade, and other concessions. But now they were cast in a new light. The fiery Algiers statement was a declaration of war with oil leading the assault. Other regiments must be formed from the cartelized ranks of producers of jute, tea, copper, and more. The West had no choice but to yield to commodity power, or so at least Algiers argued. The third world agenda had found new life.

A month later, the Middle East was in a real war, and excitement over the oil weapon reached a new pitch. OPEC, now acting as one, proclaimed an embargo to shut off oil from Israel and its supporters, the Netherlands and the United States. However, the intended victims were largely untouched because OPEC oil was still transported, refined, and marketed by the same small group of Western companies with global connections. Since their interests lay in maintaining customers and unchanged market shares, the embargo halted little oil, if any. But this apparent lack of effect did not subdue third world enthusiasm. It reached a fever level when the price of oil was doubled and doubled again.

Inevitably, these high spirits spilled over into the U.N., although the tone there was usually more decorous than at Algiers and other third world headquarters. The Algerians called for a special U.N. session in the spring of 1974 to translate their declaration into a New International Economic Order. The President of Ecuador, Leopoldo Benites, opened the assembly, called it a "milestone" and stressed the "unexpected effect that a single economic measure has produced in the entire working of international relations . . . this event has proved the vulnerability of power relationships, both economic and political, which are based on the idea of the dependency of producers of basic raw materials."[7] He was talking, of course, about the seemingly limitless power of oil to extract any price.

President Houari Boumédiènne of Algeria foresaw a new order, with the rich trembling at the prospect of other OPECs for copper, iron ore, bauxite, rubber, coffee, cocoa, and even peanuts.[8] Tunisia said with satisfaction that the oil price increases "are still shaking the old economic order."[9] Guinea predicted that the International Bauxite Organization, newly launched at Conakry, "will achieve similar brilliant" victories as OPEC.[10]

There were a few disquieting notes. Nearly all developing countries import oil, and they were faced with staggering bills. Zambia said its development would be hurt because it must find $156 million to buy oil in 1974 against $37 million in 1973. Ghana noted that its oil bill had quadrupled. Shridath Ramphal, later to become Commonwealth secretary, said that the price rise has created "special hardships" for all developing countries, including his own, Guyana.[11] Nevertheless OPEC has provided "a long needed catalyst" to change the system, and so the suffering is nothing compared to the joy.

The third world presidents, ministers, and ambassadors clearly expected wondrous things from OPEC. It would not only serve as a model for other commodity cartels but use its demonstrated strength to break down the West's resistance to everything else the South wanted—aid, markets, technology, the Fund, the Bank, and more. The South was to be disappointed.

Perhaps the most significant statement at the special session was made by Ahmed Yamani, the Saudi oil minister; it went all but unnoticed in the cries for pelf. Yamani said, "The oil exporting countries shall not entertain any suggestions that aim to impose upon them a trusteeship for determining the prices of their oil."[12]

This was subtle but unambiguous, evidently thought out with care. It meant that the Saudis would make no deal exchanging control over the price and supply of oil for Western concessions to the South. It meant that the one genuine weapon in the third world arsenal had been disarmed. Very few believed in the commodity power of peanuts or even bauxite. But oil was something else, and in the oil world, the Saudis mattered most. They are the residual supplier, the nation that can afford huge production cuts to support a given price level. Unlike Iran, Nigeria, or even Iraq, with substantial populations hungry for the better life, the Saudis are under no pressure to pour out billions on new housing, highways, and other costly development projects. If the Saudis would not entertain any curb on their freedom of action, how could oil power be deployed to force concessions from the North? A year later in Paris, the West was to test Saudi determination; it found that Yamani had meant what he said—and the last serious effort to satisfy Southern demands collapsed.

Nevertheless, prominent personalities, writing in influential Western organs, excited fears that the world was undergoing a vast transformation. Walter Levy, a leading consultant to oil companies, warned of "tremendous and lopsided shifts in the balance of power" because of OPEC's strength.[13] Writing in *Foreign Affairs,* the oil negotiator for the Shah of Iran, Jahangir Amuzegar, asserted that "the raw materials producing nations (and the oil exporters as their early pioneers) have come of age —politically able to defend their sovereign rights, economically equipped to pursue their national aspirations."[14] C. Fred Bergsten, soon to be an assistant secretary of the treasury in the Carter administration, announced, "It is clear that an NIEO, or at least a significant change in the old order, is already emerging."[15] Bergsten claimed that the new bauxite cartel (soon to become little more than a tame trade association) had lifted prices seven times, that a copper group had raised the metal's price 20 percent, that more cartels were on the way for phosphate, tin, chrome, natural rubber, iron, mercury, tungsten, and even timber. "Commodity confrontation is likely to escalate. Time is on the side of the producers . . . their ability to manipulate markets will grow."[16] The West, he said, must build stockpiles, form a common front and negotiate commodity agreements with the producers.

NIEO is the shorthand for the New International Economic

Order, the label used since the 1974 U.N. special session for the catalogue of third world claims. It has a commanding ring, a hint of revolution. It is also remarkably imprecise. Its contents vary from time to time and place to place, depending on the political needs of the third world caucus and the fashion of the day. If Niger, bordered on all sides by other nations, has become restive, special provisions for landlocked nations are brought to the fore. When predatory imperialism is the topical theme, demands for expropriating the expropriated gain pride of place. There is no single document that describes the New International Economic Order or the claims it makes. The 1974 session solemnly proclaimed "The Establishment of a New International Economic Order" and added a "Charter of Economic Rights and Duties of States" for good measure.[17]

However, no vote was actually taken on either. The West, still uncertain about the way to contain the very real dangers of oil, accepted a third world proposal to forgo a ballot. Instead, the United States and others described at length, for the record, their many differences with the two NIEO documents. This enabled the South to claim that they had been adopted by consensus.

Even the two documents do not fully cover the NIEO. It is possible, however, to extract the essence of the New Order from these papers and three others: the declaration of the third world government chiefs at Algiers in 1973; the chastened third world resolution adopted at a second U.N. special session in 1975; and the Lima Declaration pronounced at the 1975 gathering of the United Nations Industrial Development Organization, a U.N. subsidiary. Careful reading of this collection yields twenty-four different if not necessarily consistent claims posed by the South.

The twenty-four, in turn, can be divided into two groups of eight central and sixteen peripheral topics. The division is admittedly arbitrary. The eight major topics are those that turn up most frequently in third world debates, appear to have the broadest economic implications, or contain some features that might appeal to the North.

They are:

Aid. Grants and concessional loans from individual Western nations, usually called "transfers of resources" in third world documents, should be increased substantially with fewer economic and no political conditions. The U.N. target, 0.7 percent of each industrial nation's output, should be reached by 1980.[18]

TRADE. Industrial countries should remove all barriers, tariff and nontariff, against imports from the third world. The South does not offer any reciprocal removal of its trade obstacles. Preferential tariffs should be broadened and deepened, protected against loss of value by tariff cuts that industrial nations give each other. There should be compensation for Africans and others who lose their exclusive preferences in the Common Market.[19]

COMMODITIES. Agreements should be made between producers and consumers, buttressed by buffer stocks or stockpiles, to stabilize and raise the prices and purchasing power of the raw materials that developing countries export. A common fund should be established to finance the buffer stocks of each commodity, stocks that shall be bought or sold to support the desired price levels.[20]

INTERNATIONAL MONETARY FUND, WORLD BANK. Third world nations should enjoy equal power with the West in the decision making of both bodies. The present system, basing votes on quotas, condemns the South to a perpetual minority.[21]

COMPENSATORY FINANCE. IMF loans should be made to compensate for any decline in the export earnings of the third world. The existing IMF outlays in this sphere are too feeble.[22]

LINK. An extra helping of Special Drawing Rights should be issued to third world nations for their development, thus linking global reserves to growth.[23]

DEBT. The burden of debt that third world nations owe the North should be eased, either by cancellation, declaring a moratorium on payments, stretching out payments through rescheduling, or subsidizing the interest charged.[24]

TECHNOLOGY. The North must transfer its technology more widely and cheaply to the South to promote third world industry. The South should acquire industrial knowledge by outright gift, cheaper patents and licenses, and other devices.[25]

These eight central measures build largely on the Prebisch triad, aid, preferences, and commodities—familiar themes from the earliest days of the U.N. The peripheral sixteen defy easy summary because of the many constituencies to which they appeal, from ideological foes of foreign investment like Cuba (Algeria frequently mouths the rhetoric but welcomes the plant) to the Ivory Coast which gained some measure of prosperity through foreign firms. They are:

Cartels.* Encourage producer cartels to match the achievements of OPEC. Consuming nations shall take no military or political action to weaken them (a reference to the United States withdrawal of preferences for OPEC members).[26]

Private foreign investment I. Control it rigorously; limit the profits a foreign firm can send home. Any third world country can nationalize any foreign firm, paying what it regards as appropriate compensation. Multinationals (transnationals in UNese) are particularly dangerous and must be subjected to a code to insure they do not interfere in the host country's affairs.[27]

Private foreign investment II. Third world nations should promote it, both public and private.[28]

Shipping. The South should own more of the world's fleets, and costs for transporting third world goods should decline.[29]

Landlocked and least developed nations. Increase their aid, cancel their debts.[30]

Treaties. Third world nations should tear up those signed under duress.[31]

Drought. The North should give aid to halt the spread of the desert over fertile land in sub-Sahara Africa and to stop locusts everywhere in Africa.[32]

Food. Industrial nations should provide cheaper food and fertilizer to developing countries.[33]

Duties. Customs on third world imports should be returned to third world exporters.[34]

Synthetics. Regulate the production of synthetics and other substitutes that compete with third world raw materials.[35]

Southern currency reserves. Preserve their purchasing power by halting inflation and exchange depreciation. (This

*After the excitement of OPEC, it may seem odd to relegate cartels to the periphery. But it soon became clear, however, that OPEC was one of a kind, and the cry for cartels became a ritual chant.

claim reflects the 1970s when United States inflation was high and the dollar low. By the 1980s, third world dollar holders were no doubt pleased with their appreciating reserves.)[36]

INDUSTRY. Northern nations should finance industry in developing countries. The North should transfer its uncompetitive industries like textiles to the South.[37]

WORLD BANK AND INTERNATIONAL DEVELOPMENT ASSOCIATION. The North should increase their funds.[38]

SUNFED. Create a genuine, U.N.-controlled development bank and endow it richly with Northern funds.[39]

RESERVES. Make Special Drawing Rights the central reserve asset. Phase out the use of national currencies like the dollar as national reserves.[40]

BRAIN DRAIN. Stop the flow of talented emigrants from third world nations to the North.[41]

The peripheral components of the New Order are a curious blend of the inconsistent (simultaneously threatening and welcoming private investment), the Luddite (the dream of turning back the technological clock to halt synthetics), and the outmoded (Sunfed). The eight central topics, however, deserve a closer look. The striking feature of this group is that all its components, with the single exception of trade,* boil down to pleas for aid, direct or indirect. Each of these seven is a claim on Northern resources, a demand for goods and services with nothing offered in exchange.

This is a description, not a judgment. Some of the proposals may have merit and yield dividends, political or economic, to the North. But the essential character of the New Order should be understood for what it is: a plea for resources at no cost to the South.

The request for more grants and concessionary loans is self-evident. Attempts to rig commodity markets and seek higher

*Preferences might be described as a form of involuntary aid. The Swiss maker of digital clocks who loses an equal opportunity to compete in the United States market against a Taiwanese manufacturer has been compelled to provide assistance of sorts. From the standpoint of the preference giver, however, there is no direct cost and a clear benefit: lower prices for consumers. This is quite unlike the one-sided transaction of aid.

prices than would otherwise prevail is simply a form of disguised aid; it does not appear in any government budget, but comes from the higher prices paid by consumers. The volume of this aid equals the excess earnings above those generated by unregulated markets. If the New Order merely sought to stabilize prices at levels set by the long-run balance between supply and demand, no aid would flow. But the demand for cartels and commodity agreements aims at much more.

The IMF proposals are less obviously aid, but aid nonetheless. Linking Special Drawing Rights to development would convert the IMF into a distributor of grants. Reserves would no longer be created exclusively to ease international credit and finance more trade. Instead the third world would receive an extra helping of SDRs, beyond those all IMF members now divide. This additional slice is a free and nonrepayable claim on Northern goods.

Similarly, the proposal for a more liberal Compensatory Finance Facility is a call for aid, although quite different from an outright gift. Loans from the Facility are made in hard times, when export earnings drop through no fault of a third world borrower. The borrower must, for larger loans, accept some form of IMF supervision. But the concessionary interest charges are a species of gift. So is the credit itself, since no borrower would go to the IMF if commercial banks would provide the money.

Again, the demand for an equal third world voice in the Fund and Bank sounds political but is economic. It is a preliminary to more assistance. The equal voice would be exercised to promote larger, less costly, and less restrictive loans at both institutions. The notion of a bank jointly controlled by debtors and creditors is imaginative; it has little to do with banking and much to do with aid.

The proposal to ease or cancel outstanding debt is an obvious request for assistance. Like some of the other claims, it may have value for the North and its precarious banking structure. But whether or not the North's interests are served, debt relief is another form of aid for the South.

The technology notion is the vaguest in the catalogue but has become part of the litany at almost every third world gathering.

The South is convinced that Northern wealth depends in part on arcane industrial knowledge denied the third world. If only the codes were broken, great cities would rise in arid plains. The plea for cheaper licenses and patents, for the cut-rate transmission of know-how is another demand for a gift. Third world emotion over the theme of technology transfer is so strong that it led to still another U.N. conference and another U.N. agency.

At the 1974 special session, the preamble to the New Order urged a system based on "sovereign equality, interdependence [thus dismissing de-linking as a solution for *dependencia*], common interest and cooperation among all States."[42] When the package is broken open, however, it contains a mix of claims on the wealth of industrial nations. "Common interest" is what interests the South. This is less a formula for equals than a mandate for givers and takers. The New Order is largely a string of devices to secure aid without conditions. In return, the putative recipients pledge nothing—least of all anything touching on the management of their own societies.

Despite its rhetoric, the New Order is a curiously conservative program. It does not call for the global socialization of property; it leaves untouched existing property arrangements, from the feudal land tenure of India to private corporate ownership in the West. The expropriation of multinationals has a radical ring, but they are at risk anywhere. A radical program would have called for nationalization without compensation, and this the New Order does not do. There is no call for global planning, although the suppression of synthetics and the transfer of obsolete Northern plants to the South are a rudimentary form. The market price system is largely maintained, with a few kinks for commodities. Makers of the New Order do not even call for an automatic tax on the rich, a proposal advanced by the Brandt Commission, although the plea for an aid target is a distant cousin. In short, the New Order is the present order, with extra helpings for the flag bearers in the South.

Karl Sauvant, a sympathetic commentator on the New Order, has written that if its proposals were adopted, "the structures of the international economic system would not be changed appreciably. . . . The NIEO program is essentially reformist; it aims at improving the existing mechanisms, not changing the existing structures."[43] Reform may be an inappropriate word, but Sauvant's appraisal, and its distance from the revolutionary promise of Algiers, is accurate.

After the 1974 U.N. session embracing the New Order, third world enthusiasm for the oil cartel began wearing thin. There was more talk of the pain than the pleasure OPEC had brought. This was hardly surprising. In 1974 and 1975 alone, the rise in oil had cost the third world $40 billion, 60 percent of the deficit in its collective balance of payments. OPEC hastily launched its own aid program to offset the damage and retain third world support; the sums granted amounted to about one tenth of the increased bill and were spent almost exclusively in Muslim countries.[44] So another special U.N. session was called in 1975. This time the South's tone was notably restrained. India complained that its energy bill had tripled since 1972, that 80 percent of its export earnings were now spent importing food, fertilizer, and fuel. That left little for imports of capital goods to spur industrial development. Zaire loyally asserted that OPEC had lifted oil prices to their genuine market value. But in the process, Zaire observed sadly, third world countries without oil had been damaged. Unfortunately, the oil brothers had not consulted consumers. Costa Rica said that it too supported OPEC, but the cost was heavy.[45] The new prices reflect justice and decolonization, but Costa Rica wanted justice for all.

The second special session ended with the inevitable and lengthy encyclopedia of requests, but the style was far less assertive. Most significantly, there was neither praise for OPEC nor a call to form more commodity cartels. Commodity power was clearly less than its promise; OPEC had failed to breach the West's defenses and had become a menace to its friends. The promised land was still not in sight, and little manna had fallen on the way. The IMF further liberalized its Fund for lost export earnings, but that fell far short of the gleaming towers envisioned by New Order architects.

Whatever satisfaction the West gained from the softer words from the South was more than erased by OPEC's destructive impact on industrial economies. Controlling the price and assuring the supply of oil was a constant preoccupation of industrial countries throughout the 1970s. Outside the U.N. and at the initiative of the United States, the West tried to build a defense. Industrial nations hurriedly put together a new International Energy Agency, agreeing to pool their resources to meet any genuine interruption in the flow of oil. France held out, chiefly to cultivate more favored treatment from Arabs, but this mattered little. IEA's members accounted for eight of every ten barrels of imported oil. As it happened, the first working cartel created by the New Order was one for the consuming rich. This was not what the third world had in mind.

Now the North could turn its attention directly to OPEC, to seek lower oil prices or at least less explosive increases. Those already in place had imposed a heavy cost in inflation, unemployment, and reduced output. The billions flowing to OPEC frightened financiers who did not yet understand that cautious Arabs would deposit most of their new dollars in Western banks.

So in December 1975, the French president, Valéry Giscard d'Estaing, invited nineteen third world nations, including six from OPEC, to meet with seven industrial countries and the Common Market six. At Paris, the tables were turned. In the language of diplomacy, the West—not the South—was the *demandeur,* seeking something but unable to offer much in return except generalized warnings of disaster.

Henry Kissinger, the U.S. Secretary of State, told the gathering, "We are here because two years ago the international structure was gravely tested by a crisis in energy. No problem on the international agenda is more crucial to the world economy. . . . The crisis—caused by a combination of the 1973 embargo and the fivefold increase in the price of oil—has dealt a serious blow to global stability and prosperity. . . . A lower oil price would make possible more rapid economic recovery around the globe. . . . A lower price, along with stability of supply, would also benefit producer nations" by shielding them from a search for alternative sources.[46]

This was clear. The West wanted an agreement to control oil prices and an unbroken flow of crude to any buyer. If both were not forthcoming, new energy sources would be found, a threat for some remote future.

OPEC's objective was equally clear, and it had been stated by Yamani: uninhibited OPEC decision making over oil price and supply; no agreement to curb OPEC's unilateral determination of the price of oil, how much shall be produced or who can be barred from buying it. That meant nothing could be agreed in Paris, and the conference would become another dialogue of the deaf.

To frustrate any deal, OPEC relied on a simple blocking tactic: Insist on third world solidarity. The conference must also discuss commodity agreements, aid, and other financial measures and development generally. In other words, place the items of the New Order on the table. Moreover, the OPEC representatives insisted that any discussion of oil prices must consider ways and means to preserve the real income of producers from United States inflation and dollar depreciation. That agenda guaranteed the deadlock OPEC sought.

The meeting limped along for eighteen months until June 1977, agreeing on nothing. At the end, the West said it would create a new aid fund of $1 billion for the poorest Southern nations. Despite the conspicuous failure, this was as close as North and South have ever come to negotiating the bundle of third world claims. The stalemate reflects an obvious principle: Neither in diplomacy nor in trade is very much given for nothing.

Nevertheless, the South was slow to learn the lesson. It clung to the belief that OPEC would trade some of its power to press Southern claims; it believed that this power was permanent, could be replicated, and would remake the world. So nations heeded the New Order's advice and rushed to imitate the oil model. None succeeded even in copying OPEC's temporary success. Jamaica, the leading member of a new International Bauxite Association, imposed higher taxes and royalties on its foreign-owned miners. But unlike the collaborating oil companies, the six large aluminum concerns who extract more than half the world's bauxite, resisted the embryo cartel. They cut production where they faced higher charges and increased it in more accommodating places, Australia and Guinea. They began working clays and shales for substitute ores and opened new smelters where energy was cheaper. In time, the bauxite nations gave up cartelization and turned their association into a trade center, exchanging information, suggesting prices.[47]

Other cartels were tried in iron ore, rubber, mercury, tungsten, phosphate, bananas, coffee, Southeast Asian lumber, and copper. All sought the OPEC road to riches, but in vain. A successful cartel must not only produce a large share of the world's output, as Carmine Nappi has observed. It must also enjoy an unresponsive or inelastic demand for its prices, face no near-term substitutes, enlist disciplined members, willing to abide by price and output decisions, and control most of the world's known reserves.[48] To Nappi's list add a buyers' cartel with a parallel interest in higher prices.

Oil and OPEC were unique because they met all those requirements. Over a considerable range above the prices prevailing before 1973, the demand for oil was inelastic. Doubling, tripling, or even quadrupling the price caused little fall in demand. But a 10 percent rise in the price of coffee or copper or bauxite will send customers searching for substitutes or doing without. In oil, substitution is difficult and costly; nuclear plants are expensive and take years to build; shifting a power plant to coal or redesigning an auto engine takes time and money. If bananas are dear, it is simple to switch to pineapples. Expensive aluminum, which is refined from bauxite, can be replaced by tin or steel.

Oil also enjoys the advantage of unpopulated deserts. The Gulf producers, with small populations, could afford to enforce a price by cutting their output drastically—at least until new wealth turned them into large spenders. But producers of bauxite, copper, coffee, and the rest have large numbers of needy people to satisfy. They want export earnings and cannot easily agree on limiting output, the *sine qua non* of any cartel. Their failure to make even watered-down agreements, merely to stabilize commodity prices, underlines the problem.

Petroleum, moreover, is a remarkably pervasive commodity,

used in hundreds of industrial and consumer processes and products. Synthetics, fertilizer, plastics and much more—apart from oil as an energy source—depend on a petroleum base.

Finally, and perhaps most importantly, as Fred Hirsch said, "was the existing cartel structure . . . built by the international oil companies."[49] They could and did work to make OPEC price edicts effective through their grip on shipping oil, refining it into products, and selling the products at the tank wagon, pump, or factory. The seven great concerns had long experience in joint action in producing consortia, in allocating markets, and in controlling prices. For exporters of copper, bauxite, and bananas, there are no Seven Sisters or four Aramco partners benignly enforcing producer price objectives. The handful of firms who buy bananas, copper, or bauxite may cooperate covertly with each other. But they will not admit third world governments to their partnership in oligopoly. Oil shows that arrangements to push up commodity prices are unlikely to succeed without the support of consumers, particularly the great multinational buyers.

Even the union of Arab producers and cooperating multinationals, however, could not repeal economic law indefinitely. The cartel overreached itself, and its prices inspired a search for new supplies, energy saving, and substitutes. Oil was found and brought on stream in quantities in the North Sea, Mexico, the North Slope of Alaska, and elsewhere. This oil was British, Norwegian, American, and Mexican, none of it OPEC. At the same time, high prices encouraged car buyers to insist on autos that consumed less fuel; homes were insulated to cut heating bills; power plants replaced oil burners with coal; nuclear power replaced both. Market forces were working.

To be sure, OPEC remained a power, at least until the early 1980s. The new oil exploiters, moreover, had the same motive as Asian or African producers—to push prices higher. So did the great companies drilling for oil. Their combined pricing power was displayed one more time in 1979–80 with painful consequences for South and North. But ensuing slump and all the opposing forces that had been building in the 1970s finally made themselves felt. Oil prices slowly slid back from their peak of $37 a barrel to $26 a barrel by 1985 and then plunged below $15. The traditional defense, deep production cuts, as much as 50 percent by the Saudis, failed.[50] The cartel's members quarreled among themselves over price levels and ceilings on their output. Some reneged on their price and supply pledges, "cheating" to a cartelist. They were running into problems common to all commodity agreements.

If the oil cartel is not dead, it has been grievously wounded, perhaps beyond resurrection. In the early 1980s, the industry complained of an oil glut, meaning that available supplies could not be sold at the hoped-for price. The actions of the great oil companies themselves pointed to a new state of affairs. Unwilling to seek new, price-depressing sources of oil, they satisfied their needs for reserves by swallowing each other. Chevron or Standard Oil of California spent $13.3 billion to purchase Gulf. Texaco laid out $10.1 billion for Getty.[51] Both deals helped prop tottering prices. Exxon and others used surplus cash to buy their own shares in the stock market, a price-supporting technique sounder than searching for more oil.

By 1984, there was so much oil at falling prices that the war between two major producers, Iran and Iraq, which cut off some of the flow, brought relief to the industry. Ten years earlier, a war around the Gulf would have panicked France, West Germany, and Japan, the major importers. Now they were unruffled. The world was awash with oil and other forms of energy. King Fahd of Saudi Arabia may have signaled OPEC's death in September 1985. He said the Saudis would no longer serve as the swing producer, cutting production to hold up prices. "We are never the guardian of anyone," he said, and doubled Saudi output.[52] This led to extraordinary discomfort in the Reagan administration and among its Texas and Oklahoma constituents. So the White House dispatched Vice President George Bush to the Saudis to seek what Bush called "stability" or an end to the "free fall" in oil prices. Bush, in effect, was charged with urging the Saudis to revive OPEC, to slash their output and restore prices. But the self-evidently benign effects of the fall aborted Bush's missions. With almost mathematical precision, the cuts had reversed the malign effects of the increases: Wealth shifted from the

Arabs to the West, supporting sluggish industrial economies; oil importers' currencies strengthened; all nations were endowed with a new barrier against inflation; interest rates fell. Against such a global bonanza, the Reagan regime had to retreat and deny that Bush had been sent to do what he had been sent to do.[53]

Three months after Fahd spoke, the cartel acknowledged it was unable to defend a price, and its members would seek to sell what they could at any price. In time, Fahd dismissed Yamani, his oil minister, for failing to make water run uphill, for failing to restore oil prices.

Even before the decline of OPEC, the New International Economic Order had unraveled. Some of the threads might be serviceable, but the fabric, the package had collapsed. Bits and pieces still turn up in U.N. resolutions and debates. At Geneva, the UNCTAD secretariat struggles, largely in vain, to produce agreements between consumers and producers to limit swings in raw materials prices.

The other principal items of the New Order mostly disappeared. The one great exception, of course, was the cry for relief from the growing burden of debt. Loans to the third world in the 1970s and early 1980s soared far beyond the most vivid imagination of the framers of the New International Economic Order. When the oil-induced slump of 1980–82 threatened not only default of these loans but the existence of the largest Western banks, industrial nations engaged in very serious negotiations. But these talks did not take place in any forum controlled by the third world, or even one in which they were equal partners. They were organized by the IMF, central banks, and commercial banks; the debtors were largely put in the role of suppliant. New Order rhetoric was notable for its absence. The strategy of the West was to unite creditors and divide the third world debtors. Through at least the middle 1980s, it was a strategy that succeeded.

The New Order's peripheral claims generated paper and conferences but little else. Makers of synthetics continued to produce unhampered. Negotiators, under UN auspices, labored to write a code of behavior for multinationals; since it was voluntary, it was unlikely to alter the practices of the large corporations or their host countries. South Asian doctors moved to London and New York; skilled Pakistanis continued to emigrate to Gulf states and Haitians to the United States. If there had been jobs, Yugoslavs would have renewed their trek to West Germany, Italy, and Switzerland. No serious effort was made to halt the drain of third world labor; on the contrary, the third world welcomed it. Emigration relieved heavy unemployment at home, and provided, through the money emigrants sent back to their families, badly needed foreign exchange. The Sahara continued to drift southward; the locusts multiplied.

With hindsight, it is hard to understand how the New Order could have aroused so much excitement in the South or concern, however brief, in the North. It was neither new, international, economic, or orderly. It was essentially the Prebisch agenda, buttressed by the Prebisch argument over the distorted structure of world trade, embellished with *dependencia* rhetoric. It was not international because it omitted, except formally, any role for the Soviet Union and its allies. Its economics reduce to a variety of pleas for aid. There is no order in a series of contradictory propositions, stabilizing and raising commodity prices, promoting and discouraging private investment. Some of the third world claims, notably those for more open trade, stable export earnings, and less stringent debt terms have genuine worth for both North and South. But the precious metal of mutual benefit was all but buried in the slag. Demands for massive, unrequited transfers of resources are likely to go unanswered unless the claimant has a gun. For a brief moment, the South thought OPEC was the weapon, but OPEC's gun was not for hire, and its ammunition has been dampened, if not exhausted.

Nevertheless, the empty drama continued. Frustrated third world leaders turned to something called global negotiations, a master deal to cover everything. A call to launch the global talks was issued by the U.N. in 1979, another paper victory for the third world. At still another special session, however, the United States, West Germany, and Britain refused to accept the guidelines prepared for the talks. The three claimed that the proposed guidelines would violate the independence of the IMF and the World Bank. This was a convenient excuse; the West wanted no part of the negotiations, and Washington served again as a useful buffer for industrial states who did not want to give offense. A small group of diplomats from North and South attempted to find a formula that would launch the negotiations. After several years of intermittent exchanges, they could report no success.

Global negotiations enjoyed one last gasp. At the suggestion of the Brandt Commission, heads of government from eighteen nations and ranking representatives of four more, eight from the North and fourteen from the South, gathered at the Mexican beach resort of Cancun in 1981 for two days of conversation. The less sophisticated hoped agreement would at least be reached on the formula to begin global talks. But neither the Northern nor Southern positions changed, to the express satisfaction of President Reagan and the relief of most others present. So the launching formula never emerged.

One fresh idea aroused a flicker of interest at Cancun: a scheme to relieve the distress of third world oil importers. Around the table, leaders seemed so enthusiastic that François Mitterrand, the French president, told a skeptical press conference that the plan had been agreed.[54] Its credentials were impeccable. President Robert S. McNamara of the World Bank proposed a fresh fund to finance a search for oil in the third world. The money would go to nations with deposits too small to interest the large corporations but big enough to supply domestic markets.[55] That could free perhaps a score of Southern states from the heavy foreign exchange costs of importing OPEC oil. The Bank estimated that as much as 15 percent of the world's extractable oil reserves lay in developing countries outside OPEC.[56] What was needed was money to explore and exploit. Since the third world's oil bill in 1982 was $60 billion, this seemed a sensible idea.

But Clifford C. Garvin, chairman of Exxon, insisted that the Bank was the wrong vehicle for such risky loans, and that private oil companies should have first crack at any undrilled acreage.[57] Such a judgment from the world's premier oil man, understandably reluctant to find oil outside the companies' traditional pattern of control, impressed the Reagan administration. Despite the interest at Cancun, the Bank's oil window was slammed shut before it opened.

There is a neat symmetry in this endnote to the negotiations over a New Order. Oil had aroused the excited talk; oil punctuated its quiet close. Oil states had provided the initial spark; the leading member of the Sisterhood extinguished the last feeble flare.

For all practical purposes, the South's grandiose ambition is dead. The North will not remake in one bundle global trade and aid rules for the exclusive benefit of the third world. The long clash, however, has illuminated issues of real concern to both camps, issues whose resolution could increase the wealth of all nations. The wild swings in the export earnings of the third world are a problem. They frustrate not only development in the South, weakening its demand for Northern goods, but discourage investing by peasants and banks in each hemisphere. The pursuit of stable or rising commodity prices is futile and even damaging; but a steadier flow of receipts from minerals, fiber, and produce can yield advantage everywhere.

The third world's long quest for tariff advantage has gained little for either North or South. Instead, it has contributed to a great increase in a far more insidious form of protection, physical limits on imports. In the industrial world, protection shrinks trade, freezes labor and plant in less efficient industries, and promotes inflation by reducing import competition. In the developing world, protection frustrates industrialization by closing off the South's richest markets and striking directly at the capacity to service debt. A return to a more open system, envisaged if never fully realized by GATT, would benefit both hemispheres. Achieving a more rational, wealth-enhancing trading world is likely to preoccupy politicians to the end of the century.

The South's insistent demand for more economic aid and from every conceivable source has been rejected by the North in formal negotiations and, more importantly, by the actions of aid-giving nations. The demand rests on the little-examined assumption that aid spurs development and confers benefits on the South's impoverished people. The validity of this assumption, indeed whether aid should continue at even the relatively reduced levels now in vogue, are still unanswered questions.

Chapter 4

Law at Sea

In the long and largely sterile engagement between South and North, one event stands as a signal exception to the record of frustration, stalemate, or marginal concession: the eight-year struggle to establish a new law for the seas, an agreement to divide up the immense mineral and fishing resources of the oceans and to fix rules of the road through, above, and below the waters that cover two thirds of the earth's surface. Unlike so many South-North issues, freighted with abstract process and uncertain result, sea law governs the concrete and measurable. It determines who shall own billions of barrels of offshore oil, billions of tons of nickel, cobalt, and other metals in the deep sea bed, and most of the world's fish catch. It embraces great strategic issues, the mobility of superpower navies and air forces. With the conspicuous exception of metal mining, economically the least significant ocean resource, nations engaged in the long negotiation put aside ideology and fiercely pursued national interests. East and West, North and South were far less important than the possession of submarine-launched ballistic missiles, control of a narrow strait, and the presence or absence of long coastlines. Those with something to trade traded. Those without won only promises of doubtful worth.

In the end, the treaty was disowned by one of its godfathers; a nationalist American administration rejected international control of seabed mining. But the document exists, the product of nearly every nation, and these states, including the United States, appear willing to accept most of its other new rules. Some measure of order has replaced more than thirty years of conflict at sea. These were not mere diplomatic duels. Gunfire and death marked efforts by some nations to drive fishing vessels from waters they asserted were theirs. Beyond this lay threats of far greater dimensions. Neither the Soviet Union nor the United States would permit their great sea and air fleets to be barred from straits that other nations claimed as territorial waters. This raised the specter of a superpower forcing its way through a choke point against the armed opposition of a bordering state.

The Law of the Sea Treaty offers a peaceful solution to these dangerous problems. Although it is flawed, it holds out hope of a somewhat less bellicose world. The unique way in which it evolved, moreover, helps explain the total failure of many other North-South talks.

Like much contemporary economic history, oil was the initiating force. In 1945, President Truman abruptly proclaimed United States sovereignty over the resources of the continental shelf, the underwater floor that extends seaward for about 200 miles from United States coasts and is rich in oil and gas. The President, as usual, was plainspoken. "Aware of the long range worldwide need for new sources of petroleum and other minerals," his proclamation said, "efforts to discover and make available new supplies of these resources should be encouraged." American oil companies could now exploit the deposits, sure that their title was vested in the United States and that the profits would flow to them.[1]

With one stroke, Truman had torn up three centuries of history embodied in the doctrine of freedom of the seas. Since 1609, when Hugo Grotius, a Dutch lawyer, wrote his *Mare Liberum,** nations had followed the principle that all states in peacetime had equal, unfettered access to the seas and their wealth except for a narrow ribbon eventually established as three miles wide. This thin band was the territorial sea over which nations exercised sovereignty as they did on land.

*Like any lawyer, Grotius was working for a client, the Dutch East India Company. The company wanted a rationale to overturn a Papal Bull that had reserved the wealth of the East Indies for Portugal. Grotius supplied it, asserting that the sea is common to all and that "every nation is free to travel to every other nation and engage in trade with it." Quoted in Eric Bain Jones, *Law of the Sea: Oceanic Resources* (Dallas: Southern Methodist University, 1972), p. 9.

Technology overtook Grotius. By 1945, oil companies could bring up petroleum under the sea, at least in the shallow part of the shelf but well beyond the three-mile limit. Under Grotius' doctrine, anyone could exploit this oil, just like the fish outside the territorial sea. That served the interests of neither the American companies nor the Navy. Harold L. Ickes, Truman's Secretary of the Interior, saw the oil's value as a great reserve for the Navy, and he urged the president to issue his proclamation. Neither Ickes nor Truman foresaw they were creating a vast new range of problems, not least for the Navy they were trying to serve.[2]

Other nations with other concerns swiftly followed the American lead. States with coasts adjoining the rich fishing waters of the Eastern Pacific and West Africa became alive to the promise and the threat. They too were impelled by technology. Fishing factories from the Soviet Union and other European countries, modern boats with new equipment, were making huge inroads into their traditional catch. Freedom of the seas must go.

Just a year after the Truman proclamation, the Mexican coast guard seized American shrimp fishermen thirty miles offshore and fined them for invading Mexican waters. So much for the three-mile limit.[3] Ecuador, Peru, Chile, Brazil, and El Salvador all claimed national jurisdiction over a sea of 200 miles. In Africa, Nigeria announced a thirty-mile zone and Sierra Leone 200 miles.[4] The old agreement had collapsed and incidents multiplied. Sometimes there was violence, and patrolling coast guardsmen fired on unarmed fishing ships. An American sailor was wounded in one affair, and seizures became routine.[5] By 1954, twenty American tuna boats had been captured and fined by Peru, Ecuador, Colombia, El Salvador, and Panama, straining relations in the Hemisphere.[6]

Nations everywhere scrambled to enclose fish-laden seas and fought off those asserting traditional rights. Iceland established a fifty-mile zone to protect its cod and other fish, an enterprise accounting for the bulk of its exports. Fishermen from Hull and Grimsby ignored the limit and insisted on plying their historic trade. London sent out armed patrol boats to protect them and frequently exchanged rounds with Icelandic vessels. The cod war was no comic matter for NATO. The United States ran an important base in Iceland at Keflavik; the fight over fish threatened to close it.[7] In time, and acting on Truman's separate and companion proclamation for fish, the United States hauled in Soviet and other European boats in waters off New England. Argentina fired on a Russian ship, and Cuban planes strafed a Bahamian fishing boat as late as 1980. Wars of tuna, lobster, and cod pitted friend against friend, as well as foe; the rule had become each for himself.[8]

The intermittent anarchy at sea posed an acute problem for the great powers and their navies. They seek to assert power throughout the globe and rely on the freedom of their warships to sail the oceans everywhere. A three-mile limit to national sovereignty was well-suited to this strategy. But anything larger could choke off vital passages from one sea to another. Although the newly proclaimed territorial limits of 200 miles were too vast to be taken seriously, a new and more reasonable convention was being established, and it threatened naval power. By the middle sixties, there was growing recognition that the territorial sea should extend twelve miles—this was the limit fixed by the Soviet Union for its coasts—and that raised troublesome questions for admirals and even air marshals. If national sovereignty extends twelve miles, the global map must be altered drastically. Critical sea lanes are cut off, become national waters barred to the unlimited passage of war vessels and planes.[9]

Geographers count 116 choke points or straits less than twenty-four miles wide, some of major strategic importance. They include Gibraltar, the entrance to the Mediterranean; Bab al Mandeb, the Southern entrance to the Red Sea; Hormuz in the Persian Gulf; Makassar, Sunda, and Lombok, passages through the long Indonesian archipelago; and Singapore and Malacca, short routes from the Pacific to the Indian Ocean.[10]

Under a twelve-mile rule, these international straits become territorial waters. In a territorial sea, navies are inhibited by the rule of "innocent passage," a vague doctrine prohibiting actions "prejudicial to the peace, good order, or security of coastal states." This has come to mean that no planes shall fly over them without the consent of the nations in which they lie, and no submarines, whose safety depends on the secrecy of the opaque seas, can pass through them submerged. For great navies, the conversion of open straits to national waters would be an intolerable burden.[11]

The move to a twelve-mile limit and the threatened disappearance of open straits would also mean longer, costlier trips for commercial shipping, particularly the great oil tankers. Nations, fearing a spill would damage their coasts, could invoke "innocent passage" to bar tankers from straits or prohibit the passage of vessels carrying poisonous gases or lethal chemicals.

But above all, it was the Soviet and American admirals and air force generals who fretted over the creeping jurisdiction at sea and the danger of open straits falling under sovereign control. Elliot Richardson, who directed the effort in the Nixon administration to write new sea law, described the Navy's needs. "To fulfill their deterrent and protective missions," he said, "these forces must have the manifest capacity either to maintain a continuing presence in farflung areas of the globe or to bring such a presence to bear rapidly. An essential component of this capacity is true global mobility."[12] His chief was even more emphatic. It is a "fundamental security interest," President Nixon said, to break the choke points created by a twelve-mile limit.[13]

For the Soviet Union the need is even more intense. The United States, after all, has two long coastlines and open waters that wash the shores of its principal allies. But two major Soviet fleets, in the Baltic and the Black Sea, are hemmed in by narrow passages. This fact has led some cruder cold warriors to contend that the two sides have no common interest, that the United States should let the Russians suffer with their geography and keep the straits closed. But such a course is perilous. The Soviets would never accept damaging choke points. If they remained, the Soviet Union would be tempted to fight for control of these waters, waging war that could embroil Europe from north to south.

In the 1960s, there was an added strategic reason for assuring that submarines could travel submerged through straits. The ultimate deterrent, the one nuclear weapon that cannot be destroyed, is the missile fired under the seas by submarines. When these weapons had a range of only 2,500 miles, they could quickly cover the entire Soviet Union only by sailing underwater through straits. With their current range of up to 6,000 miles, this is no longer the case. That is why straits passage is now regarded as essential largely for local conflicts rather than the ultimate, strategic war. In 1972, for example, the United States rushed a warship from the Pacific to the coast of Bangladesh through the Indonesian straits. In fact, the show of force did not, as it was supposed to, deter India from aiding Bangladesh against Pakistan. But the principle remained unimpaired. Open straits are critical chiefly to bring power to bear in conflicts between proxies, not the superpowers themselves.[14]

The Air Force concern over straits is largely linked to supplying allies. In the 1973 Middle East war, a reeling Israel was revived by an Air Force lift of weapons. Britain and other Western allies refused permission to fly over their lands, and the airlift could reach Israel only through the Strait of Gibraltar. Arab nations urged Spain to deny overflight. But Francisco Franco, the Spanish dictator friendly to the United States, looked the other way and the lift flew unimpeded. Unless overflight rights are established in straits, another Spanish government might be less accommodating.[15]

With so much at stake, it was inevitable that the Soviets and Americans would quietly get together. On the Russians' initiative, they met in 1967 and 1968 and fixed a common stance. They agreed that the territorial sea should run twelve miles. Innocent passage through straits, however, must be abandoned; instead there should be a right of unimpeded passage, just like that on the high seas. Overflights by planes would be guaranteed; so would unrestricted travel by warships and submerged passage by submarines. As a lure for agreement from the rest of the world, coastal states would win generous fishing rights off their shores.[16]

The talks cemented a partnership that was to last for the next fourteen years, until the treaty was nearly completed. A striking feature of the sea law negotiations was the sight of American and Soviet admirals, usually in ill-fitting business suits, huddling together in corridors and private conference rooms whenever a sensitive point arose. The cooperation was so close that Washington and Moscow sometimes worked out their joint position even before the United States consulted its allies.

The Soviet-American decision to restore order at sea was one major force for a treaty. The other was a 1967 speech at the U.N. by Arvid Pardo, a Maltese diplomat and lawyer. He electrified the third world by describing the mineral wealth in the oceans. Pardo said:

> Ocean space beyond the limits of national jurisdiction is the common heritage* of mankind. The resources of ocean space, beyond the limits of national jurisdiction, must be explored and exploited with a maximum of international cooperation, for the benefit of all mankind.[17]

He held out the hope of a vast treasure trove for the poor, innocently suggesting that national jurisdiction could be halted at the edge of the territorial sea, twelve miles from shore.

Pardo's eloquence brought an excited response from frustrated Southern diplomats, who saw in the riches of the sea a chance to close the gap between North and South. Like him, they feared that national jurisdiction would spread across the seas, that even their own governments would insist on appropriating much of the "common heritage." All this was for the future. What was now clear was that great powers wanted something, a limited territorial sea and free passage through and above the straits it would encompass. Very well. The great powers must then give something, something that would provide the poor with fish, oil, and those metals in the deep sea. But that was all the third world nations could agree upon. Each nation separately calculated how to assure itself of the maximum oil and fish. Since metal mining was still in an exploratory stage, however, and could yield no one

*Pardo's "common heritage" was the theme of a 1970 resolution of the General Assembly. The document proclaimed that exploitation must take special account of the developing countries. The United States joined in the 108–0 vote for this pious sentiment, regarding it as a cheap price to pay if it would halt the enlarged claims of coastal states. ("Law of the Sea Capsule History," reprint from *The Interdependent,* United Nations Association of the United States. See also Mohamed El-Baradei and Chloe Gavin, *Crowded Agendas, Crowded Rooms,* New York: Unitar, 1981, p. 2.)

anything soon, the third world could and did build their customary common front over a seabed regime.

One thing was clear: All these matters must be linked, all resolved together. The great powers would have preferred a treaty limited to straits, territorial seas, and fish. But on this, the third world was adamant. And it won the day, a comprehensive treaty covering everything from mining to the sovereign waters of archipelagoes, because it had something to trade.

There were preliminary talks, more talks in a U.N. committee, and finally in 1973, a Law of the Sea conference that ran for eight years. One hundred sixty-three nations took part; the affair was larger than the first UNCTAD and far more rooted in matters of substance: oil, fish, and nodules of copper, cobalt, nickel, and manganese.

The nations, rich and poor, scrambled to assert national claims over this wealth in the earliest talks. That broke up the synthetic unity in the third world as a whole and even within regions. Early on, the nations adopted what might be called the Truman principle: What lies off my coast is mine; what lies off yours is yours. Even before the Law of the Sea conference officially opened, the coastal states had staked out their claims to separate Exclusive Economic Zones stretching 200 miles from their shores. All the fish and any resources on or in the seabed below, metal and oil, would become the sole property of the proprietor of each zone.

This was splendid for states with long coastlines: the United States, Soviet Union, Canada, Australia, New Zealand, Argentina, Chile, Peru, Brazil, Mexico, Norway, Nigeria, Venezuela, Tanzania, Kenya, Indonesia, and India. It was disastrous for about thirty states with no coast at all, the landlocked, who include some of the world's poorest countries: Bolivia, Mali, Niger, Chad, the Central African Republic, Nepal, and Afghanistan. It damaged another twenty with short coastlines (Guinea-Bissau and East Germany), on inland seas (West Germany and Singapore), and those who could not reach the open sea without crossing another nation's watery preserve (Poland and Belgium). It would also cramp Polish, Japanese, Soviet, and American tuna boats who fish far from home in what would become the waters of another nation. But Poland is kept on a short leash in the bloc, and Russia, the United States, and Japan had other, larger strategic interests to consider. So the distant-water fishing fleets swallowed their complaints.

Landlocked Bolivia and Paraguay protested this split of the spoils. That divided the Latin bloc, just as the landbound in Asia and Africa spoiled any common front in their regions and within the Group of 77 as a whole. The inland states were fobbed off with vague promises of winning access to the sea, of somehow sharing in the resources of the newly enclosed ocean space. These vague promises were faithfully translated into equally vague provisions in the treaty that finally emerged.

The diplomats made a ritual bow toward conserving fish. The proprietors of each zone should catch only "the maximum sustainable yield," a volume no larger than that required to preserve each species.[18] But this too is general enough to give any proprietor an open license. If a proprietor nation catches less than the limit, it is enjoined to let its landlocked brethren take part of the catch—always providing that the landlocked can find some way to get to the sea.

The agreement on the 200-mile economic zone, embodied in the treaty of 1982, is sweeping. It covers 40 percent of the seas, the richest 40 percent. It embraces about 90 percent of the fish and up to 95 percent of the offshore oil. It adds 2.2 million square miles to the United States, 1.4 million to Canada, 1.3 million to the Soviet Union, 1.1 million to Japan, 600,000 to Norway, and 300,000 to Britain. Most importantly, about a dozen developing countries with long coasts led the fight, enlisted allies among the rich, and made the resources zone new law. In the Pacific, the 200-mile zone led to some bizarre results. The Pitcairn Islands with a population of sixty acquired a maritime area several times the size of West Germany, population 60 million. Kiribati, a speck in the sea, was awarded a larger area than China. But the clear winners were the rich. The United States, Australia, New Zealand, Canada, Japan, Norway and the Soviet Union, with 15 percent of the world's population, gained 44 percent of the new monopoly resource regions.[19]

The zone's proponents had rarely found common ground in

the loftier reaches of the North-South debate. Here, some extremely odd alliances formed: the United States again with the Soviet Union; Tanzania and India with Canada and Australia. Self-interest over the particular had mended fences broken by grander disputes.

In return for their amiable assent to the resources zone demanded by third world coastal states, the United States and Soviet navies (as well as those of Britain and France) could now win the unimpeded passage through straits they had so eagerly sought. But the new resources zone threw up a fresh problem; it must not create a new barrier for the great fleets. The treaty accommodates them. They can fly over, sail through, or under the 200-mile zone, just as if they were on the high seas.[20]

The division of the seas into monopoly resource zones of 200 miles was matched by the generous award to archipelagoes. Indonesia is an archipelago with several straits, and its bargaining power was impressive. Thanks to their peculiar geography, Indonesia and other archipelagoes won the right to enclose the waters around all their islands as if they were a solid land mass. With 1,300 islands, Indonesia added 2.2 million square miles to its internal waters, an area equal to the United States zone.[21] This, however, gave the navies another concern, assuring navigation through what had become the "inland waters" of archipelagoes. The diplomats promptly invented "archipelagic sea lanes" to provide a high seas passage and allay any naval anxieties.[22]

Once the resources zone and the archipelagic waters had been agreed, the rest was reasonably smooth sailing for the admirals. Cyprus, Greece, Yemen, Spain, and some others resisted the proposed arrangements for straits, but they were overwhelmed.

By the time the 1973 conference formally opened, sixty-nine countries had claimed territorial seas of twelve to 200 miles.[23] Thanks to the monopoly resources zone, the twelve-mile limit was enshrined in the new law. The sovereignty of nations over straits less than twenty-four miles wide was solemnly proclaimed; it was promptly shattered by the new right of "transit passage" that assured unfettered travel for vessels and overflight for planes. The admirals and air marshals, despite an inconspicuous public role, had secured through the negotiating diplomats the objective that had brought the Soviets to Washington in 1967. (In the past, it had been suggested that the United States should avoid a treaty and rely on friendly regimes for passage: Spain and Morocco through Gibraltar, the Shah of Iran through Hormuz, and the generals currently in charge of Indonesia. Unhappily, regimes and friends are fickle, and their perpetual existence cannot be guaranteed.)

To be sure, even without a treaty, no force can resist either the Soviet or American fleets. In a crisis, both would damn the torpedoes and push through any choke point. But this sort of behavior carries a political price: more or less universal condemnation. It is much more agreeable to have the right of unimpeded passage spelled out and then use force if necessary. Colonel Qaddafi discovered as much in 1981 when he sent up two planes to challenge the U.S. Sixth Fleet well beyond the twelve-mile zone. Qaddafi lost his planes and won no sympathy in the world.[24] (Libya later won considerable global support when its towns were bombed by the United States but no sea law issue was involved.)

The division of the seas did not stop with the creation of the 200-mile resource zones. Oil demanded more. Most of the offshore oil, perhaps 90 to 95 percent, lies in the continental shelf, a terrace sloping gently underwater from the shore to a depth of about 600 feet and extending out up to 200 miles and sometimes beyond. This was the rich region Truman took, and all coastal nations were ultimately awarded their shelves under the treaty's monopoly resource zone. By the late 1960s, however, oil technology had advanced beyond the possibilities of Truman's era. Oil could be extracted at depths greater than 600 feet. The companies pressed for national sovereignty over the seabed beyond the shelf, to the last 5 to 10 percent of the known oil.

At the end of the shelf, the sea floor falls off sharply and becomes the continental slope. Then it declines slowly as sediment builds up from the seabed floor. This last segment is called the continental rise and marks the end of the underwater geological mass of the continent. Together, the shelf, slope, and rise make up the continental margin. Both the slope and rise contain oil—far less than the shelf, but still a prize worth having. Since total recoverable offshore oil is estimated at 2.7 trillion barrels, even 5 percent comes to 130 billion barrels or about $2,500 billion at the 1985 price of oil.[25]

The major companies were eager for this prize. They pressed for still another exclusive zone, one that would grant each nation monopoly exploitation of the resources in the continental margin, the entire formation of shelf, slope, and rise.

The oil majors were asking for a lot. In some places, the margin reaches as far as 1,000 miles from shore. But any other solution except sovereign national rights was distasteful not only to the companies but every nation with a large continental margin.[26] Pardo's "common heritage" suggested that some U.N.-type of international regime should produce the oil beyond the shelf. The oil companies, with OPEC nations as an example, calculated they could make profitable deals far more easily with individual states than with some international agency guided by a "common heritage" principle. Moreover, the United States itself possesses a substantial continental margin. It would be a pity to lose the oil in the slope and rise to some global body. Every nation with a wide continental margin supported the companies' view. Argentina, Australia, Brazil, Canada, India, Japan, Mexico, New Zealand, Norway, Britain, the United States, and the Soviet Union all in time saw the logic of exploiting what nature seemed to offer them.

One scholar, R. P. Anand, counted only twenty-eight states with wide continental margins. In contrast, there are sixty-two with narrow margins and another sixty suffering from no coasts or blocked ones. International exploitation would have benefited 122 countries.[27] But matters of substance were at stake, and one nation, one vote is typically reserved for more abstract issues. So the twenty-eight with wide margins carried the day and won through the treaty a qualified right to monopoly control of the oil in the margin. The outcome might be described as the Truman corollary: He who has gets.

The twenty-eight, moreover, erased traditional bloc lines, North and South, East and West. Once again, an unlikely coalition had formed, this time for the sake of oil. Some of the developing countries, notably India, had first argued that the resources should be exploited for the poor generally. But national interest and a large margin in the Bay of Bengal convinced New Delhi, a leader in the Group of 77, that charity begins at home.

The biggest obstacle to the oil companies' ambition was the U.S. Defense Department. The Navy worried about enlarging national sovereignty tens and even hundreds of miles beyond the continental shelf. Its high seas freedom was guaranteed, but the best of guarantees can be rewritten or ignored. The admirals waged a brisk bureaucratic fight to limit national control over oil and gas to a depth of 200 meters, perhaps 150 to 180 miles out.

But the five major oil companies—Exxon, Mobil, Texaco, Gulf, and Standard Oil of California—and their surrogates, the American Petroleum Institute and the National Petroleum Council, were too strong for the Pentagon. The oil industry was "the most powerful private interest in the seabed debate" in Washington, according to Ann L. Hollick, a keen-eyed academic analyst of the proceedings.[28] Oil's seaward push was strengthened by the OPEC price increase and endorsed by the Nixon administration, and the nations with continental margins won exclusive rights over the oil. The treaty did make some concessions, however, to the less endowed. Nations and companies could not extract oil more than 350 miles from the coasts. Beyond that, a U.N.-type agency could have what was left. Moreover, all the oil and gas taken beyond 200 miles was subject to a royalty or tax that would reach 7 percent after eleven years. This money would be distributed by an international agency to the less fortunate, a useful device to buy off their opposition to the rapid disappearance of the "common heritage." The payments are also a vestige of the fading belief that resources beyond territorial waters are the property of all.

The conviction that at least some of the sea's resources are common property never died completely, however. There was still a large area of the oceans that had not been allocated to anyone, the deep seas beyond the territorial waters, beyond the monopoly resources zone, and beyond the continental margin. They belonged to no one, and so, the third world argued, their resources belonged to all. As it happens, there are metals in the deep seas, nodules of manganese oxide, some as big as a basketball and others the size of a grain of sand. Since the 1960s, Western mining companies had been exploring the largest belt in the Northern Pacific, developing techniques to scoop up these nodules from the ocean floor.[29] Their volume is enormous, 1.6 trillion tons, according to one estimate. They contain about 1.5 percent nickel, 1 percent copper, 0.25 percent cobalt, and about 30 percent manganese.[30] Their worth, however, is unclear. All are in abundant supply on the mainland. The U.S. Geological Survey calculated in 1977 that domestic supplies in the United States alone would last for twenty-five years.[31] In the early 1980s, moreover, the prices of all these metals were sinking for lack of demand. To bring up the enormous supply on the seabed might almost make the metals a free good.

But the nodules glistened like an El Dorado for the South, which saw at last the first building block in its New Order. For opposite reasons, the nodules aroused the West, particularly the Reagan administration, which determined that seabed mining shall not yield to international socialism. The nodules re-formed the blocs that had been shattered by practical questions of oil, fish, and navies. Mining became the one exclusively North-South question at the Law of the Sea conferences. It is still unresolved and could yet sink the elaborate set of rules agreed upon for navigating and exploiting the rest of the oceans.

National self-interest, pursued so scrupulously in other parts of the treaty, was dumped overboard in the ideological scramble over mining. Few nations produce nickel, copper, and cobalt. (The manganese in the nodules is so plentiful that most is likely to be thrown away.) Most nations consume them. But the third world insisted that production from the seabed—improbable before the year 2000, if then—should be cartelized to protect the earnings of the handful of producers on land. This control, moreover, shall be in the hands of a U.N.-type agency dominated by the South. The overwhelming majority of Southern states said, in effect, we will pay higher prices for metal we must import to establish the principle of a commodity cartel under an international regime. For the most part, the South wrote the treaty sections governing mining as a model for the stalled New International Economic Order. A sympathetic commentator, Elizabeth Mann Borgese, wrote: "The principle of the common heritage, first applied to the resources of the seabed beyond the limits of national jurisdiction . . . could become the foundations of a new economic order."[32] It was just this that inspired Reagan to refuse to sign the treaty and raise even greater doubts whether the metals will ever be extracted.

The third world, invoking Pardo's "common heritage," relied on the common sense principle that resources at the bottom of the high seas belonged to no one and therefore must be exploited for the benefit of all. Among Western governments, at least, there was little quarrel with the principle although much disagreement over practice. From the Nixon through the Carter administrations, it was taken for granted that some form of international supervision would govern nodules mining.*[33]

On this edifice, the third world built an elaborate bureaucratic structure into the treaty. There would be an International Seabed Authority with a one-nation, one-vote Assembly to lay down general policy. There would also be a Council, the real rule-making body, with thirty-six members carefully balanced among rich and poor, East and West, and geographical regions. Whether or not this gave the United States and its allies a blocking veto over critical questions has touched off a debate that will not be settled until and if the Council ever meets.

Other commissions and the inevitable secretariat were established. Above all, there is the Enterprise, an arm of the Authority that is supposed to mine the seabed, just like Lockheed, U.S. Steel, Kennecott, Royal Dutch Shell, and the other large concerns already exploring in the Pacific. Unlike the private companies, the earnings of the Enterprise would be distributed largely to the third world. There are even elaborate provisions for the

*The countervailing legal theory for the Reagan administration was produced in two volumes by Theodore G. Kronmiller, a deputy assistant secretary of state for oceans and fisheries. Relying on Grotius, he argued that what belongs to no one becomes the property of him who takes it. "Thus, under international law, it is permissible for a State or private enterprise unilaterally to appropriate the resources of the seabed and subsoil beyond the limits of national jurisdiction," Kronmiller wrote. Theodore C. Kronmiller, *The Lawfulness of Deep Seabed Mining* (London: Oceana Publications, 1980), p. 521.

Enterprise to hire private firms, and precise rules for how much these subcontractors shall be paid. "The amount of detailed regulation being developed for an industry that is yet unproved and basically unknown is staggering," said Thomas A. Clingan, Jr., a sometime member of the United States delegation and a professor at Florida Law School.[34]

Third world radicals like Algeria pressed for a seabed monopoly by the Authority. No private firms, particularly the Western multinationals already at sea, would be entitled to anything. They could serve as Enterprise contractors; they must divulge their technical know-how to the Authority. That was enough. The North vigorously fought this all-and-nothing approach. Indeed, the eight-year conference spent more time on the economically minor issue of mining seabed metals than any other subject.

It was the United States and Secretary of State Henry Kissinger who, in 1976, suggested a compromise to reserve some ocean space for the private concerns. Kissinger proposed that each private miner should select an area twice the size of a potential minesite, about 150,000 square kilometers. The Authority would then choose half for itself and the Enterprise; the other half would stay in private hands but must be exploited under Authority rules. As a further inducement, the private concerns would agree to sell their know-how to the Enterprise.[35] So the radicals were turned back, and this parallel system was written into the treaty.

Perhaps the most troubling section of the treaty embodies the third world dream of controlling if not raising commodity prices. The document's third world architects professed concern for the copper in Chile, Zambia, Zaire, Peru, and the Philippines, the nickel of Cuba and Indonesia, and the cobalt of Zaire and Zambia. If the seabed nodules were mined without limit, it was thought, these developing countries must suffer lower prices and lower export earnings, the usual fate of the third world. Under international control, so unhappy an outcome will be prevented, and the world will gain a model for all the other raw materials produced in the South.[36]

Another set of elaborate provisions was written into the document, strictly controlling for twenty years how much can be brought up. The limit is tied to a predicted demand for nickel at current prices. A complex formula was developed to assure that the miners, private and international, would produce no more than 60 percent of the increase in nickel demand in any year. Canada, urged on by its International Nickel Company, the world's largest exporter, thought this was splendid and joined the third world as a delegate to the West for production curbs.[37] The American mining companies, aghast at any international control over their deep sea ventures, were strenuously opposed. "Multinational corporations [have the] ability to plan and execute national market entry without spoiling markets," Richard G. Darman observed.[38] Darman, later a central White House figure in the Reagan decision not to sign the treaty, meant that Kennecott and other United States copper producers are far more skilled at restraining production to hold up prices than any fledgling international organization.

Nevertheless, the production curb became part of the Treaty. Just how higher prices for copper wire or steel alloys could benefit the impoverished of the third world, to say nothing of consumers in rich countries, was not discussed. Compromises were possible over a mining area for multinationals; none was admissible for commodity prices. V. K. S. Vardaman, director general of India's geological survey, expressed the third world's view. "Unregulated prices and production can spell disaster in the short run to some of the land-based producers," he wrote, "and we must take necessary steps to avoid such a catastrophe."[39]

In fact, the principal beneficiaries of attempts to prop the price of nickel, the most valuable constituent of the nodules, are Canada, the Soviet Union, French New Caledonia, and Australia, not the third world. Indeed, Australia joined Canada and the Group of 77 to battle for the mining provisions, a breach in the unity of industrial nations.[40] Once again, specific self-interest cracked traditional blocs. But the decision of the treaty makers had less to do with economics and more with philosophy. On paper, the third world had now constructed an international agency that could generate its own income, govern the behavior of multinational corporations, control production to prop up prices, and compel the transfer of Western technology. The New Order lives, at least in the words of the treaty's mining provisions.

Nature and geography, however, have played a cruel trick on the great hopes that the third world has invested in the nodules. Even larger and richer metal deposits have been found under the seas and outside the jurisdiction of the treaty's Seabed Authority. These are the polymetallic sulfides, strong in copper and iron, containing lead, molybdenum, zinc, silver, tin, and traces of gold and platinum. The Commerce Department valued one Pacific find alone at $3 trillion, although the figure made no allowance for what might happen to prices if this treasure reaches the market. An area of hot brine in the Red Sea is estimated to contain enough zinc, copper, lead, silver, and gold to make a pool of only ten square meters worth $2 billion. Under the Treaty's exclusive economic zone, Saudi Arabia and the Sudan, not the Authority, will exploit this lode. The metal-rich sulfides have also been detected in the monopoly zones of Chile and Mexico, and more deposits may lie off Hawaii. Unlike the nodules, there is no known technology to recover polymetallic sulfides. But if the Authority succeeds in supporting or increasing metal prices, it will provide an incentive to insure its own undoing, much as OPEC has done.[41]

The Authority's greatest problem, however, is the complex of private mining companies who have been discovering how to scoop or suck up nodules from the seabed. The most aggressive are the American firms: Lockheed, U.S. Steel, and Kennecott. Their partners from Belgium, Holland, Britain, West Germany, and Italy support the cause of uncurbed mining at sea with varying degrees of enthusiasm. Unsurprisingly, the companies want a free hand to reap whatever profits lie in the nodules, restrain production to prop up prices through their internal decisions, and safeguard their technical know-how from any international authority. The American firms in the groups or consortia mining the sea provided most of the arguments that persuaded Reagan against signing the Treaty.

The private mining companies claim to be particularly irked by the treaty's provisions for the transfer of technology. Neither the Authority nor its Enterprise know how to mine the sea; the companies do. So the third world's treaty drafters inserted provisions requiring the private concerns to sell to the Enterprise at "fair and reasonable prices" their technical knowledge.[42] Unless they agreed, the companies would not get a license from the Authority. From the Authority's standpoint, the provision is a practical solution. Moreover, it embodies the New Order belief that possession of Western industrial secrets is a key to the modernization of the third world. For the companies, this is another red flag, the surrender of hard-won experience on which profits are based. In fact, according to several studies, there are neither secrets nor equipment in seabed mining that can't be bought in the open market.[43] But the technology issue has acquired an emotion-charged life of its own in both camps.

Oddly enough, the miners have gained the great oil companies as allies in their fight against the treaty. This seems peculiar since the oil firms are assured of national control to the edge of the continental margin, as far out as any oil is known to exist. But the companies are prudent. What if oil can be found and recovered in the deep seas beyond the treaty's award of national jurisdiction? This oil would be assigned to the international Authority; the companies prefer dealing with states. A political consideration was also involved. The companies unleashed their trade associations to attack the mining provisions because international control of mineral resources could set a dangerous precedent. Nations someday might want to erect a similar system for offshore oil.

The combination of mining and oil, with their supporters on Capitol Hill and inside the Interior Department, proved irresistible for the Reagan administration. The president said he was satisfied with everything else in the treaty; the mining sections, however, would not do.[44]

In a last bid to win United States support, the third world wrote in a special section protecting the interests of the "pioneer investors," the eight consortia already at sea—French, Japanese, Soviet, and Indian groups plus four led by or including American firms.[45] But even this was not enough for the miners or the White House. At the close of the Law of the Sea conference in April 1982, the United States (with Turkey, Israel, and Venezuela) voted against the treaty. One hundred thirty nations approved it, and seventeen abstained, including technically advanced miners like Britain, West Germany, and the Netherlands, as well as the Soviet Union and some of its allies. Typically, the Soviet Union will not bind itself to a global treaty that does not equally constrain the United States.*[46]

In the closing weeks of the conference, Reagan described the United States objections. He could not accept provisions that did not assure future private miners access to the seabed, that compelled firms to yield their technology, enabled the treaty to be amended in twenty years without Senate approval, placed curbs on output, and did not guarantee the United States a stronger voice in the Authority's decision-making. He also objected to clauses providing Authority funds for "liberation movements," which he feared might go to the Palestine Liberation Organization. (His worry on this score was groundless. The United States had been assured a veto in the Council over any such largess.)[47] Above all, the president complained that the treaty would set an undesirable precedent.[48]

This last was the crucial point. The administration knew, as the third world knew, that the mining provisions were a trial run for the New Order. Control of markets by private firms was one thing; control by some international agency violated the creed of good conservatives everywhere. Reagan would not launch a New Order at sea that might someday creep ashore.

But what of all the provisions that Reagan approved—the twelve-mile territorial sea, the 200-mile monopoly zone for fish, the 350-mile monopoly shelf for oil, and, above all, the freedom for the Navy and Air Force to cross strategic straits and regions reserved for national economic exploitation? Were these to be thrown away because of the miners and a faith in markets domi-

*A sterner test of intentions came a few months later when the treaty lay open for signature. By the end of 1984, 155 nations had signed, including the Netherlands, who had abstained in April, and such mining states as Japan and France. This was not the last hurdle, however. A nation must ratify its signature, usually through the approval of a legislature. Only then is it bound. Sixty ratifications are needed to bring the Treaty into force, but only fourteen had been delivered at the start of 1985. The United States refusal was clearly discouraging others. *Ocean Policy News* (Washington, D.C.: Citizens for Ocean Law, December 1984), p. 1.

nated by large corporations? Certainly not. All this, the administration claimed, had now become "customary law" because all nations had subscribed to it.[49] The United States, in effect, argued that it can enjoy everything it likes under the treaty while rejecting the treaty itself.

This position created a field day for lawyers. Legal journals across the country debated the nature of "customary law," the rights of treaty signers, the legality of going it alone in the seabed. A layman might agree with Leslie M. McCrae, in the *California Western International Law Journal*, that custom involves the clear, continuous habit of doing something believed obligatory or right, that it rests on a practice uninterrupted for years.[50] Again, duration, uniformity, general application, and the perception of obligation are the elements of customary law, at least according to George B. Pierce in the *Virginia Journal of International Law*. How can novel matters be transformed into custom? Under that simple rubric, everything of consequence in the Treaty is novel, from unimpeded passage through straits to a national shelf of 350 miles for oil.[51]

Lawyers, like Humpty Dumpty, are capable of investing words with the meaning they want. At least in the United States, a large number accepted the administration's view. The American Law Institute Restatement of the Foreign Relations Law concluded that the Treaty codifies customary law—except, of course, for the disputed mining sections.[52] The prolonged negotiations, the agreements by consensus rather than formal vote, had transmuted innovation into custom. The third world had insisted that all agreements were provisional, that only a package deal was acceptable. But this was inconvenient, and so it was ignored.

For at least the first few years after the United States refusal to sign, no one tried to put up an oil platform on another nation's shelf, and no fishing boats were seized inside a 200-mile zone (although an Irish patrol boat sank a Spanish trawler in 1984).[53] Nor was any Soviet or American submarine traveling submerged through Gibraltar forced to the surface. The nonmining provisions were observed. There was no will to challenge the treaty, despite its ambiguous state. But if American planes fly over Hormuz, will Khomeini's Iran accept the American Law Institute's view of their rights? What if the wheel turns again in Indonesia, and a violently anti-American regime takes power. Will Lombok and Sunda still be open? For Darman, who as White House assistant shaped the American rejection, these are unreal questions. As early as 1978, he urged scrapping the treaty draft and said that, if necessary, the United States could simply force its way through a previously open passage.[54] But the whole point of the negotiations were to avoid such costly incidents, incidents that threaten not only American lives but also American standing as a civilized, law-abiding nation.

The Reagan administration was also facing problems with its plans to mine the sea through private enterprise. As a practical matter, it needed at least a treaty with other advanced nations, especially West Germany, France, and Britain, under which each would recognize the claims staked out by the others. In two agreements after the Law of the Sea conference, the United States persuaded other industrial nations to move toward Washington's goal.[55] But some, notably the French, are reluctant to go further. They are unwilling to jeopardize the treaty's concession to pioneer miners, an assured site and production rights for more than thirty years. This is attractive bait, something courts would recognize as legal. To follow the United States route to its conclusion, to set up an independent mining regime, would deprive the advanced countries of their pioneer sites; the treaty denies its awards to nations making pacts with nonsigners.

A treaty of industrial powers, moreover, may sound attractive, may give the appearance of assured titles to its members. But in fact such an agreement is incomplete. The Soviet Union is capable of mining. India may be soon and Brazil tomorrow. They would not be bound by any United States pact, and nothing could prevent them from encroaching on the claims. The industrial nations might recognize each other's space, but no one else need do so.

The investment in a minesite is conventionally put at $1.5 billion.[56] Only the most reckless banker would put that kind of money into a venture that rests on a legally questionable title. If negotiation and agreement turned the novel notion of unimpeded straits passage into customary law, can the mining provisions of the treaty be regarded differently because one great power has rejected them?

The question of finance much agitated the congressmen who supported the American mining firms. They were not soothed by a General Accounting Office report in 1982 that said:

> The principal financial institutions that underwrite seabed mining ventures told us they would not finance further technological development of actual mining operations . . . without a satisfactory Law of the Sea Treaty, and that they did not consider the reciprocating states agreement [one of the U.S. accords] as a viable alternative.[57]

A Kennecott Copper official testified that his company would supply the needed funds from its own resources—provided that the United States guaranteed the company's title. The very firms who rejected the treaty in the name of free enterprise can now be expected to press for public insurance of future seabed investment.[58]

The real point, of course, is that nobody—except perhaps consumers—really wants to bring up the nodules, not at least as long as metal prices are low. Instead, the miners talk vaguely about possible commercial production in the next century. Cartel-minded third world nations are equally reluctant and for the same reason. This is King Midas in reverse. To touch those metals is to turn them into dross.

If some day there is a profitable demand, it is not likely that the United States or its partners will go it alone. The risk of sinking billions of dollars on a disputed title is too great. If the United States still has not signed the treaty, its mining firms will simply seek French, Dutch, or some other parentage from a signing nation and fly a foreign flag.

The struggle over mining rights has much of the unreal flavor that characterizes so many North-South talks, evoking intense passion over an object that cannot be realized in this century, perhaps never. The treaty, however, will have some very direct and often baleful consequences for the here and now. It offers little or nothing to the largely impoverished citizens of nations with no seacoast, landlocked Uganda, Chad, Afghanistan, Paraguay, and some twenty-five others. It provides only uncertain protection for millions of tourists who might have expected a strict regime to control pollution on beaches. It frustrates marine scientists who had hoped to explore freely all the waters beyond the narrow territorial sea.

The landlocked need, above all, to reach the sea, a guaranteed right of passage through their more fortunate coastal neighbors. Once afloat, the landlocked need a promise to share in the fishing of their neighbors' monopoly zones. Having nothing to trade, the landlocked got nothing. To cross a neighbor's land, the treaty directs them to reach an agreement with a coastal state, an agreement that can be spurned if the neighbor believes its undefined interests are harmed. Moreover, if this high hurdle is overcome, the landlocked may catch only those fish unwanted by the coastal state, provided that this unwanted portion does not exceed the coastal state's definition of a catch that will imperil a species' ability to reproduce itself.

Ibrahim J. Wani, a Ugandan delegate, eloquently summed up the prospects for Rwanda, Burundi, Mali, and the other landlocked. We were, he said, betrayed by our fellow developing countries.[59] Since coastal states determine whether or not passage harms their interest, "the freedom of transit seems devoid of meaning."[60] Even if transit is granted, the landlocked can still be barred from fishing. They may share in the earnings of oil found beyond the monopoly resources zone, but most oil lies inside it. Wani said:

> The zone is primarily for the coastal state. In this respect, the convention completely forsakes the common interests of understanding, cooperation, and equitable economic order that takes into account the needs and interests of mankind as a whole.[61]

At least, said Wani, any revenues generated by the Enterprise, the mining arm of the international regime, might have gone to the poorest. Instead, they will be carved up among all developing countries. But no matter, said the realistic Wani. It is not clear that the Enterprise will ever yield revenues; it can't compete with the consortia of multinational firms. The bleak fact, he concluded, is that the landlocked are reduced to a "humiliating dependence on aid."[62]

Despite this indictment, Wani and Uganda support the treaty. At the very least, it constitutes the first formal recognition that there is a class of markedly disadvantaged states. Perhaps, he said, negotiations between the landlocked and their geographically more fortunate neighbors will someday yield something.

Environmentalists, worried about dumping at sea, oil spills, or sewage pouring into the oceans, did somewhat better. The United States and France, with support from Bulgaria, Australia, West Germany, Tunisia, the Netherlands, and New Zealand, urged strong powers for coastal states, largely to regulate tankers. But other states with tanker fleets firmly resisted. This crusade against regulation linked such strange brothers as Algeria and Israel, India and Pakistan, Tanzania and Liberia. Chile, Colombia, Brazil, Turkey, Singapore, Nigeria, and the United Arab Emirates joined them. Even the deepest political conflicts within the Group of 77—Israel is always and Chile sometimes a pariah —were submerged by the threat of economic handicap.

In the end, the quarrel was resolved with a compromise. Pollution from a nation's shores, the biggest source, is largely uncontrolled. Coastal states are piously enjoined to write appropriate rules conforming to uncertain international standards. Pollution at sea is treated somewhat more stringently. The treaty directs states to hold a conference that will write international rules, and such a gathering had been at work. The pact, moreover, gives coastal nations limited powers to investigate and even to seize ships suspected of polluting. Thus, a nation dumping sewage and chemicals from land into the waters is left largely unrestrained. But a modest start has been made on a code to curb tankers and others polluting at sea.[63]

"The brutal truth is that most delegations . . . are unconcerned with the quality of the marine environment except in the negative sense that they wish to be sure protective measures will not inhibit their economic development." This judgment came from James L. Johnston, a U.S. Treasury representative at the sea law conference.[64] Most third world nations regard environmental curbs either as a luxury only rich nations can afford or a trick by rich nations to stunt the growth of the poor. Jamaica's foreign minister, Allan Kinton, frankly urged a double standard, one excluding developing nations from pollution controls. "The ability of the sea to absorb pollution is regarded as an important resource," he said. This view may yet haunt his nation, so heavily dependent on its beaches for foreign exchange.[65]

Seagoing scientists fared as poorly. Their objective was a clause promising the maximum freedom of movement for their vessels beyond the twelve-mile limit. They were all but pushed 200 miles further out to sea, practically deprived of any rights in the Exclusive Economic Zone. This area, said David Ross, director of marine policy and the ocean management program at the Woods Hole Oceanographic Institution, is "the most scientifically and economically interesting part of the ocean."[66] The treaty commands scientists to ask every coastal state for permission to bring their ships inside the zone. The coastal state can reject the request if the mission touches on resources in the region, a loophole large enough to bar virtually all seagoing scientific expeditions.

The plain fact is that third world states do not like seagoing scientists. They suspect that the missions are secretly engaged in spying or some other military purpose. Since 50 percent of all marine research in the United States is paid by the Defense Department, there is some substance to this suspicion.[67] Above all, developing countries fear that the research will somehow deprive them of resources. They are unimpressed by arguments that the study of ocean currents will lead to better forecasting of monsoons or that an examination of currents off the Pacific coast of South America will help disclose why Peru's rich fishery suddenly shrinks.

"I know no one in the United States oceanographic community who is happy about the present state of negotiations on marine scientific research," said John A. Knauss, provost for Marine Affairs at Rhode Island University.[68] But unfortunate as the treaty may be, David Ross of Woods Hole, like Wani of Uganda, argued that it should be adopted. Some countries have even more restrictive legislation, he said, and at least the convention promises uniform treatment.[69]

Taken as a whole, the Law of the Sea Treaty falls far short of a model of justice, and offers neither the promise of a better qualitative life nor a rational exploitation of ocean wealth. Its expansion of national boundaries on and below the sea, its division of oil and fish, provide a bonanza for wealthy and near-wealthy nations with large coastlines. "Far from promoting this objective [to narrow the gap between rich and poor], the new Law of the Sea Treaty is likely to widen the gap between the rich North and the poor South," said Tommy T. B. Koh of Singapore, who presided over the final conference and is one of the treaty's sturdiest advocates.[70] It is even possible that the treaty will provoke rather than minimize disputes. There may be fierce struggles over uninhabited atolls or even rocks if they lie in a region rich in minerals or fish. Harsh quarrels over fixing boundary lines for resource zones could break out between neighboring coastal states. The treaty creates machinery to settle disputes; it is feeble. Any nation engaged in a quarrel of consequence can escape a binding judgment and choose to settle through "conciliation." This is merely guided negotiations. In effect, no arbitrator or court can impose on a sovereign nation without its consent. Ann Hollick has forecast that "the inability to agree on strong provisions for the settlement of disputes will result in a high level of friction in the oceans and the sporadic resort to military force."[71]

Indeed, the treaty is so defective that it has been almost disowned by its intellectual godfather, Arvid Pardo:

> An understanding of contemporary principles of equity is not visible in the present negotiating text. . . . Coastal states will appropriate not less than one-third of ocean space together with 90 percent of presently exploited fish stocks, all known commercially exploitable hydrocarbon resources and even a substantial portion of commercially exploitable manganese nodules of the abyss; the greater part of these resources will be appropriated by less than two dozen states. . . .[72]

Again Pardo warned:

> Even the partial division of ocean space now contemplated will . . . enormously increase present inequalities between states and consequently will give rise to acute tensions and conflicts which will not be easy to resolve.[73]

Nevertheless, he declined to toss the treaty overboard. Although the convention is "fundamentally flawed," Pardo concluded, it must be accepted "to maintain some semblance of a global law of the sea" and to introduce the principle of common heritage.[74]

From both a global and an American standpoint, his judgment is sound. The treaty, for all its sins of omission and commission, does provide a framework for order on, above, and below the seas. It creates international rules to replace those torn up by Truman in 1945. The rules, however inequitable and incomplete, were written after hard bargaining by negotiators representing 163 states.

The treaty assures superpower navies a freedom they might otherwise feel compelled to take at gunpoint. A second Arab attempt to close Gibraltar and halt an airlift to Israel is less likely because of the treaty. A United States administration, tempted to seal off Nicaragua's access to the Gulf of Fonseca, must consider whether it will undermine the global agreement on territorial waters. The convention provides no simple solution to the Greek-Turkish quarrel over oil in the Aegean; it does offer guidelines for what could be a peaceful settlement.

The treaty may end decades of disputes over fish that were sometimes accompanied by the crackle of gunfire and poisoned relations between friends and allies. Peru might still challenge American tuna boats 250 miles at sea, and the Soviet fleet may attempt to poach in New England waters. But a code has been established that is likely to serve as a restraint.

The treatment of scientists, the landlocked, and the marine environment is sadly inadequate. But those whose interests have been directly damaged still support the treaty as a first step toward recognizing that the problems exist. There is no assurance that amendment will cure the defects, but there is provision for amendment, for orderly change, and a happier outcome is possible.

If the peculiar mining section pays tribute to the principle of consumers-be-damned, there is no need to fear that this is a precedent, that it will weaken Western resolve to oppose similar schemes on land. The nodules are unique. In time, the sheer volume of seabed minerals is likely to overwhelm any cartel and bring down prices after all. Economic forces, new discoveries, a glut on land, will curb the ambitions of the international Authority.

The United States administration after Reagan should sign the treaty and undertake the hard fight for Senate ratification. It may be argued that no law is better than bad law. But the treaty's strengths far outweigh its weaknesses. The economic zone, for example, is defective because it gives too much to too few and excludes too many altogether. However, the notion of a defined resources zone, like the definition of territorial waters, is useful because it provides an orderly means to settle conflicts. No matter how thin the provisions for the marine environment and marine scientists, they are an incremental gain over the separate determination of these matters by every flag. The unhampered passage of submarines and planes is a common sense recognition of the reality of power. Less can be said for the mining sections, although there is merit in the concept that what belongs to no one shall belong to all.

The treaty, for all its defects, represents order and law, principles to resolve disputes, and rudimentary machinery to solve them peacefully. It replaces a world in which law at sea was what each state said it was. That was no law at all. Treaties, like domestic law, are broken; domestic law, nevertheless, is rightly regarded as a touchstone of civilization, a curb on the behavior of the vast majority. The world is better off with the treaty, no matter how imperfect, than with the unrestrained appetites of nations.

There is something peculiarly outrageous in the United States position. The treaty is the end product of secret talks between Moscow and Washington; for fourteen years thereafter, the United States played a central role in shaping the text of the convention. Many of the world's governments think that the United States has acted in bad faith; since concessions were extracted and given in nearly every section, compromises endorsed or even proposed by United States negotiators, these governments are justified in their view. A great nation proclaiming its belief in the rule of law makes an unsightly rogue elephant. A nation that picks and chooses the international rules it will observe is a menace to itself and the world it lives in.

From the point of view of narrow self-interest—zone, shelf, margin, and unimpeded passage—the concrete gains far outweigh the theoretical losses of a mining regime that anyway assures American firms more metal than they want for up to fifty years.

There is another danger in the United States decision to sail its lonely course. Leigh Ratiner, probably the best-informed American critic of the treaty and the *de facto* chief of the United States delegation in the final weeks of negotiation, observed:

> The costs of isolation are far higher than the costs of accepting some of the rhetoric of the North-South dialogue. . . . Once leadership is abdicated and the world finds that it can proceed without us, it will not be easy for the United States to reclaim its influence.[75]

The struggle for the treaty offers some lessons for North-South negotiations. Global bargaining on a wide range of related matters can produce a result, but only under certain conditions. States must follow Adam Smith and act in their own interests. They must abandon artificial blocs in which they give lip service (but no more) to propositions that violate their own well-being. Global negotiations on commodity prices or trade are doomed if third world states are compelled to support projects that would make them poorer, not richer.

Another critical and obvious condition is the need to have something to trade. There can be no agreement between sets composed exclusively of givers and takers. Here, third world states had much to give—free passage through straits, the width of oil-bearing continental margins, the extent of territorial seas, and monopoly resource zones. Nations of the South shared in some of these gains, but to a lesser extent than the industrial world. This is why they claimed a modest version of their New Order for seabed mining. In bargaining terms, the demand was not outrageous, no matter how deformed the provisions that finally emerged. This is also why Western negotiators, even from the United States, were willing to accept the arrangement, the price for more significant matters.

So there were genuine trades and trading within trades. The trades, moreover, dealt with particular objects and not with vague doctrines. They concerned specific national boundaries for fish and oil, not abstract support for commodity agreements in general, the appropriate level of foreign aid, or a code of behavior for multinationals. The absence of specificity makes other global talks hollow.

Above all, nations could see the advantage of rule as opposed to no rule. It was this that persuaded those who won the least, the miserable landlocked states, to accept the treaty. No deal can be struck between sovereign entities unless each is convinced of some gain in the bargain.

Chapter 5

Aid for Whom?

The misery of famine-stricken Africans flickers across Western television screens—children too weak to brush the flies from their eyelids, men with matchstick legs and exposed ribs, walking skeletons, wailing infants sucking at dry breasts. What the small screen cannot show is that this horror is largely man-made, not just a caprice of nature but the predictable result of policies pursued by Africa's new governments and reinforced by Western programs labeled "development aid."

Around 1960, when many nations south of the Sahara gained their independence, most could feed themselves, and some even exported surplus food. The new rulers, largely formed in the European universities of former colonial masters, were eager to imitate the European style, to modernize, to build industries, airlines, and other trappings of Western civilization. They poured taxes at home and funds from aid-giving agencies abroad into highways, dams, factories, airports, harbors, great conference centers, and imposing ministerial edifices. Many of the new rulers and their Western patrons ignored the continuing costs to maintain these projects and their place, if any, in a rational development scheme. Above all, they ignored the peasants in the bush, the food producers, most of Africa's population, who account for anywhere from 30 to 60 percent of each sub-Saharan nation's total output.[1]

Then the bills came due. In the 1970s, farm output began falling behind Africa's growing numbers. Alarmed aid givers drastically changed course. "Rural development," cash for schemes to help farmers, became the new catch phrase in both Africa and Asia. Agricultural assistance from the West and the new Arab aid givers in OPEC quintupled between 1973 and 1981, reaching $12.3 billion.[2] Africa alone absorbed $5 billion in farm aid, almost half from the World Bank.[3] But the results were perverse; the dangerous trend continued. Produce from Africa's farms stagnated, and the number of mouths to feed increased. For thirty-one countries, food output increased each year by a bare 1.3 percent.[4] Population grew twice as fast, 2.7 percent.[5] For twelve nations, the results were even more shocking. By 1984, they were producing no more than they had at independence a generation earlier. A Malthusian nightmare had stricken the continent.

This turns common sense on its head. No matter how wasted or mismanaged, grants of foreign money for agricultural development in the 1970s should have expanded farm wealth and output. African wars, civil wars, and drought surely contributed to the dismal result. But the stress on farming, no matter how belated, and the new foreign funds to encourage it should have mitigated these disasters.

Aid money, however, supports governments, not farmers. The funds may be earmarked for "rural development" but they are first filtered through capitals. Quite simply, African rulers, with the mindless assistance of the West, squeezed their own farmers to benefit the politically potent cities. Many of the new regimes destroyed the farmer cooperatives that had marketed the maize, sorghum, coffee, and other produce. Cooperatives, as Julius Nyerere, the president of Tanzania, had observed, are politically unreliable.[6] In their place, Africa's rulers installed government-run monopoly marketing boards. Farmers were—and many still are—forced to sell their crops to these boards at low prices, sometimes less than the cost of production. This practice serves the regimes in two ways. They pocket the difference between the prices they pay and those they charge for food sold in the cities, a far easier way of supporting government than painful taxes on income. The monopoly boards also ensure cheap food for politicians, military officers, bureaucrats, and unionized labor that might be restive in capitals. The capital is where coups are made and unmade, where today's ruling general is toppled by tomorrow's ruling colonel or sergeant. Peasants threaten no one's power. They may on occasion passively resist the petty bureaucrats who descend upon them, but they are effectively excluded from political life. Their only recourse is to grow less food, enough for themselves and their families, as little as possible for the extortionate marketing boards. So agricultural output stagnates or declines, and in times of drought, there are no food reserves.

The new governments discovered another device to make life in the capital more agreeable. They maintain overvalued currencies. They demand more francs or dollars for their nairas and cedis than these currencies would fetch in a free market. This discourages farmers from producing crops for export, from investing their own labor on irrigation works or buying seed and fertilizer. The return from export crops in cedis, nairas, and the rest is painfully small. For the period 1976 to 1980, the World Bank calculated that Ghana paid its cocoa farmers 40 percent of what they would have received in world markets; Tanzania gave its coffee producers 23 percent; Mali made cotton growers accept 43 percent, and Malawi its tea planters 28 percent.

Conversely, the overvalued currencies make imports a bargain in the cities. Elites can enjoy cheap Audis or a Mercedes-Benz, inexpensive air conditioners, television sets, and even food from abroad. If the overvalued currency created a gap in the balance of payments, foreign aid filled it.

The combination of low, state-enforced agricultural prices at home and artificially depressed export prices abroad is a form of exploitation that Prebisch overlooked. Africa's peasants confront ever-worsening terms of trade imposed by their own regimes. In Zambia, for example, inflation raised the price of soap, kerosene, pots and pans, and the other items farmers purchase by 200 percent between 1965 and 1980. Farm prices were held so low that peasant buying power dropped 65 percent. The system, in other words, drains incomes from poor farmers to the better-off city-dwellers.[7]

"The result has been a sort of indigenous colonialism," said Rutherford B. Poats, "extracting surpluses from the peasants for urban or industrial uses."[8] Poats is chairman of the Development Assistance Committee of the Organization for Economic Cooperation and Development, the official promoter of aid from the West. His judgment is a remarkable admission of the failure, indeed the malign consequences of Western aid in Africa.

In Asia and Latin America, the systems are different, but the results for those at the bottom are much the same. Most African peasants own their land, small plots that could yield more if incentives rather than disincentives prevailed. Land ownership in Latin America and Asia, however, is concentrated among a relatively small number who employ wage laborers or rent to tenants who pay a share of the crop. Here, land tends to be underused because low-paid workers or tenants with uncertain tenure lack any motive to extract the maximum yield. A large number of Asians and Latins toil on tiny plots they own; their holdings are too small for the investment needed to raise output. Again, aid tends to perpetuate misery because it leaves these systems of land ownership untouched.

Aid givers, particularly the United States, make one other important contribution to rural poverty. They give away or sell at low cost surplus wheat and other produce to help prop prices for farmers at home.[9] This food, sold cheaply in cities, further holds down farm prices in Africa and elsewhere and provides more revenues for third world governments. Surplus foods have drastically altered the eating habits of Africans. Instead of the traditional corn, sorghum, and millet, city dwellers now eat foreign wheat and rice. Overvalued currencies make these grains cheap even when they must be purchased abroad.[10] The amounts of such surpluses are significant. The United States, for example, dumped 6.1 million tons of surplus grain around the world in 1983 alone. To be sure, some of this was emergency aid, a humane act to feed starving Africans. But the surplus is dumped in years when the rains come as well as in drought. It thereby helps insure that not enough will be grown so that Africans can once again feed themselves.

The World Bank rarely admonishes either aid givers or recipients, at least in public. Like Poats and the Development Assistance Committee, it has a strong institutional interest in expanding aid. But Africa's plight is so stark a rebuke to the assistance culture that the Bank has felt compelled to speak out. A Bank study warned:

> External assistance can weaken the resolve of governments to tackle developmental problems in general, as much as food aid can weaken their will on agriculture in particular. . . . Aid is no substitute for domestic programs that provide the incentives and create the efficient institutions required to increase domestic production more rapidly.[11]

In a series of reports, the Bank examined not only the aid-supported disincentives for farmers but all assistance to the continent. The verdict was damning, particularly for the givers of aid. The "donors . . . allow commercial or strategic considerations to outweigh considerations of priority, efficiency and relevance," said the Bank.[12] Thus donors implicitly endorse African policies that lower living standards. Empty or underused factories, cracked highways, rusting tractors, and unusable airports bear silent witness to how much has gone wrong. Donors, said the Bank, should put their money into rehabilitating this wasted investment. They prefer, however, new projects that yield contracts for their businessmen or prestige for client governments. Donors like to finance large, modern hospitals and universities in capitals. Neither money nor prestige are acquired from clinics in the countryside or secondary and technical schools. Donors will finance new highways in Nigeria, ignoring 5,600 miles of damaged trunk roads that frustrate the movement of goods. "Almost without exception, the Bank's reviews have revealed that a good deal of the pressure to undertake new investment or continue with low-priority projects derives from the inflexibility of foreign donors. The more the program is externally financed, the harder it has been to maintain national control over priorities," the Bank said.[13]

The studies all but imply that Africa might be better off without foreign aid. The Bank, however, is not about to declare its own bankruptcy or that of the Western nations who finance it. Instead, it urges even more assistance, but of a new kind that deserves a closer look.

The unrelenting squeeze on Africa's farmers is dramatic but neither unique nor uniform. There are signs that some nations, Kenya, the Ivory Coast, and a few others, are trying to change the order of things, to scrap policies that discourage output and give farmers incentives to grow.

In Asia and Latin America, different forces are at work but the outcome is much the same. Since the mid-1970s, India has achieved what appears to be a striking success in agriculture. India's farm output has grown faster than its rapid gains in population, and food imports have given way to modest exports. But this balance has been reached at a low level of consumption for most Indians. Moreover, the persistent misery in the countryside, particularly among landless and tenant farmers, the poverty of tens of millions in fetid city slums, demonstrate the inability of India's farm growth to reach the population's lower depths.[14]

In Latin America, the rapid industrial expansion of the 1970s, fueled by foreign commercial bank loans, left largely untouched the impoverished of the *favelas, barrios,* and other squatter cities on the outskirts of cosmopolitan capitals or the army of tenant farmers tilling huge estates. In Latin America and Asia, as in Africa, mass poverty suggests that governments pursue policies that improve life for a relative few. The foreign aid they receive strengthens their resolve to pursue this course.

Third world governments demand redistribution of wealth from North to South. But they rigorously disdain this formula at home. Even in times of disaster, the largest share of any pie is divided among the privileged in cities and the countryside. "Who has ever seen a starving military officer or merchant, let alone aid worker?" asked the commission that wrote *Famine.* "It is a question of who has access to that food."[15]

A Bank study directed by Paul Streeten concluded: "Poor countries tend to tax poor farmers and subsidize food such as high quality wheat and rice that is consumed by better-off urban groups, though among the poorest are landless laborers and urban dwellers who have to buy food."[16] Throughout the third world, a persistent bias favors the best-placed city dwellers. Administrators of foreign aid frequently deplore this state of affairs.

But its survival suggests that their concern is largely limited to wringing hands.

Foreign assistance—wealthy governments taxing their citizens to provide resources for poorer governments—is a relatively novel notion. Nevertheless, it has penetrated every corner of the world. By 1983, more than sixty third world nations each received from $100,000 to $1.6 billion, with India at the head of the list. The funds came from seventeen Western donors, OPEC, and the Soviet bloc. In all, these aid givers distributed $36.2 billion, with three quarters from the West and nearly one fourth or $8 billion from the United States. Washington provided funds for no fewer than sixty-five nations.[17] Every self-respecting industrial country has an aid agency and missions abroad to watch how its money is spent. The World Bank, a cluster of international lending and virtual grant-making institutions, has been created. There are smaller models in Africa, Asia, and Latin America.

All this arose from relatively modest origins. One strand goes back to Harry S. Truman's 1949 inaugural address. Its fourth point urged, "a bold new program for making the benefits of our scientific advance and industrial progress available for the improvement and growth of underdeveloped areas." Truman envisioned a cooperative effort, engaging all states, working through the United Nations. This was to be small-scale, confined to technical assistance, not the financing of dams, telecommunications, road networks, and other large outlays of capital. Only $211 million was sought for this limited program.[18]

But by far the strongest root of foreign aid was Truman's Doctrine of March 1947 to resist the Soviet Union. The Doctrine provided $400 million in military and economic assistance to repel communist subversion and Soviet pressure in Greece and Turkey. The Greek government was fighting a civil war against communists; Turkey was resisting Soviet demands for partial control of the Dardanelles. Both were to form NATO's southern flank, on the front line of the Cold War struggle. These were matters too serious to be dealt with by an international agency. Moreover, a Republican Congress, suspicious of aid, could not resist a plea to arm nations fighting the Soviet Union. The same logic won Congressional support for the far more ambitious, $13 billion Marshall Plan to rebuild and rearm Western Europe.[19]

From the very start, then, aid's objectives—military, economic, and political—were tangled. Aid is described as a disinterested gesture to help poor nations spur their own economies by financing investments and imports they could not otherwise afford. Aid is an element of high strategy, to strengthen regimes in the Cold War competition.

The confusion over aid's objectives have multiplied in the years since Truman. By 1961, the Congress declared that the United States has "provided assistance to strengthen the forces of freedom by aiding peoples of less developed countries to develop their resources and improve their living standards." Aid would not only spur economic growth but shrink mass misery and win people to Western values.[20]

Distinguished private citizens have attempted to supply a rationale, usually to encourage more aid. One group, led by Lester Pearson, a former Canadian premier, warned, "There is no greater danger to peace than that from two thirds of mankind remaining hungry, disillusioned, and desperate."[21] Peace, therefore, "will depend to a large extent on what the rich are prepared to do to help." But Pearson's commission was forced to acknowledge that "it might be easier to secure general and firm acceptance for a commitment to aid if it could be shown that failure to give it and carry it out would produce catastrophic and immediate consequences. This is not the case, however. . . ."[22] The Pearson commission had simultaneously raised and deflated the claim that aid and peace are linked. Ten years later, another group led by Brandt produced a fresh argument. It said: "Above all, we believe that a large-scale transfer of resources to the South can make a major impact on growth in both the South and the North and help to revive the flagging world economy."[23] This was a Keynesian echo. Its hidden assumption was that aid stimulates economic development or output in the third world. Its open assertion held this would then create new markets for the depressed industries of the North.

Perhaps it will. But there are more direct ways to put idle men and plants to work in the North. The most efficient would enlarge industrial demand by increased government spending or tax cuts. This in turn would expand imports from the South—as happened in the 1983 recovery—thereby increasing the third world's ability to buy from the North. Lower interest rates would also stimulate demand directly in both hemispheres. In contrast, there are leakages in any aid program, a peculiarly indirect device to put the North's jobless to work.

The Reagan administration, cool to aid giving through international agencies, still finances the world's largest national program. It is defended by a long array of arguments. Aid is said to be a good thing because the third world is a big United States market. But this Brandt-like contention is undermined by the skewed outpouring of funds; nearly a third of all American economic assistance flows to Israel and Egypt, markets of marginal importance. Poor countries, it is said, supply critical materials, bauxite, chromium, cobalt, and manganese; this is true but uninteresting since they would be sold on world markets with or without aid. M. Peter McPherson, the Reagan aid administrator, has even claimed his agency will promote "private sector initiative and ingenuity."[24] But it is unlikely that the promise of aid will convert a socialist third world economy to an open system, and it is unclear that the administration means what it says.* The United States conspicuously declined to contribute to a new European fund designed to lift the heavy hands of African governments from their farmers.

Third world poverty, the aid administrators warn, "create[s] violence, political instability" and so "U.S. security interests are therefore often closely linked to the internal political, economic and social health of individual countries and regions in the developing world."[25] There is little evidence that aid promotes the

*In one sensitive sector, oil, the administration most emphatically means what it says. It insists that public agencies shall not finance the search for crude in the third world. The United States has not only blocked the World Bank's special loan agency for oil, it frequently votes against even conventional Bank loans for oil. Instead, the United States provides money for firewood or renewable energy resources, activities unlikely to harm the great companies. "Most resources for energy investment must . . . come from private sources," McPherson has said. Major oil companies, struggling to keep up prices, can only agree. (M. Peter McPherson, *Development Issues: U.S. Actions Affecting Developing Countries, 1983 Annual Report*. Washington, D.C.: Development Assistance Committee, 1983, p. 110.)

"social health" of recipients; to the contrary, it reinforces the status quo of third world regimes whose nations' social health depends on large-scale reforms.

The heart of the United States aid program lies elsewhere, in the reasoning that buried Truman's Point Four in billions for Greece and Turkey. Washington now runs an Economic Support Fund "to promote economic and political stability in regions where the United States has special security interests and has determined that economic assistance can be useful in helping secure peace or to avert major economic or political crises."[26]

More bluntly, the United States and other nations, East and West, give money to shore up friendly third world rulers, keep neutrals neutral, and gain political influence. Strategic, not economic considerations, determine who gets the funds and how they shall be spent. If this leads to self-sustaining growth, economic development, so much the better. If an appeal can be made to taxpayers on ideological or humanitarian grounds, that too is useful. But the overriding concern is military and political. The aid from great nations is a weapon in the great global contest; among lesser donors, aid is a tool to extend influence.

An earlier generation of aid givers was more direct. The Canadian Prime Minister John Diefenbaker said: "$50 million a year . . . would be cheap insurance for Canada . . . to halt Communism in Asia."[27] The U.S. Secretary of State, Dean Rusk, approvingly quoted a report by the Senate Foreign Relations Committee. It said, "Foreign aid is both an unavoidable responsibility and a central instrument of our foreign policy. It is dictated by the hard logic of the Cold War and by a moral responsibility."[28]

W. Averell Harriman, then assistant secretary of state for Far Eastern affairs, was almost as blunt. "The Communist threat of aggression and subversion against the free nations of the area and the overriding poverty and lack of development . . . These are the twin and closely related problems which the foreign aid program seeks to meet."[29]

Words like "responsibility" and "development" inevitably work their way into the language, but neither Rusk nor Harriman left any doubt where primacy lay.

The political-military potency of aid has often been overestimated by both sides in the Cold War, but this has not inhibited the donors. A strikingly blind prophecy was made by Robert S. McNamara, Defense Secretary in 1964. He testified that "the foreign aid program is the best weapon we have to insure that our own men in uniform need not go into combat."[30] Within a year, more than 500,000 Americans in uniform were fighting in Vietnam, and McNamara ultimately left the Pentagon to run the World Bank.

The struggle for Indochina, of course, was decided on the battleground. But its fate still raises difficult problems for those who defend the political efficacy of aid. A large United States program did not widen support for unpopular governments in South Vietnam or Cambodia. (In fact, the United States helped overthrow Prince Norodom Sihanouk, who led a relatively secure but insufficiently anti-Communist regime in Cambodia. Such are the vagaries of political judgment that Washington eventually backed—and still backs—the movement nominally led by the Prince to topple his communist successors.)

The defeat in Vietnam inspired fresh thinking about aid in the U.S. Congress. Senator J. William Fulbright, chairman of the Foreign Relations Committee, warned that the program not only fails in its stated aims but actually undermines peace. A modest program to El Salvador, for example, develops a momentum of its own. Aid officials, the Pentagon, and the State Department develop a vested interest in a "success" to justify themselves and extract more funds from Congress. Soon success is equated with the survival of the regime receiving aid. Its perpetuation is deemed critical to American interests. If the regime is challenged from within, the challenge is communist-inspired or serving communist purposes. More rather than less money and guns are needed to help a free world ally, to support a good friend. Preservation of the aid-receiving government becomes an objective of American strategy and money.[31]

Fulbright argued that these self-entangling involvements should be avoided by abandoning the national aid program and channeling development assistance exclusively through the World Bank and other international or regional agencies. His advice was not followed. The bureaucratic stake in things as they are is too strong. The persistence with which aid officials defend their budgets is illustrated by Robert H. Nooter, an assistant aid administrator. A month after the 1973 ceasefire that marked the end of the American struggle in Vietnam, Nooter was still pleading with Congress for another $15 million to enable the beaten Saigon regime to carry out "a sweeping land reform program." With chaos at hand and North Vietnam's takeover imminent, Nooter called this "the most significant social program carried out by the government of South Vietnam." It came a little late.[32]

Throughout the 1970s, however, the argument that aid is a Cold War weapon was heard less frequently. It was regarded as crude or inappropriate, particularly while the memory of Vietnam was so fresh.

As aid came under increasingly critical scrutiny, it became clear that economic as well as political goals had gone astray. Even nations with encouraging rates of growth had failed to translate higher output into a better life for most of their people. If new dams created power, an electric light illuminated misery in the villages and city slums where most lived.

In Washington, where styles of assistance tend to be set for the West, Congress attempted to seize the initiative and redirect the program. From now on, Congress ordained in 1973, the money would go to meet "basic human needs," reach the impoverished who had failed to share in the distribution of the gifts.[33] This "new directions" legislation was supposed to end aid as an instrument of politico-military policy. Instead of bolstering regimes for the strategic purposes of the day, the funds would provide slums with sanitary water, cheap housing, and sewage. The rural poor were to benefit from low-cost credit, seeds and fertilizer, irrigation, clinics, schools, and a network of advisers teaching better farming methods.

But even in a era of reaction against imperial presidencies, the executive and not the legislature determines policy. At most, the Congress can block a program by denying funds. Even then, a determined executive can usually find some way to spend what it wants. So strategic considerations soon dominated the United States program again. Congress itself failed to show any lasting enthusiasm for its "new directions"; it has none of the political appeal of a war against communism.

The aid program was divided in two. One portion, labeled Development Assistance, was designed to satisfy "basic needs." The other, the Economic Support Fund, was for business as usual, money to governments whose survival was thought critical to strategic interests. These outlays can be spent for virtually anything that satisfies Washington, including deficits in the payment balances of favored governments. Any contribution to development or the improved living standards of the recipients is incidental.

The relative importance of aid for human needs and for support to sensitive regimes is reflected in their budgets. For the fiscal year starting in 1985, the Reagan administration planned to spend $3.5 billion on the Economic Support Fund and $2.2 billion on Development Assistance: Military concerns won $3 for every $2 directed at "basic human needs."[34]

From the standpoint of a government dispensing funds, aid should have a political purpose. Money must further what presidents, premiers, and ministries regard as national interests. The national interest in making life bearable in a squatter city is difficult to measure. As a general proposition, increased food production in Asian nations will strengthen a client government and is desirable, but if the measures to increase that output threaten the government's existence, they are undesirable.

Money, moreover, must be distributed discriminatingly. Those in the enemy camp are obviously ineligible—Libya, Cuba, and Vietnam for the United States. So are those who affront the donor by perhaps an ill-timed vote at the U.N. Those who get the most are thought to matter most.

The 1985 United States aid plan scrupulously follows the rule of political discrimination. Three nations, Israel, Egypt, and Turkey, take all their economic aid from the unfettered Support Fund and consume over half its money. Israel, receiving $850 million, is Washington's principal ally in the Middle East and is seen as a bastion of democratic order in a turbulent region. Egypt, the strongest Arab power, is rewarded with $750 million for severing its Soviet links and insuring Israel against a war on two fronts—at least as long as Cairo's policymakers do not shift again. Turkey's generals, who rule directly or behind a civilian facade, are fiercely hostile to Moscow and qualify for $175 million. Together, the trio accounts for more than a third of all economic aid* without drawing a dollar of Development Assistance designed for the poor.[35]

Economic aid to other nations also reflects the program's political contours. Leading recipients are Pakistan $250 million (for its almost unbroken support of American policy in Central Asia, its supply routes for arms to anti-Russian Afghanis), El Salvador $290 million (to battle against domestic leftist forces), Costa Rica $180 million and Honduras $120 million (for their help in Washington's attempt to overthrow a leftist government in Nicaragua), the Philippines $134 million (for the struggle against its own guerrillas and for providing the United States with a naval and an air base). These nations draw on both the Support Fund and Development Assistance.

The figures, moreover, count only what is defined as economic aid. Except for Costa Rica, they all receive large quantities of American weapons in amounts that sometimes exceed their economic assistance. Direct military aid under the 1985 plan provides arms worth $1.4 billion to Israel, $1.175 billion to Egypt, and at the end of the scale, $61.3 million to Honduras. Most of this arsenal is financed by soft loans at concessional or less than market rates of interest, and these loans have more recently been replaced by gifts.[36]

The United States is not unique, however. Other national aid programs also follow what is thought to be the path of self-interest. In the West, Britain sends most of its money, 62 percent, to its former colonies in Africa, South Asia, and the Caribbean. Now that the Empire has vanished, the funds give Britain political influence and economic advantage for its businessmen.[37] France counts as aid the money it sends its overseas departments

*Economic aid is defined here as Development Assistance plus the Support Fund. Shipments of surplus food worth $1.7 billion were also scheduled. But this is chiefly a program to dispose of surplus crops, an aid scheme for American farmers. Dumped surpluses cannot be counted as aid.

and territories, much as if Federal projects in Puerto Rico or Hawaii were assistance. Most of the rest goes to ex-colonies, chiefly in Africa, retaining a French hold that independence threatened.

The Soviet Union got into the aid business in 1954, after Pakistan joined an American-organized military pact. Moscow feared that its neighbor, Afghanistan, might slip into the Western orbit, and began its program to keep Kabul close to the Soviets. The initial Soviet effort was cautious, a $3.5 million loan for some grain mills. By the 1980s, Russian aid was far more ambitious, about $3 billion a year, with Cuba and Vietnam joining Afghanistan as the biggest recipients. The Russians might better have heeded Fulbright's warning that aid can become a fatal trap. Despite the large investment in Afghanistan, more than 100,000 Soviet troops were fighting an endless battle in the 1980s to put down the resistance against Moscow's chosen regime for Kabul.[38]

Arab aid from rich oil states also furthers political and military ends. Most goes to Jordan and Syria, on the front line with Israel. Egypt once drew heavily from OPEC and the Soviet Union until it switched camps, made peace with Israel, and came to the West. OPEC has also given money to Africans, mostly Muslim states, to sustain an anti-Israel bloc at the U.N. Not surprisingly, the volume of OPEC aid has faithfully followed the price of oil. From a peak of $9.6 billion in 1980, it fell to $5.5 billion in 1983.[39]

The three largest aid donors, then, the United States, the Soviet Union, and OPEC, put their money where their guns are. Aid is largely an extension of military policy, to contain or defend Israel, to support an invasion of Afghanistan or bolster a Pakistani neighbor whose border is open to weapons for anti-Soviet insurgents, to suppress or encourage Cuba and its allies in the Caribbean.

The noble rhetoric—self-sustaining development, basic human needs, eradicating misery—is not taken seriously in capitals where decisions are made. (Sweden claims to run a disinterested aid program and gives money to Cuba and Vietnam in the belief that these police states foster egalitarian societies. This is more of a commentary on Stockholm's political judgment than its good will, since aid to policemen strengthens the police.) But even if aid was severed from political interest, its chances of making an impact on mass misery are not very bright. After all, the money never goes directly to the citizens of a country; it is always transmitted through their governments. Third world rulers and their high officials propose or assent to projects and programs. Within each country who gets what from foreign aid is decided by those in charge.

A small group is usually in charge—the ruler of the day, the president for life, or an ambitious sergeant, higher military officers, some businessmen, large landholders, a core of high civilian officials, themselves often substantial landholders. They cannot be expected to undermine their privileged status, to pursue policies that would weaken their grip. Those in power, said Paul Baran, a Marxist economist, "are those who benefit most from the status quo—politically, socially, and economically. It is no good expecting those who enjoy the benefits of the present system to bring about fundamental changes in it."[40]

The third world governments receiving the billions run risks in using aid for their poor. Secure tenure for tenant farmers might create a new, self-confident group that would make demands. Transforming slum shacks into livable dwellings could increase political pressure in cities. But outlays for great conference halls, highways, and national airlines can bind contractors, politicians, and the higher civil service more closely to those in power. Money for arms pleases officers, enlarges their commands, and may postpone a coup. P. T. Bauer, a conservative economist, has said, "Aid increases the power, resources and patronage of governments compared with the rest of society and therefore their power over it."[41]

Only a government that believed its fate depended on the mass of its citizens would feel compelled to use aid on their behalf. Pakistan, Zaire, Egypt, Vietnam, Cuba, Syria, Indonesia, and most big aid recipients fall outside this class. India may come closer to it, but caste, ethnic, religious, and linguistic division all reduce the threat from below.

The discovery that aid had bypassed most of the third world's population troubled McNamara when he took over the World Bank. The Bank is not committed to the strategic or commercial concerns of Western donors nor to the survival of particular third world regimes. Freed from the Pentagon and the United States administration, McNamara could and did speak out forcefully. Economic development had taken place in the 1960s. But it was a skewed development, and averages concealed the static fate of the impoverished, he said. With his characteristic penchant for statistical precision where no precise count can be made, McNamara asserted that 2 billion live in poverty and 800 million of these in "absolute poverty." This he defined as "a condition of life so degrading as to be an insult to human dignity."[42] There had been growth in third world nations, but "a very large proportion of their people have not shared in its benefits." Under his leadership, the Bank would change its development strategy to better the lives of these absolute poor.*

McNamara's global poverty estimates could neither be proved nor disproved, but there was an abundance of studies to support his thesis that growth had failed to better the lives of many. The International Labor Organization found that despite growth in South and East Asia, poverty was actually increasing in the rural areas where most live. By the ILO's standard, an Asian is impoverished if he consumes fewer calories than needed for a minimum level of health.[43] In Pakistan, the percent of impoverished rose from 72 to 74 in the 1960s, although the nation enjoyed a brisk rate of total economic output. In three large Indian states of four that were measured, the share of impoverished jumped five to eighteen percentage points; no change was recorded in the fourth. For Bangladesh, the undernourished in the countryside rose from 40 to 62 percent; for Malaysia, it was 40 to 47 percent, and in the wealthier Philippines, from 10 to 12 percent. An Indian commentator, C. P. Bhambhri, concluded: "The benefits of development in India have been cornered by the urban elite and the rural rich."[44] Some economists, notably Jagdish N. Bhagwati, cite other studies to suggest that the lot of India's rural poor has been bettered both absolutely and relatively under a "pull

*Until the end of his tenure in 1981, McNamara insisted that his aides identify the exact number of poor whose lives would improve from each Bank project. The hopelessness of this task led some to invent a plausible number and trust this would satisfy their chief.

up" effect from a steadily rising output of grains. But Bhagwati readily acknowledges that the data is incomplete, and the authorities are divided over its interpretation.[45]

More recent surveys agree with Bhambhri. The World Bank documented great misery even in lands where the supply of food is greater than the consumption. One is Egypt, where 25 percent of the children in rural areas are stunted. For Indonesia, the estimate is 20 to 30 percent. In Brazil, one of the richest third world nations, 37 percent of the children suffer from malnutrition.[46] In Sri Lanka, however, far less elitist than the other three, only 5 percent of the population receives less than 1,900 calories a day, and this is a country that must import food.

A serious attack on rural poverty in Asia and Latin America touches the most sensitive of political nerves, the ownership of land. Many of McNamara's 800 million absolutely impoverished are landless laborers, working for wages, tenant farmers with no certainty they can stay on the land they rent and holders of dwarf plots. (Africa's rural poor, it will be recalled, are victimized differently, by the grasp of government.) From the first report of the U.N. experts in 1951 to the more recent studies by the Bank, thoughtful observers have warned that farm living standards and output will be held back or even ground down without land reform.

Reform means breaking up large, underworked estates in Latin America and Asia and distributing land to the landless and poor farmers. It means assuring tenants they can remain on the land they work. Both groups will then have an incentive to invest time and effort for greater yields. They will also need water and cheap credit to buy seeds, fertilizer, and pesticides. All this, along with technical advice, constitutes the essential ingredients of reform. The first step is the redistribution of land. Wolf Ladejinsky, who helped plan the highly successful land reforms in Japan and Taiwan, said: "Unless those who work the land own it, or at least are secure on the land as tenants, all the rest is likely to be writ in water."[47]

But as McNamara, Ladejinsky's boss, observed, "Such programs are difficult to carry out for they affect the power base of the traditional elite groups in the developing society."[48] (The successful reform in Taiwan, Japan, and South Korea, moreover, suggests that land tenure and ownership can be changed only in societies dominated or heavily influenced by a foreign army.) The large landowner whose land would be redistributed is a ranking member of these elites. Even modest landlords, with ten or twenty acres, will oppose any scheme to give their tenants more security or raise the wages of landless workers by reducing their numbers. In India, the higher civil servants often own sizable parcels of land in their native villages. They can't approve change. Nor can the moneylenders, politically important in Asia and sometimes in Latin America, welcome competing and cheaper government credit. An irrigation scheme for a large property is enthusiastically endorsed by its holder; providing water to small plots will only make the land he hopes to buy more expensive. A tube well on a judge's land is a useful aid project; he will oppose wells for his small neighbors, or, as in Bangladesh, appropriate those designed for them.[49] The urban elites and their supporting networks in the countryside can and will block reform.

Apart from the direct economic cost is the question of status. The gap between rich and poor, far greater in the third world than in the West,* brings prestige to those on top. A more egalitarian society would diminish their standing. They will resolutely oppose it, whether they call themselves Socialist, Congress, Christian Democrat.

Many third world nations have enacted land reform laws—India, Pakistan, Malaysia, Burma, Bangladesh, the Philippines, Indonesia, Venezuela, Chile, Colombia, the Dominican Republic, and more. Typically, they begin with a flourish: photos of a

*One calculation of this gap appeared in the *Journal of Development Economics* in 1976. While the most prosperous 20 percent in the United States enjoy incomes six times that of the poorest 20 percent, the ratios for some third world countries are as follows: India, ten to one; Brazil, twenty to one; Kenya, eighteen to one; Tanzania, eleven to one. A similar result was reported by the Agency for International Development in 1972. Then, the richest fifth in the United States enjoyed incomes eight times as great as the poorest fifth. But the ratio for developing countries was twenty-five to one for the most unequal and ten to one for the least unequal. Cited in John W. Sewall and the staff of the Overseas Development Council, *The United States and World Development Agenda 1977* (New York: Praeger Publications, 1977), pp. 4–5.

minister handing a land title to a landless laborer, reports of tens of thousands of acres distributed. But these laws usually become dead letters, tokens, unenforced and neglected. Little redistribution takes place, and rural misery remains unrelieved.

The Bank's renewed concern with the poor and Congress' "new directions" have colored at least the language of American aid programs. The United States effort now embraces projects labeled Village Mother/Child Welfare in Indonesia, Low Income Housing in Liberia, Small Irrigated Perimeters in Senegal.[50] How much of this aid gets past capitals to reach people on the ground is questionable.

Just as rural poverty increases, so do the miserable squatter colonies growing daily on the perimeters of great cities. The two are intimately linked. The landless farmer in Bihar, if he has the energy, moves to a ramshackle bustee in Calcutta, hoping for a better life. Workers flee large coffee estates in Brazil to cluster in the shacks above Rio. For all the talk of satisfying "basic human needs," aid does little for urban misery.

Ruling groups want highways for their cars, not lanes through muddy settlements; they want airports for flights abroad, not bus service to bring squatters to jobs. They demand water for houses with plumbing, not for those in shacks. Hospitals and schools must be built where the well-off live; clinics and classes in the slums can wait.

"The obstacles" to satisfying McNamara's "basic needs," a report to the World Bank said, "are not physical but political . . . and cast doubt on the possibility of growth first and redistribution later. . . . Governments in societies in which power is concentrated have no interest in eradicating poverty. . . ."[51]

The fact of undiminished and possibly increased poverty contrasts strikingly with the eloquent promises of third world governments. The Philippines development plan for 1978–82 spoke of "the conquest of mass poverty" as "the immediate, fundamental goal." India's 1979 plan asserted that "what matters is . . . whether we can insure within a specified time frame a measurable increase in the welfare of the millions of poor." Indonesia called in 1979 for "a more equitable and just distribution of welfare."[52] But the evidence of increased misery among the third world's poor underscores the judgment of Charles R. Frank and Richard C. Webb: "The almost exclusive concern with extreme poverty among aid givers today is rejected as a foreign conception by the elites in most LDCs [less developed countries]."[53]

If bolstering client regimes is the principal purpose of national aid programs, why should donors concern themselves with mass poverty? The conventional answer is that discontented people may overthrow their rulers and threaten the peace. But the postwar experience demonstrates that this is unlikely, that third world rulers are infrequently upset by mass revolts but rather by revolts of those close to power. There are, however, at least two other reasons why taxpayers supporting foreign aid have a legitimate interest in who profits from it.

One is ethical. The world of mass misery that intermittently appears on Western television screens is disturbing. There is a sense, no matter how fleeting, that something is wrong, improper, unjust. The quick public response to pleas for emergency aid in disasters reflects this impulse. Charity and generosity are characteristics rarely associated with government; the emotions of ordinary citizens, however, can be touched. Indeed, the absence of strong popular opposition to aid probably depends on its ethical appeal.

The second reason is economic. Third world systems that discourage farm output, that neglect tens of millions of unproductive slum dwellers, are producing far below their capacity. The malnourished, the illiterate, and the diseased can extract from the land and the mines and the factories only a fraction of their potential yield. Many third world nations are richly endowed with natural resources; they lie idle or underworked because human labor is so heavily handicapped. Here the Brandt commission argument applies. A richer third world could enrich the West, providing not only larger markets but an expanded stream of goods and services to free those in industrial nations for new, more rewarding tasks. Both justice and economics, then, argue for attempts to improve the lot of the world's 2 billion impoverished.

Despite aid's failure to touch the overwhelming majority in the third world, it is widely believed that assistance has at least made some contribution to economic growth, to total production. The new highways, telephone lines, and factories surely added to the net investment and output of developing countries. Robert Asher, writing after the growth decade of the 1960s, concluded: "American aid has contributed to the substantial, indeed remarkable economic improvement that has taken place in the less developed world since 1950."[54]

This, however, is far from clear. There is some evidence that aid has actually impeded growth, or at least prevented third world economies from producing as much as they could. Aid agencies typically favor large rather than small projects because they are more impressive, easier to supervise, and offer greater prospects to exporters in the aid-giving nation. The smaller schemes may save scarce resources—skilled local labor, imported materials and managers. But they are tedious to administer and create no monuments to impress visiting, aid-giving legislators. So, in Brazil, a sober proposal to build four generators separately over seven years was transformed by the U.S. aid agency into an all-at-once project crammed into five years.[55] World Bank funds for sugar cane mills in Indonesia inspired the military to force farmers at gunpoint to grow cane instead of their traditional rice.[56] Tanzania, with Bank money, built eleven cashew processing plants that are largely idle; their capacity is three times the nation's entire yield.[57]

The anecdotal evidence is endless. The statistical evidence is inconclusive. Even the Pearson commission, organized to urge the case for aid, conceded that the "correlation between the amounts of aid received in the past decades and the growth performance is very weak."[58] Gustav Papenek, examining eighty-five countries in the 1950s and 1960s, calculated that aid not only propelled growth but was more than twice as important as domestic savings and foreign investment.[59] But a decade later, Paul Mosley, a British aid official, stood Papenek's thesis on its head. "[T]he positive and significant relationship between aid and growth noted by Papenek in the 1960s appears to have collapsed . . . ," Mosley wrote. Indeed, he found that the most heavily aided countries grew least. At best, Mosley said, aid spurs growth only for the very poorest nations.[60] But his own scatter diagram, plotting aid and growth, rebuts even this. Poor countries with the greatest aid per person, Chad and Niger, advance much more slowly than those with the least aid per person, India and Pakistan.

For all the studies, speeches, and documents, the disturbing fact is that little is known about development. There is no adequate theory explaining the forces that promote growing output in the third world. There is instead a cluster of views, some of them expressed in the pioneering study of the U.N. experts in 1951 describing the preconditions and obstacles to growth. These are sociological, psychological, and cultural as well as economic. One on which there is wide agreement is the need for an orderly state, where laws governing land or tax reform, the availability of credit, and equitable distribution of import licenses or rationed food are executed faithfully by officials and their subordinates.[61] But most third world nations are, in Gunnar Myrdal's phrase, soft states. They are characterized by a lack of social discipline, starting at the top. Officials ignore or breach rules and collude with the powerful; official authority is undermined by its own slackness.

Another barrier to development is vested privilege, binding men to traditional inherited tasks, preventing the expression of a free or entrepreneurial spirit. Caste in India is a strong fetter. It has been outlawed by the nation's constitution, but it survives and flourishes in the villages because the proscription is not enforced. It condemns men to assigned roles and prevents the development of their full productive powers.

Still another barrier is tribal or ethnic partiality. The new African states drove out their Asian minorities, losing their best entrepreneurs. Tribal rivalries preserve jobs for one group, exclude another, and cost society a resource, a talent. The lack of education is another major obstacle to growth. Cuba, South Korea, and Somalia have mounted successful campaigns to wipe out illiteracy.[62] But most third world regimes are either indifferent or fear a better-educated population. So schools and elaborate universities rise in cities, and the countryside is largely ignored. Fatalism is another powerful force constricting growth. Whether induced by religion or the guns of the state, third world people tend neither to expect nor demand a better life. This further softens the soft state and helps insure that laws will not be enforced.

The web of corruption that runs all through soft states blocks development. Most regimes impose a great battery of controls over exports, imports, farm output, manufacturing prices, scarce materials, and many other forms of economic activity. Administrators grow wealthy bending these rules, selling permits, turning their backs on landlords with holdings above the reform-dictated level. Uncertainty marks every transaction; the only certainty is that some payment shall be made. If a farmer must pay an extortionate bribe for the fertilizer and water that will make his high-yielding seeds grow, his green revolution turns dusty gray. Growth, Bauer said, "depends on people's attributes, attitudes, motivations, mores and political arrangements." These are not qualities that aid can create.[63]

It is frequently argued that poor nations suffer from excess population, that living standards would rise if the number of infants was curbed. Few propositions are less susceptible to proof. Crowded Singapore is a high-income, high-growth state; most African countries regress despite low ratios of people to land space. Efforts to curb population by force, as in India and China, ignore some critical points. In the third world, an infant often becomes an economic asset to its family and nation in eight years or less, working in the fields or streets, producing more than it consumes. In any event, life at the bottom is so miserable for most, bureaucrats who interfere with procreation, one of the few available pleasures, reflect the arrogance of very old and very rigid caste societies.

One point is clear: Despite or because of thirty years of foreign aid, there is a growing gap in well-being between the rich and poor in the poor nations. The indifference toward or even exploitation of poor third world citizens by privileged ruling groups reinforces the sense of hopelessness and holds back production. A striking example comes from Tanzania and its president, Julius Nyerere, who lectures the West on its duty to provide aid "as a matter of justice." In the name of African socialism or *Ujamaa*, Nyerere forced several million small landholders living on scattered plots to abandon their huts and move into villages to cultivate cooperative farms. The villagers knew what Nyerere did not, that their soil was suitable only for extensive cultivation by individual growers, not to the intensive farming of collectives. Crop output fell swiftly. Despite Nyerere's use of an armed militia and the burning of recalcitrant peasants' huts, the farmers drifted away from the settlements and back to their plots. Nyerere was forced to abandon *Ujamaa.*[64]

Can aid be used as a lever to reduce mass poverty? Could gifts and loans be given on condition that nations undertake genuine land reform, scrap state monopolies crippling farm output, and build clinics in the countryside rather than hospitals for an urban elite? The question almost answers itself. Rich nations give money to support third world governments, not to transform the societies over which they rule. If third world recipients fear land reform, or if other measures for the poor threaten their power, they will successfully resist these conditions for aid. Since the aid-giver's first priority is winning governments, the conditions will be quietly forgotten. Pakistan and India have proclaimed ceilings on the land any large farmer can hold. The ceilings are regularly violated, with land held in the names of dozens of relatives. But no national donor would consider stopping aid to enforce the land laws; that would damage relations with two important governments over an issue that could overturn both.

A test of this proposition came in the 1960s when the Kennedy administration launched its Alliance for Progress. With great fanfare, Washington announced that it would provide Latin America with $20 billion over ten years to promote land and tax reform as well as housing, health, and schools for the urban poor.[65] Kennedy feared that Fidel Castro would infect Latin America's impoverished with the communist virus unless there was a major change in the continent's maldistributed wealth. The Latin governments applauded, and a few, notably Chile and Colombia, actually redistributed some land. But as the Castro threat faded, Washington ignored its stated aims. Money went to nations adopting programs of financial rectitude. A Chilean plan to expand schools, increase the taxes of the better-off, and redistribute land was deemed economically unsound by Washington.[66] Brazil's president announced the expropriation of landholdings of more than 120 acres; he was quickly overthrown by a military junta who killed the project.[67] Brazil then became the largest recipient of Alliance aid. A recent survey found Brazil's 342 largest landowners held nearly ten times as much land as the poorest 2.5 million. Unsurprisingly as much as 40 percent lies uncultivated.[68]

"Nowhere did AID [the U.S. Agency for International Development] make progress in agrarian or educational reform a condition of its major lending . . . or consider it relevant whether a country closed a fiscal gap through regressive or progressive taxes." So wrote Jerome Levinson and Juan de Onis in *The Alliance That Lost Its Way*.[69] The promise of reform was abandoned by the United States and its clients. The political security of Latin regimes came first. The Alliance demonstrated that an aid-giving nation cannot simultaneously demand change that threatens those in power and seek to strengthen their rule.

The World Bank, the West's international aid agency, has no army, no foreign ministry, no business interests, and no politico-strategic ambitions. At least formally, it is free from the policy constraints that guide the aid-giving of powers. To be sure, the Bank does not operate in a vacuum and must take careful account of the views of its dominant members, notably the United States. These nations supply the Bank's capital, the money raised in financial markets and the contributions to IDA. The Bank's board, which approves each loan, is composed of national representatives whose ballot is weighted according to national economic strength. A 1982 Treasury study for the Reagan administration noted with satisfaction that Washington had succeeded in cutting off bank loans to the radical Allende regime in Chile, had partly stopped loans to Vietnam, and had persuaded the Bank to resume loans on easy terms to Indonesia, Thailand, and the Philippines, although they were no longer eligible to receive them. On the whole, the Treasury concluded, the Bank contributes to long-term American political and strategic interests. (But not enough for the nationalist Reagan-Regan Treasury. It recommended reducing the United States contribution for both hard and soft loans.)[70]

But even this weighted structure gives the Bank some margin for maneuver, because the political interests of the United States, France, Britain, West Germany, and Japan are not identical, and the Bank is not the exclusive instrument of any one. The United States is the most powerful, but it is not all-powerful, and it can and has been outvoted.

The Bank, then, appears better placed to raise the sensitive subject of reform, even to insist on reform as a condition of its assistance. McNamara spoke out, and eloquently, on the theme of reform. Nearly every developing country has promised or written a land reform law, he said. "But the rhetoric of these laws has far outdistanced their results. They have produced little redistribution of land, little improvement in the security of tenants, and little consolidation of small holdings."[71]

McNamara, too, stopped short of action. "The Bank cannot force structural change," he said.[72] Its funds have "played a minor role in the financing of land reform programs."[73] Its projects for change in the countryside are frustrated "where the government itself is dominated by special interests unsympathetic to the objectives of rural development."[74]

This is the voice of national donors. Even the Bank, according to McNamara, can't tie aid to reform that third world elites consider a threat to their power. I. G. Patel, India's former central bank governor and Secretary of the Finance Ministry, agreed. "Even multilateral institutions have to remain in line with the hard realities of economic and political power," he said.[75]

For all McNamara's insistence on directing aid to the impoverished, he had tacitly acknowledged that the Bank's loans must serve growth in general, increased economic output needless of distribution. Without reform, this output would be produced by the many to be consumed by the few.

John White has contended that this approach freezes the structure of third world societies and blocks development itself. He said:

> The emphasis on growth can be seen as an emphasis on support for those elements which are already most active within soci-

> ety, and the bias of international agencies is seen as a bias against change, except in the crudest quantitative sense of more of the same. Where this bias operates without modification, international agencies constitute a force opposed to development.[76]

But the second surge in oil prices and the desperate plight of Africans led the Bank on a new course in 1980. For the first time, it began insisting on some reform as a condition for some loans. African governments could now get funds only if they freed farmers from their paralyzing grip, offering incentives instead of imposing disincentives. Paper promises were not enough. The Bank distributed its new "structural adjustment" loans in slices, depending on performance. Every twelve to eighteen months, recipients must show measurable progress to qualify for more aid. They must raise crop prices, devalue their currencies, weaken or abolish their monopoly buying boards. This was painful, and by 1983 only six African nations were receiving structural adjustment[77] money—Kenya, the Ivory Coast, Malawi, Mauritius, Togo, and Senegal. Senegal, however, fell behind its promised pace of farm reform, and the Bank cut off its funds.

Despite the crisis in food, "powerful political interests have developed around existing policies," the Bank said.[78] Nevertheless, the barriers against peasants were cracking. By 1984, sixteen nations had lifted their ceilings on farm prices or freed them entirely from control.[79] Egypt raised wheat prices 37 percent and enlarged its yield by 4 percent; the Sudan doubled its cotton output with higher prices and the distribution of seeds, fertilizer, and pesticides to tenant and other farmers.[80] Zimbabwe recorded the most spectacular performance, but without the carrot of a structural adjustment loan. It more than doubled corn prices over five years, gave credit to small farmers, and despite the drought, raised farm output 30 percent in 1984.[81] Each step forward, however, was offset by another step backward. If sixteen nations achieved a real devaluation of their currencies, sixteen more raised their exchange rates to cheapen imports for the elite. Reform, the Bank said, has been "patchy and tentative" and "progress remains inadequate."[82] The West's Development Assistance Committee reached a similar conclusion. In nearly every country that has promised to stimulate farming, the plans "are yet to be completed and implemented."[83]

The new approach, however, was promising enough for thirteen industrial nations. They raised $1.1 billion for a new African fund. The money would go to countries that encouraged farmers, that ended the traditional exploitation of the countryside for the capital.[84] The United States saw no political advantage in a joint effort and refused to contribute.

There is, of course, no assurance that the good intentions of either the African recipients or the aid donors will last. If the United States can persuade several allies that Zaire's regime must be supported regardless of how it treats its farmers, Bank money for Zaire will be forthcoming. After a good harvest or two, Africans may reject money that menaces their political control. The failure of the Alliance for Progress to link reform and aid is sobering. The Bank, moreover, is reluctant to press its own initiative. "You can't buy yourself into a policy change," said Ernest Stern, the Bank's senior vice president for operations. A $50 million loan is simply not large enough to encourage major reform.[85] Opposition from borrowers has led the Bank to substitute sectoral for structural adjustment loans, promoting change in a single area like power, transportation, or trade rather than economy-wide reform. Stern has forecast that at most both kinds of loans will not exceed a fifth of the Bank's funds. "There's a good deal of policy weariness," he said, one way of expressing the deep-seated opposition to change and the Bank's traditional caution toward politically charged issues. Indeed, under prodding from the Reagan administration, the Bank has turned to an entirely different structural loan. An echo of the IMF's credits, this loan aims at strengthening market forces and is linked to the reduction of subsidies, lower tariffs, price incentives, shrinking state enterprises.[86]

Nevertheless, a new form of tied assistance has now emerged, no matter how timid. If pursued with conviction and money, it could offer some prospect of bettering the lives of the hundreds of millions bypassed in the aid of the past.

For governments giving aid, economic and distributional

consequences are secondary. The prime concern is strategic, strengthening regimes to oppose Communism (or the West or Israel for aid givers in Moscow and OPEC). Unfortunately, the money buys neither loyalty nor obedience. Client governments are concerned chiefly with their own interests, interests that may not coincide with their patron's. Today's friendly, aid-supported regime often moves tomorrow into the enemy camp. Egypt was a favorite Soviet client and a major recipient of Arab aid until Anwar Sadat decided that his interests were better served by the West and peace with Israel. Now, Egypt, with Israel, is one of the two biggest United States clients. But Sadat's successors, urged on by Muslim fundamentalists, may conclude that they should lead rather than oppose the Arab camp and that a militant anti-Israel stance would further that end. The American investment would then become bankrupt.

A coup in Israel, where elected governments engage in an orderly exchange of power, is unlikely. Moreover, Israel's dependence on American aid is so great—the precarious Israeli economy needs dollars for imports of nearly everything, especially weapons—that it is reasonable to believe that the Jewish state would accept Washington's prescription for peace in the Middle East. It has not, rejecting United States pleas to reduce its settlements on the West Bank of the Jordan as a preliminary to some form of Palestinian autonomy. Israel's *de facto* annexation of the West Bank is one of the single greatest sources of tension in the region, a tension that weakens Washington's objective of stability. The massive American aid, moreover, did not stop Israel from invading Lebanon in 1982 (although some high American officials may have tacitly approved the adventure), an invasion that further increased turbulence in the Middle East. Lebanon's new president, Amin Gemayel, was hailed by the Reagan administration as a pillar of the West and promised abundant aid. But when Israeli, American, and other Western troops left Beirut, Gemayel turned 180 degrees and aligned himself with the strongest presence in his domain, Syria, a close ally of the Soviet Union.

Even the most dependent client can frustrate its patron's declared objectives. The Soviet Union has discovered as much.

Cuba relies on Moscow as heavily as Israel on Washington. Nevertheless, Fidel Castro sent troops to fight rebels in Angola, embroiling the Russians in an area where they apparently sought a far less conspicuous role.

Morocco, among the surest of American supporters, shocked Washington in 1984 by making an accord with Libya, an arch villain in the United States catalogue. Morocco wants to put down the guerrilla Saharawis in the western Sahara; Libyan oil money and an end to Libyan arms for the Saharan nationalists will further this goal. Aid from the United States is useful to King Hassan, but his war makes more pressing demands.

The United States once poured aid into Ethiopia, strategically placed on Africa's horn. Emperor Haile Selassie was backed in his fight against neighboring Somalia, a Soviet client. But the Emperor was overthrown by a colonel mouthing Marxist formulas. Here the switch is complete. The United States now gives money and guns to Somalia, while Moscow places its new bets on Lieutenant Colonel Mengistu Haile Mariam.

The fragility of political friendship was nowhere better demonstrated than in Iran. There the United States maintained one of its largest aid programs, sending weapons and money to the Shah on a grand scale. In time, and partly because of the aid —it created a veneer of Western culture offensive to fundamentalist Muslims and increased Iran's maldistribution of wealth— the Shah too was overthrown. The new regime of militant clerics is hostile toward the Soviet Union and much of the rest of the world, but Iran has now joined the American list of least-liked governments. Or did until Washington inexplicably switched and, at Israel's urging, secretly armed Iran against Iraq. Since Iraq is Israel's enemy, Jerusalem's motive was clear. Washington's was less so, but the bizarre episode raised anew the question of who is client, who patron.

Pakistan also reflects the mischievous consequencs of aid. United States assistance to President Ayub Khan increased at the rapid rate of nearly 30 percent a year in the first half of the 1960s. Growth was impressive, but the new wealth, as in Iran, flowed largely to the few.[87] So Ayub was overthrown. His successors, despite American support, were unable to suppress a revolt in the country's East Wing (now Bangladesh), a revolt inspired in part by the West Wing's successful monopoly of the gains from aid. In time, a general-dictator came to power, eager to strengthen ties with the United States, presiding over a shrunken state in a regime of uncertain life.

The affair is another cautionary tale. The absence of legitimate power in most third world countries means all alliances are fragile. Aid can buy support of a regime as long as its rulers think it is in their interest. But their notions of interest may change drastically; even more likely, they will be displaced by other men with other motives.

Some seemingly more stable countries, like Jordan and India, carefully draw aid from rival camps. India's foreign policy pronouncements more often gratify Moscow than Washington, but it claims neutrality and is too big to be ignored. Jordan walks a careful line between Arabs determined to contain or destroy Israel and the United States, Israel's great friend. So, making gestures to each, Jordan successfully pockets Arab and American aid.

Some aided regimes are obviously ripe for overthrow. One such is Zaire, rich in copper, cobalt, and other minerals, once self-sufficient in corn, its principal food. But under Mobutu, 24 of its 27 million suffer from malnutrition, and at least a quarter of the country's corn is imported.[88] Aid can't overcome the disincentives to output from Mobutu's rule, described by one scholar, Guy Gran, as a "kleptocracy" or the rule of thieves.[89] A kleptocracy may be anticommunist; it is hardly stable. Whether the officers who may overthrow Mobutu turn to Washington or Moscow is an open question.

Similar dangers threaten the recently enlarged aid programs in Central America. The United States nurtures regimes in El Salvador and Honduras to wage war against leftist guerrillas and Nicaragua. But the present rulers in San Salvador or Tegucigalpa could disappear in a coup or civil war, and new men may bitterly resent their predecessors' dependence on Washington. There is ample precedent.

The United States richly rewarded Somoza, Nicaragua's dictator, until his crusade became hopeless. Much of the stress between Washington and the new left regime in Managua flows from this history. To be sure, Central America is nearer Washington than Zaire or Iran, and American power is correspondingly greater. Haiti, for example, is a habitual aid client, and a succession of kleptarchial rulers have sat in its presidential palace despite a steadily declining standard of living for the Haitian people. Although Washington's power close to home is not absolute, it helped bring down the most recent kleptarch, Duvalier, and oversaw the installation of friendly successors. However, the survival of Castro, despite many United States attempts to overthrow him, open and covert, reflects the limits of even a superpower.

Aid, then, is an uncertain instrument of foreign policy. The ruling groups who receive it are dubious clients. They will do what they think serves them; if this coincides with a patron's desires, all the better. Aid, after all, is yet another source of their wealth and power. But if clients believe their interests demand they must flout donors, they will do so. This is as true for Vietnam and Cuba as it is for Israel and Morocco.

Aid neither guarantees stability within a recipient's borders nor beyond them. Sometimes, it helps create tension or even disorder. The more imaginative third world politicians like Nyerere have warned that without larger helpings of aid, miserable third world peasants and slum dwellers will rise up to wage war on the North. "The rich nations," he has said, "will either accept the principle of international equality and move in that direction, or they will have to control the poor nations by force."[90]

Apart from the questionable assumption that a Nyerere or many third world rulers would use aid to better the lot of their people, the prospect of a mass uprising in the South is almost inconceivable. In most nations, the poor are too miserable, too beaten to rise even against the elite groups that exploit them at home. On those rare occasions when they do, their anger is turned inward against their own rulers, not the distant North.

Myrdal has said:

> This idea—that poverty-stricken masses, feeling hopeless about their future, would be prone to revolt—stems from Marx's

> simplistic theory about class struggle and the proletarian revolution.
>
> As a matter of historical record, really impoverished peoples have seldom revolted. When there was a crop failure in some district in India, the poor who had no food usually just went hungry. Some contracted disease and some died. Some took to the road with a hope of finding food somewhere else. They did not revolt.[91]

There are, of course, fringe political benefits from aid. The ambassador of an aid-giving nation has an assured and easy access to ranking ministers and even the ruler of an aid-receiving state. The course of diplomatic life and the contents of cables run more smoothly. In the late 1960s, the aid mission in New Delhi was more than twice as large as the embassy, clearing a path to the top for both the ambassador and the aid mission director.[92]

Governments do worry about U.N. resolutions, no matter how slight their consequences. A third world nation receiving aid from the United States is likelier to accept Washington's language, sometimes. The Soviet Union obtains similar diplomatic triumphs. Again, third world speeches denouncing outrages by one superpower or another probably vary in intensity depending on the volume and source of aid.

Apart from diplomats, there are other beneficiaries. A vast army of officials among donors and recipients, buttressed by battalions of consultants and academics, draws up projects and administers programs. They are all engaged in a ceaseless struggle for more. Tibor Mende, a former U.N. official, described the aid purveyors as

> an administrative-academic complex of unsuspected dimensions. . . . It has become one of the largest industries in the world. It provides a livelihood and a career to more people than do any of the giant international corporations, yet it turns out no goods. Moreover, it is the sole industry in the world which, though in decline, continues to expand its personnel.[93]

The local contractors who mix cement, pour concrete, and erect steel all gain from aid. So do the exporters of machines, tools, and food financed from aid funds. Led by France, Western nations now offer aid in a package, as an inducement to buy goods. Botswana, for example, was promised $4.2 million by the United States if it bought locomotives from General Motors or General Electric.[94]

Evidently, the rulers of governments who receive the checks and the elite circle near them profit from aid. In the countryside, larger landlords, officials, and small merchants also gain.

The Brandt commission asserted:

> The overwhelming proportion of aid money is usefully spent on the purposes for which it is intended, and aid has already done much to diminish hardship in low-income countries and to help them provide a basis for progress in rural development, health and education.[95]

The evidence is otherwise, and this is to be expected. Aid from governments is only tangentially concerned with diminishing hardship. Its central purpose is political, gaining the allegiance of those in power whose prime objective is their own perpetuation.

The strategic arguments for national aid programs are equally unconvincing. Checks to third world governments can purchase allegiance temporarily, open a military base, produce desired votes or speeches at the U.N. But rulers and interests change in the third world with startling rapidity. Its politicians follow Palmerston's rule of no permanent friends, only permanent interests.[96] Indeed, aid can increase instability by widening the maldistribution of wealth. The absolutely impoverished may remain passive, apathetic. But the lavish living of ruling generals can rouse the envy of sergeants, priests, and politicians excluded from the spoils. So today's emperor or president-for-life prudently banks funds for his exile in Switzerland or buys real estate in New York.

In a rational world, programs of bilateral or national aid would be wound down, phased out gradually to avoid abrupt shock, but brought to a final end. The more commercially oriented programs of France, Britain, West Germany, and Japan are less of a threat to their own citizens. Japanese aid to encourage orders from Thailand is unlikely to engage Tokyo's arms in an attempt to preserve a particular regime in Bangkok. But aid for commercial purposes is a hidden subsidy for exports; it distorts the flow of trade and makes more difficult a return to an open trading order. These programs, as well as the more dangerous politico-strategic projects of the United States, the Soviet Union, and OPEC, should also cease.

This proposal is admittedly quixotic. Defense, foreign, and commerce ministries in all rich nations easily convince themselves that aid yields large dividends in influence and control over clients. They will not easily surrender what they think is power without a struggle. Some Western legislators, in the Congress and parliaments, have traditionally been skeptical of aid's worth and more conscious of its dangers. In time, the legislators may be asked to send troops to preserve some falling client, or they may hear a new regime denounce them for having buttressed the tyrant who just fell. Then the legislators may gather their strength and refuse further supplies for executive ambitions. The prospect, however desirable, is probably remote; the most that can be expected in the near future is that aid funds will be cut back.

Technical assistance—supplying the South with experts, model farms, or advice on housing, industry, sanitation—is unobjectionable. This was Truman's original idea; it can do no damage and might even do some good. Converting national aid programs to technical assistance agencies could ease the pain for displaced aid administrators and those who serve them. The United Nations Development Fund purveys technical assistance, and some of it is used fruitfully sometimes. The Fund, spending about $800 million a year, could well be expanded.[97]

The World Bank does not furnish aid in the conventional sense. Its loans, financed by bonds sold in commercial markets, carry market rates of interest, and repayment is demanded on schedule. The Bank, in other words, serves as a middleman between private markets and the South, using its good name to obtain loans that third world regimes could not get on their own. To be sure, there is an element of aid in this since the Bank substitutes its impeccable financial standing for the peccable rating of the borrower. But this is essentially intermediation and should continue. Indeed, at a time when commercial banks are retreating rapidly from the third world, the Bank should expand its lending. It now provides only one dollar in loans for each dollar of its capital, a remarkably conservative ratio. In contrast, commercial banks lend about $20 for each $1 of capital, but as the world has seen, that borders on the reckless. If the Bank increased its ratio to two to one, a Brandt Commission proposal, it could double its loans. The large private lending institutions would probably demand higher interest payments on Bank bonds, and this means higher charges to borrowers. The shortage of loans for the third world, however, may be so great that the extra cost would be worthwhile. Whether or not the loans promote growth is, in the end, up to the borrowers. But the South and its rulers ought not to be cut off from capital for which they pay.

The Bank, moreover, should launch one new venture, the special window for oil urged by McNamara and vetoed in Washington. Despite United States opposition, the Bank does deploy some of its existing funds to find and develop oil and gas. The total reached $1 billion in the 1983 budget year but has slipped back since.[98] "When your largest shareholder makes a lot of noise, you have to pay attention," one official said wryly.[99] He meant the United States, whose major oil companies fear new discoveries in the third world would further reduce prices and profits. A substantial increase rather than a decrease in oil lending, however, would benefit all consumers, North and South. Loans at less than market rates to find new deposits could depress the cost of energy everywhere and provide some insurance against the resurrection of OPEC and its corporate supporters. The world economy still suffers from the damage they inflicted in the 1970s. Fresh discoveries hold out the prospect that an abundant resource might again sell at somewhere near its cost of extraction on land.

The International Development Association, IDA, is the Bank agency that does give aid. Its loans carry no interest charge and fifty-year maturities. Many of these loans suffer from the same disabilities as national aid programs. They reinforce regimes whose policies stifle farm output and neglect the human resources squatting in great cities. But they need not do so. If all IDA money was conditional, like the new structural adjustment loans, the agency's aid could raise output and living standards for the disenfranchised in the third world. IDA should provide funds only in return for visible reforms in land tenure, taxes, slum housing, and sanitation, and the spread of literacy. Money should be granted only in return for those major changes that promise fuller use of resources, human and physical. Failure to perform, continuing exploitation of farmers in favor of city elites, would cut off the funds. An IDA promoting reform would then fill the gap left by the abolition of national aid programs and would deserve a substantial increase in contributions from the rich.

There are two obvious objections to this course. If reform threatens the power of third world rulers, they will not commit what they believe is suicide for the sake of IDA's money. They will prefer to press their traditional patrons. This, of course, is another powerful reason to end the bilateral programs. The second difficulty lies with IDA's financiers. The agency must reflect the policies of the industrial nations. The United States, Britain, France, and Japan may not agree entirely over El Salvador, Nicaragua, Cuba, Chad, Grenada, or China. But these differences can be composed. Members of IDA's board may engage in logrolling. If El Salvador has failed to meet the test of land reform, France can be persuaded to vote for aid in return for Washington's support in Burkina Faso. IDA, then, would simply become a surrogate for dismantled national aid agencies.

There is no answer to this. The resistance of even the most high-minded international civil servants has practical limits. Publicity could act as a deterrent of sorts, alerting legislatures and publics to abuses. But only limited reliance can be placed on public indignation over a loan to a Tanzania that failed to scrap its monopoly marketing board. The Alliance for Progress was turned on its head, and barely anyone noticed. Nevertheless, the experiment is worth trying. Some hard-pressed African rulers believe they can survive and may even benefit from reform. There could be others. The aid givers are at least as great an obstacle as the recipients. Their interest in a more humane and hence more productive third world is far less than their strategic or commercial concerns.

There is no possibility of substituting conditional IDA assistance for national programs as long as the crude economic nationalism of the Reagan era prevails. But this posture is the result of a specific set of forces, the defeat in Vietnam, feeble economic policymaking since the 1970s, the lack of clear executive purpose, the humiliations of a superpower by lesser regimes, and the disgrace of a president. In time, new lessons will be drawn from the events triggered by United States nationalism and its analogues in Europe and Japan. The next turn of the political wheel could leave the United States and other industrial nations persuaded of the folly of bilateral aid, of the possibilities that lie in the international institutions they control.

Aid in its present form defeats its intended goals, both strategic and economic. The strategic objective is a chimera. The economic goal is possible only if assistance is used to undermine the institutions that perpetuate poverty in the cities and countrysides of Asia, Africa, and Latin America. This means rejecting, politely but firmly, the pleas of Southern rulers for more aid and fewer strings. Aid of that stripe is a contradiction in terms.

Chapter 6

The Uncertain Flow of Trade

At the heart of the third world's quarrel with the global economic order lies the price of raw materials. Copper, rubber, jute, bananas, coffee, iron ore, and more provide a major share of earnings from abroad, hard currency for developing countries. Their command over imports of tools, machines, technology, consumer goods, and even food largely rises and falls with the prices of the commodities they export.[1] About a dozen nations—notably Mexico, Brazil, the four "baby tigers" of Taiwan, Singapore, Hong Kong, and South Korea, Malaysia, the Philippines, Thailand, and India—are escaping from the commodity trap and draw an increasing part of their earnings from new manufacturing industries, exporting steel, autos, and other products. But these new industrialists are the exception, and several still earn much more from raw materials than from finished goods. For Brazil, three fifths of its foreign receipts in the early 1980s came from commodities, Malaysia two thirds, and the Philippines three quarters.[2]

As late as 1981, 42 percent of third world exports were raw materials. Sixty-eight nations still earned more than half their foreign exchange from commodities. Unlike prices for imported machines, however, the prices of raw materials fluctuate wildly, swinging up and down with drought, pest, or flood, slump or prosperity in the developed world. These gyrations make orderly plans difficult and can discourage investment in the mines and crops on which so much of the third world relies. The roller coaster may promote the planting of too many or too few coffee trees or cocoa bushes; it inhibits the search for new minerals or the opening of new mines. Above all, wide swings in export earnings, feast one year and famine the next, break up the steady and increasing flow of imported goods a third world nation needs to build its own industry, to develop and expand its economy.

Although the governments of developing countries bear a substantial measure of responsibility for inhibiting their own growth, they are largely helpless in world commodity markets, unable to assure stable earnings from exports.

Since the end of the war, the developing countries have urged a simple-sounding solution to end export uncertainty. They have asked rich nations to join in agreements to flatten the swings in raw materials prices. They have proposed pacts to put a floor under and a ceiling over the price of each commodity much as industrial nations do to protect the incomes of their farmers. Indeed, the developing countries have even more ambitious goals than stable prices. They hope to use the pacts to gain ever-increasing prices, extracting income from rich consumers for poor producers.

Unsurprisingly, the rich nations have firmly repulsed all attempts to use commodity agreements as a form of hidden aid. But at least in principle, the West has not rejected agreements aimed only at dampening the swings in commodity prices. The United States has been the most openly hostile to interference with market forces, except for that by the handful of great corporations who dominate the buying of tea, cocoa, copper, bauxite, and other raw materials. This has led Robert L. Rothstein to suggest that "for market enthusiasts, administered prices are anathema—unless set by Western corporations."[3] But the United States has nevertheless taken part in several commodity agreements, promoted at least one, coffee, to stiffen Latin Americans against Fidel Castro, and publicly proclaimed its lack of religion on the subject.[4] Since 1958, the United States has said it will not oppose workable agreements and will examine each commodity case by case. If the West's enthusiasm has been limited, it has not been a significant obstacle to the pacts.

Nevertheless, twenty years after the third world organized itself economically at the first UNCTAD, only a handful of agreements are in place, and their importance is negligible. One, tin, worked with a fair measure of success until its collapse in

1985. Another, for rubber, is too young to judge. Those for coffee and cocoa have broken down with wearisome regularity. The last, sugar, covers only a fraction of the world market. All the meetings and all the talk, the resolutions, proclamations, and demands, have produced almost no change in the way the world's commodities trade. UNCTAD's efforts, said L. N. Rangarajan, amount to this: "Years of negotiation and mountains of paper may eventually produce a mouse."[5] Writing in 1983, he concluded, "The primary commodity scene is as bleak as it ever was."[6]

The third world's central global economic objective has been almost completely frustrated. Meanwhile, raw materials prices continue to gyrate. Between 1979 and 1984, copper swung between $.596 and $.998 a pound, tea from $.899 to $1.767 a pound, jute from $278 to $866 a ton. At UNCTAD headquarters in Geneva, the subject embarrasses officials. Commodity price agreements remain on the third world's agenda, but they have become part of a ritual incantation.[7]

At first glance, this failure is remarkable. The need for steadier export earnings is no less pressing, and for many nations that means stabilizing the receipts from a single commodity: coffee for Colombia, El Salvador, Guatemala, and Haiti; cocoa for Ghana; bauxite for Guyana; copper for Chile; tin for Bolivia.

Moreover, the logic of commodity pacts has, in the abstract, a certain surface appeal. Producing and consuming nations could agree on a price floor and a ceiling. When prices in the market threaten to fall through the floor—a Western slump will drive minerals down while a bumper harvest will threaten farm products—the floor will be defended. The pact members will buy up any surplus and store it as a buffer.

If market prices pierce the ceiling—a Western boom to drive up minerals, flood, frost or some other natural calamity to slash agricultural produce—the buffer stock manager will sell from his warehouse to hold costs in place. For commodities that can't be stored like bananas or meat, pact members can resort to export quotas. They will curb sales when prices fall, increase them when they rise. Several of the existing pacts, notably tin, have used both a buffer stock and export quotas, chiefly to defend the floor.

If the need exists, if the mechanism has a logic, and if—at least sometimes—consuming nations are willing to cooperate, what has gone wrong? Why are commodity agreements so rare?

The answer lies with the commodity producers of the third world. Their interests often clash, although they produce the same raw material. It is their failure to agree, not dogmatic hostility of the rich, that accounts for the lack of agreements. In tea, for example, India and Sri Lanka, the dominant exporters, face a challenge from new producers in East Africa, notably Kenya. To escape its dependence on traditional crops, Kenya has settled 100,000 peasants on tea plantations and has sought a pact to steady tea prices. But the producers can't agree; India wants to limit the export market share of the newcomers while Kenya wants to expand its sales. New Delhi favors export quotas; Kenya wants a buffer stock.[8] So New Delhi can be expected to talk endlessly and postpone indefinitely the agreement the new producers want, at least until their output threatens New Delhi's privileged position.

(To attract votes on the eve of India's 1984 election, Prime Minister Indira Gandhi sharply reduced exports and drove down domestic prices. Mrs. Gandhi did not survive to benefit from this device, but the technique worked. India's big tea-drinking voters enjoyed a cheaper brew, and world prices shot upward. Under an international agreement, India could not have played such electoral games.)[9]

For copper, Chile is India, and the story is much the same. Before an international accord was established, the large concerns who mine the metal were reasonably successful at holding prices steady in the 1950s and 1960s. A healthy fear of competing plastics and aluminum kept the lid on. Then the producing countries tried their hand at an agreement and very soon fell out. When prices collapsed in the mid-1970s, Peru, Zambia, and Zaire obeyed the rule to cut production. But Chile, whose copper can be extracted cheaply, ignored the agreement and expanded output, destroying the infant pact.[10]

In the same way, cost differences persuaded eleven iron ore producers to abandon their attempt to make an accord in 1977. Physical and chemical differences in ores, the gap between efficient and inefficient ports meant different production costs and made agreement difficult. A low cost producer like Brazil wants no part of a deal that places a high price umbrella over less fortunate miners.[11]

The tin agreement, once regarded as a model, has run into similar problems. Bolivia is one of the biggest producers, but its costs are high; Malaysia, a low-cost producer, wants low prices to discourage substitutes. So Bolivia dropped out of the accord in 1982. The agreement survived partly because of a skillfully managed buffer pact and partly because of a *deus ex machina.* When the buffer stock was exhausted and prices threatened to burst the agreement's bounds, the United States strategic stockpile sold tin to hold things in place. When the buffer ran out of money to prop tin prices, the agreement's pragmatic members clamped on export quotas, physically limiting sales.[12]

Other special factors enabled the tin producers to hold prices within the target range for most of their pact's history. There are only a few members, seven. The world market's tonnage is small, a fraction of copper, and so storing a buffer is not a crushing financial burden. Finally, there is a growing demand for tin plate, unlike many other products processed from raw commodities. Supporting prices is far easier in an expanding than a contracting industry. Like OPEC, the tin producers were finally undone by greed and economics. They pushed prices to a level that encouraged substitutes—paper cartons, aluminum, and glass bottles. Ancient mines began working. Late in 1985, the buffer stock ran out of money to keep tin off the market, and its manager was forced to renege on promises to buy tin. Whether the pact can be put together again is in doubt.[13]

Cocoa pacts come and go, sometimes because economic forces overwhelm the price targets, frequently because members, consumers, and producers, will not abide by the rules. The accords died twice in the 1970s because prices broke through the agreed ceiling; another agreement fell apart in 1980 when the developing countries sought a floor of $1.20 a pound while prices slid to 50 cents. The deal was remade a year later, but without the major consumer, the United States, and producer, the Ivory Coast. Moreover, cocoa agreements are plagued by the familiar high-cost–low-cost problem. Brazil and the Ivory Coast, cheaper producers, seek lower target prices and higher quotas for themselves. Ghana and Nigeria resist them.[14]

The coffee arrangement sponsored by the U.S. Alliance for Progress worked fairly well for ten years, until 1972. But then frost in Brazil and wars in Africa led to shortages and a price explosion. Coffee has had an indifferent record ever since.[15] Again, Colombia's high grade and Africa's low grade coffee leads to quarrels over prices and quotas. New producers like Indonesia and Kenya struggle for a slice of the arranged market against the established growers. The Ivory Coast has evaded quotas with an exotic device, "tourist coffee," sending its excess produce to a third country that has not exhausted its limit.[16] Importing consumers frequently refuse to play their role of enforcing quotas. Each shipment is supposed to carry a certificate of origin, attesting to the fact that it comes from a producer who is exporting within the agreed limit. But when importing firms are eager for coffee and the price is right, certificates are falsified.

Few commodities have even reached the imperfect stage of coffee, cocoa, and tin. Phosphate is typical. Morocco, the world's largest exporter with about one third of the market, simply boycotts talks on a pact. It sees no advantage in accommodating smaller, higher-cost competitors.[17]

Agreements among governments to stabilize raw materials prices are crippled or doomed because third world nations are unwilling to sacrifice a known national advantage for a hypothetical common interest. As in any cartel, members squabble over their share of the market. Even that most successful of short-run cartels, OPEC, has been riddled with internal fights over levels of production—the equivalent of export quotas—and can't, under stress, hold to bargains solemnly made at Geneva and elsewhere. When commodity agreements are reached, they are breached. A nation beset by balance of payments deficits will not hold back exports in the name of a price agreement. Gamani Corea, UNCTAD's former Secretary General, has lamented that third world commodity producers "just don't see how they can give up a presence" in markets, "especially when they are hard-pressed. They just don't see that if you want to regulate price, you must regulate volume."[18]

There are other difficulties. Producers need consumer nations, the West, to make the accords work. The consumers serve as enforcer and financier. They are supposed to import only the volume provided under the quotas, and they frequently ignore this obligation. They are supposed to contribute money for the buffer stocks that help regulate price but often balk at the amount or provide too little for effective control.

Choosing the right target for price floor and ceiling is an awesome task. In theory, these should bracket a price that a freely competitive market would set. But wars, natural catastrophes, monetary upheavals, boom, and slump almost insure that any levels set today are overtaken by tomorrow's events. There is a natural struggle between producers and consumers. Producers understandably seek high prices and consumers low prices; their failure to agree has frequently prevented accords.

The postwar history is clear. Commodity pacts have failed and can be expected to fail largely because third world producers fall out. It is easy enough to endorse resolutions at conferences embracing commodity agreements in the abstract. It is much harder for two nations to agree on how much of a world market they will share and what is the proper price for their raw material, particularly when each has different costs. The appearance of a new producer makes the task even more difficult. For brief periods, for a few commodities, the differences can be submerged. But the history of tea, coffee, cocoa, and even oil suggest that these arrangements are fleeting. "No agreement has been able to exert a significant and consistent moderating influence on the markets involved," concluded Christopher P. Brown.[19] Iron ore, copper, manganese, phosphate, bananas, meat, jute, and the others that UNCTAD has sought to bring under a price-stabilizing umbrella never reach even the dignity of a paper pact.

Encouraged by UNCTAD officials, the third world has made one last effort to pump life into commodity agreements. UNCTAD has called for a large sum of money to lend buffer stocks that have exhausted their resources. The agency believed that the buffers cannot all be exhausted at the same time, that a Common Fund could work on an insurance principle. The Common Fund was supposed to collect $2 billion from third world and developed nations and borrow another $4 billion from international organizations or commercial banks. This sum, it was reasoned, would be so attractive that somehow producers would sink their differences and draw up new pacts.[20] UNCTAD called its invention the Integrated Commodity Program. Harry G. Johnson bitingly described it as "neither integrated nor a policy, but an attempt to paper over with semantic ambiguity a variety of inconsistent policies. . . ."

In the end, a skeptical West cut the Common Fund back to $330 million, plus another $280 million for promotion and research.[21] It has made no difference. By the end of 1982, thirty-seven third world countries had not even bothered to ratify their membership, including such important raw materials producers as Malaysia, Morocco, Brazil, Nigeria, Peru, Pakistan, and Argentina. Norway offered to pay the membership price for ten nations; one accepted.[22] Before its 1985 collapse, the tin agreement broke up briefly, in part because its members feared they would be compelled to surrender their buffer money to the Common Fund.[23] If commodity agreements are largely impotent or doomed, what is the point of contributing to phantom buffers?

The death of commodity agreements is not an unmitigated blessing for industrial nations although Western rhetoric sometimes suggests as much. The pacts' professed aim, more stable prices, could have benefited the North as well as the South. Indeed, this accounts in part for the willingness of consumer nations to join the few agreements that emerge from time to time. Stable commodity prices could help contain Western inflation. There is reason to believe that raw materials costs work like a ratchet on price levels, particularly in the United States. Increases are passed on by processors and manufacturers to become embedded in final prices. A fall in commodity prices, however, is merely a windfall to industrialists. They do not lower their final prices proportionately but simply pocket the difference. So, a cutback in the upward swings would dampen consumer price increases. One economist, Jere R. Behrman, calculated that if eight of UNCTAD's targeted commodities had been kept from rising or falling 15 percent in the 1970s, total output in the United States would have grown by $15 billion. A slower rising level of consumer prices would have reduced unemployment and so expanded production.[24]

Businessmen have told Congressional committees that steadier raw materials prices would serve their interests. Stable costs would induce more efficient investment and more orderly production abroad. How much of a difference steadier prices would make to the third world has not been estimated. But spasms in export earnings disrupt local investment, interfere with imports of capital goods, and create and deepen recurrent balance of payments crises. Nevertheless, commodity pacts as a universal solution are no longer a realistic objective. They have been swamped in a morass of conflicting national interests within the developing world.

The third world's single-minded focus on commodity prices has obscured its real concern. What developing countries need and want is money, foreign exchange, purchasing power for Western machinery, skills, and materials. Commodity prices and exports are simply a means to an end, earning dollars, marks, francs, and pounds to pay for imported goods and services. The problem lies in the fact that wide swings in raw materials prices yield wide swings in export receipts. Instead of the vain attempt to stabilize prices, there is another and far more direct way of dealing with this: Insure a more even flow of export earnings by a system of guarantees. If Colombia suffers a drop in receipts because bumper harvests have depressed coffee prices, or if a frost kills Brazil's crop, lend these nations enough to make up the earnings gap. In boom times—Brazil's frost will provide Colombia with a windfall—require them to repay. Stabilizing commodity prices is simply an awkward way to achieve the same end.*

On the eve of UNCTAD's first meeting, an embryo scheme to steady the flow of export earnings was quietly adopted by the International Monetary Fund. It labors under the bureaucratic title of Compensatory Financing Facility, and its early versions

*Of course the third world had really hoped its schemes would not stabilize but raise prices and earnings. Even if this was possible, it would not be accepted by the West.

provided only a thin trickle of loans. But over the years, the Fund discovered that the payments deficits it tries to cure often flow from deep cuts in commodity earnings, cuts that have little to do with the behavior of third world nations and much more to do with slump in the West. The Fund began loosening its constraints. Between 1980 and 1984, the IMF loaned 8.3 billion of Special Drawing Rights (about $9 billion in 1985 currencies) to developing countries that had suffered a shortfall in their export receipts. About one third of the IMF's outstanding credits now come from this single source.[25]

The Facility works this way: Any nation—and the overwhelming majority are from the third world—can borrow if it suffers a drop in export earnings through no fault of its own. This means that the shortfall was caused by a natural disaster, flood or drought, or recession in the West.

The Fund calculates the gap in export earnings against a five-year trend. It computes the borrower's receipts in the two years preceding the drop and forecasts those for the next two years. The IMF assumes exports will grow at a steady pace for the five-year period. The shortfall is the difference between the sum that should have been earned in the slump year and the actual receipts.*

The Fund, however, does not finance the full shortfall, only a fraction. Each borrower is limited by the amount of its quota or contribution to the Fund. For many third world nations, this is modest indeed. Mali's quota is 50.8 million SDRs; Zambia's is

*The Common Market runs a variant of this device for sixty-five African, Caribbean, and Pacific nations, mostly former French and British colonies. It provides grants and loans for shortfalls in earnings from the Community, but only for individual commodities. Moreover, a limited number of commodities are covered. The Fund, in contrast, covers all exports of goods and services to the entire world. The Common Market's commodity-by-commodity approach tends to discourage recipients from diversifying, from trying new crops, including food. It also discourages the processing of raw materials and manufactured exports. It binds countries to the Common Market. The technique exemplifies "aid" to reinforce protectionist, parochial goals, qualities that often distinguish the European Community. The third world, through UNCTAD, is taking a belated interest in compensatory finance. Characteristically, UNCTAD prefers the commodity-by-commodity technique because it strengthens the status quo, particularly the bureaucratic and political armies running state marketing boards.

270.3 million; for Peru, it is 330.9 million, Bangladesh 287.5 million. The quota limit acts as a low ceiling.[26]

The Fund calculates that it covered nearly three fifths of its borrowers' shortfall, 58.1 percent, between 1976 and 1984. But the ceiling works perversely, providing more money in good years than bad. In 1981, when export earnings plunged, Fund loans matched only half the estimated shortfall, 49 percent. By 1983, the third world's exports were rising in step with the United States recovery. The IMF then filled three fourths of the gap, 75.7 percent. A year later, the level dropped sharply to 40.5 percent.[27]

These figures, moreover, magnify the IMF's support. They count only those nations that successfully applied for help and omit all those who did not or could not. Some had exhausted their right to borrow from the Fund. Others were disqualified because their own policies—overvalued exchange rates or large domestic deficits—were blamed for their export problems. The Fund then makes up only a small fraction of the actual drop in total third world receipts.

Louis M. Geroux, a Fund authority on the Facility, has argued that full compensation, even for qualified nations, would be a mistake, that it would encourage borrowers to delay needed reforms to prevent future shortfalls.[28] But this contention, potent for aid, has less relevance here. The loans are made to victims of a fall in earnings that takes place through no fault of their own. This is the cardinal principle on which compensatory financing rests. If the shortfall was caused by pest, drought, or Western slump, no internal reform can correct it.

The real reason for the Fund's restraint is money. Compensation in full could exhaust the Fund's resources, limit its ability to lend to third world debtors whose finances are critical for Western banks. A large increase in quotas could provide funds for full coverage of export shortfalls but governments of industrial nations are not ready for such an adventure. The Reagan administration resisted proposals to double the Fund's resources in 1982 and accepted a 50 percent increase only when it saw this was necessary to support Western banks.[29]

A more effective stabilization of third world export earnings requires loans covering a major fraction—perhaps 80 percent—of any shortfall.[30] The loan should be determined by the loss of export earnings, not the borrower's quota at the IMF. In 1984 that would have meant IMF loans of at least 1.6 billion SDRs—the total would have been higher if nations that had used up their borrowing rights had been eligible—instead of the 815 million SDRs that were disbursed. The Fund's resources should be expanded to make fuller coverage possible, to spare third world nations dependent on commodity exports from a sharp contraction in imports because of accidents of nature or Western business cycles.

Indeed, such loans could make a modest contribution to relieving slumps in the West. They would tend to expand when industrial economies declined and contract in booms. Since these loans would be spent mostly for imports from the West, they would strengthen the weakened demand among industrial economies. (This argument is quite different from the Brandt proposal for enlarged aid to cure Western unemployment. The export loans—not gifts—are countercyclical, expanding in bad times, contracting in good. Brandt urges an enlarged and continuing stream of free claims on resources.)

Until now, the Fund has relied on quotas or member contributions for its money. But it could, if its Western managers agreed, borrow in commercial markets, much like the World Bank. High Fund officials have indicated they would welcome this freedom to tap private resources. The United States and other powerful members, however, fear this would weaken their grip over the institution. That concern seems groundless. Western influence over the World Bank has not been markedly diminished because the Bank goes to Wall Street, the Euromarket, or London to borrow. The real difficulty lies with the intensified nationalism that has overtaken the leading powers, their dislike of collective decision making—even among themselves—and their illusory search for total control. It is this same spirit that frustrates the conversion of national into international aid programs. But a decision to permit IMF borrowing is a mild infringement of Western sovereignty, and the value of a genuine export stabilization plan should make up for it.

The IMF's compensatory loans carry a price and properly so. In mid-1985, the interest charge was 7 percent, well below a market rate but a real cost.[31] The loans, however, must be repaid in three to five years and this is an anomaly. Since the money is borrowed to make up a shortfall, it should be repaid with a windfall, when export receipts rise above the trend line. Commodity prices rise as well as fall. In boom years or times of slim harvests for neighbors, borrowers will earn more than the five-year trend predicts. Repayment should come from this surplus, free from an arbitrary date on the calendar.

A loan at a subsidized rate with a maturity linked to surplus earnings and covering most of a drop in exports has some of the qualities of aid. Indeed, the very fact that a third world debtor turns to the Fund is a plea for help, a sign that the borrowing country can't raise the money in commercial markets. There is no assurance that the loan will not be misused, that it won't help sustain an elite who impedes rather than spurs development. There is no special magic in money from the IMF. Unlike national aid programs with their strong political content, however, a loan from the Commodity Financing Facility responds to an objectively determined need, an export shortfall. Moreover, there is a stiff, no-fault test. The Fund must be satisfied that the shortfall did not result from disincentives to farmers, from an overvalued currency, or other failings of the borrower. The gap must arise from natural or economic circumstances over which the borrower has no control. The loan, then, is free of much of aid's taint.

The third world cannot sustain its case that the terms of trade are rigged against it; it can plausibly argue that it is victimized by gyrations in commodity prices far greater than those for manufactured goods. In the end, the possibility of abusing the Fund's commodity loans is outweighed by the gains for North and South. All benefit when developing countries can expand their imports of goods and services from the industrial world.

The most direct way in which North and South enrich each other is through trade, the exchange of goods and services. This is ritually recognized in the North by presidents and premiers, but it is no less true. Each year, leaders from the United States and six other industrial nations meet to renew their allegiance to open trade and deplore the obstacles they have recently created against its unobstructed flow. At annual summits, they solemnly warn that protectionist barriers will "foster unemployment, increase inflation, and undermine the welfare of our people."[32] They express their determination "to maintain our political commitment to an open and nondiscriminatory world trading system." At the 1985 summit, the seven declared that "Open multilateral trade is essential to global prosperity, and we urge an early and substantial reduction of barriers to trade."[33] They then return home to invent new devices to protect domestic industries from foreign competition. The leaders are not necessarily hypocrites. They are responding to what they regard as the higher political imperative. They do appreciate that in general an open trading system enhances material well-being. But there are particular steel, textile, auto, and other workers and their employers whose jobs and capital are threatened by foreign goods.

For the South, this is peculiarly ironic. Since the start of aid programs, the North has encouraged these countries to grow through diversification, develop industry, bring to world trade something more than raw materials. This is the highroad to success. For a growing number, Brazil, Mexico, India, South Korea, and others who took the advice seriously (or more likely thought it through for themselves), it has a hollow ring. No sooner do they successfully produce textiles and clothing or television sets and electronic clocks then up go the barriers; the Northern markets, where three fifths of the South's manufactured goods are sold, are ringed in or closed off. The good advice has soured.

Trade barriers had been coming down steadily through much of the postwar period, but once again, the 1973–74 oil shock and the sharp slump it produced turned history back on itself. Ever since, obstacles to trade have been rising steadily. The rich victimize each other as well as the developing world—many of the new barriers were designed chiefly to shut off Japanese competition—but this is little consolation for the South. In the 1970s and early 1980s, a time of sluggish Western growth and high unemployment, an extraordinary number of new techniques have emerged to bar or control the flow of foreign goods—Voluntary Export Restraints (enforced by the threat of compulsion), Orderly Marketing Arrangements (an order issued by importers to exporters), price floors below which foreign products may not be sold. Customary and legitimate devices to protect against unfair trade have been stretched to fight off foreign competitors. The penalty tariffs of Countervailing Duties or Anti-Dumping measures have been deployed almost indiscriminately.

The seven summit statesmen would argue that they must consider their own people first, that domestic makers of jeans, steel tubes, and television sets cannot be sacrificed on the altar of abstract trading principles. The victims are not only the makers of foreign goods who lose a market. They are also the citizens who vote the seven into office. The wave of protection has cost consumers in the industrial world tens of billions of dollars in higher prices—there is no way of accurately measuring the amount for many of the arrangements are secret—adding to the inflationary pressures that have inhibited Western governments from returning to the benign path of high growth, high employment, and low price increases.

The growing obstacles to trade stand in marked contrast to the first twenty-five postwar years, the years of general Western prosperity. Then, memories of the 1930s and the destructive role of tariff walls in the Great Depression, were still strong in people's minds. Western nations resolved to bring down trade walls (farming was and is excepted largely because farmers live in competitive markets they cannot but governments can control). To this end, the West created another remarkable international institution, the General Agreement on Tariffs and Trade. Every few years, nations assembled under GATT's auspices to swap cuts in their tariffs, a tax on imports, and the most common form of protection. After prolonged bargaining, the major trading nations came away with lower tariffs. Trade flourished. A nation with an industry damaged by a tariff cut could turn to GATT for relief from its pledge; an elaborate code of rules, of international law, grew up to govern trade. The process was so successful that tariffs have all but disappeared as a factor in the trade of industrial nations. (The South clings to very high tariffs, claiming that its young industries can't yet stand international competition, a dubious contention for those who have successfully penetrated Northern markets.) By 1987, the average tariff on industrial exports to the United States will be 4.2 percent, for the Common Market 4 percent and Japan 2.5 percent. These low averages, however, conceal some very high peaks for individual products. Chemicals in the United States have traditionally sheltered behind a tariff far above other industries.[34]

But the economic malaise of the 1970s weakened the GATT system. The rule of concerted agreement was ignored, and rich nations acted on their own to block fabrics, clothes, consumer electronics, steel, autos, and other products that newly industrializing nations export. Managed or manipulated trade now cuts into the foreign currency earnings on which these countries count to import goods and services as well as pay their heavy debts.[35] The rise of the new protectionism and the steady erosion of GATT showed no sign of diminishing well into the 1980s. Slow Western growth and high unemployment heightened fears of job loss for workers and managers in industries that could not compete.

It is uncertain how much world trade is distorted by the new protectionism. Apart from the secrecy of many arrangements, some are so effective they simply wipe out all trade in particular goods and so can't be counted. The studies then report widely varying results. One by Sheila Page estimated that about 34 percent of all imports to the industrial world had to thread their way through nontariff barriers in 1974. Five years later, this had climbed to 41 percent. In 1984, Jan Tumlir, GATT's chief economist, calculated that as much as 45 percent of all international trade was subject to cost-increasing barriers, not counting tariffs. This is a remarkable level for a world whose industrial rich profess the virtues of unimpeded trade.[36]

The World Bank, acknowledging that the new protection warps trade statistics, produced the smallest estimate. In 1984, the Bank calculated that the United States resorted to barriers other than tariffs on only 5.5 percent of its trade with the third world and 13 percent on trade with industrial nations.[37] For Japan, the figures were 5.4 percent and 19.2 percent; for the

Common Market, 11.8 percent and 15.1 percent. In contrast, UNCTAD counted nontariff barriers on 21,000 specific products and claimed that 96.6 percent of all goods face some limit on the quantity that can be sold abroad. UNCTAD included all the heavy protective devices that the third world uses against itself and the rich.[38]

"You're talking about a heck of a lot of trade," said Harold Malmgren, deputy trade representative in the Nixon and Ford administrations. New curbs on autos, steel, and textiles alone add up to "more of an increment in protection than has occurred at any time since 1929–30 and the Smoot-Hawley tariff."[39] The Smoot-Hawley bill increased American tariffs on 3,000 products, contributing to a cut in trade that deepened the Great Depression.[40]

Western economists are notorious for doctrinal division. But in matters of trade theory, nearly all subscribe to the principle of comparative advantage. It holds that each nation gains by producing goods and services in which it enjoys the greatest cost advantage and importing products in which its margin of cost advantage is smaller or nonexistent. At its simplest, the rule directs all countries to specialize in the goods they produce most cheaply and then exchange them. Comparative advantage, the invention of David Ricardo, works this way: Perhaps the United States can produce television sets more efficiently than Brazil. But if the United States manufactures computers at an even greater margin of cost savings, the United States is better off, becomes richer, by encouraging the flow of resources—labor, materials, capital, and management—into the output of computers and buying television sets from Brazil. Nations should concentrate on products that provide the largest *comparative* advantage, not a simple *absolute* gain.

This doctrine lies at the root of international trade theory. Like most principles in economics, it is refined common sense (sometimes so refined that the complexities of the real world are assumed away). Ricardo was a ghostly presence at the postwar creation of GATT and the successive rounds that tore down the most familiar trade barrier, tariffs. The new protection, however, turns his doctrine on its head. By blocking imports, nations produce less efficiently, making goods in which they suffer a disadvantage in costs. Trade shrinks everywhere, and the South's largest markets are constricted.

The problem is that the benefits of free trade are diffused over an entire nation in the form of lower prices and a wider choice of goods but the pain of trade concessions or the profits from protection are highly concentrated, among the luggage makers, shoe manufacturers, and battery producers whose plants and workers face extinction from foreign competitors. It is this that gives protection its political power, particularly at a time when other job prospects and other industries are sluggish or declining.

The new managed trade began as early as 1962, when the West was still enjoying more or less steady gains in economic growth and employment. The Kennedy administration, pressed by declining cotton mills in New England and the South, persuaded nineteen countries, mostly Asian, to curb their cotton exports to the United States. The exporters were made to understand that the withholding of their consent would lead to more drastic, mandatory action, a threat that was later used repeatedly against other industries. With unintended irony, the cotton agreement's preamble promised the arrangement would "facilitate economic expansion and promote the development of less-developed countries . . . increasing their export earnings. . . ."[41] Indeed, Kennedy believed in freer trade, and his name was given to the GATT tariff bargaining round after his death. Almost unnoticed, the Common Market, fretting over what it saw as too much steel capacity, induced the growing Japanese industry to limit its exports of some fabricated products. This too was a "voluntary" arrangement, backed by the implied threat of sterner action.[42]

The critical series of events began in the early 1970s when the system that fixed exchange rates collapsed. Now currencies could and did float more or less freely, effectively wiping out what was left of tariff protection. This hastened the decline of GATT, its orderly rules, and the relatively open markets of the rich. An American manufacturer producing behind a 10 percent tariff wall lost his advantage when the currency of a foreign competitor declined by 10 percent against the dollar. Since tariffs were disappearing anyway, this was less important than the fact that fluctuating exchange rates were now exercising a powerful influence on trade. Declining currencies gave exporters an advantage; appreciating currencies made selling abroad harder. But above all, it was the 1974 slump linked to the steep rise in oil prices that brought about the new world of manipulated trade. Slower output and fewer jobs touched off irresistible demands for more arrangements like those for cotton and steel. They grew at an exponential rate.*

The most sweeping is the Multifibre Arrangement of 1974, successor to the cotton deal, a complex web that ensnares nearly all textiles and textile products. It embraces not only cotton but wool and synthetics. It covers yarn, fabrics, and 123 specific products—socks, dressing gowns, shirts, underwear, sweaters, jeans, and virtually every other piece of clothing.[43] Every third world producer of consequence must take the pledge, promising to export to the United States or the Common Market no more than a specific quantity of each item. The arrangement limits exports from Colombia, Haiti, China, Hong Kong, Japan, South Korea, Malaysia, Mexico, the Philippines, Romania, Yugoslavia, Singapore, Thailand, Brazil, India, Egypt, Pakistan, Argentina, Brazil, Sri Lanka, and more. Thus Sri Lanka, its growth tied in considerable measure to textiles, agrees to export no more than 11 million pieces of five items to Western Europe, 17.5 million pieces of seven items to the United States.[44] Those few textile goods that somehow get left out are inhibited by so-called Orderly Marketing Agreements or pacts between Washington and a single exporter. The United States used this rubric to halve imports from Korea and Taiwan.[45]

Textiles matter to developing countries. Typically, they can be produced with little investment by low-cost, unskilled labor. A textile industry is often the first a developing country creates for foreign exchange so the Multifibre scheme is a large burden to

*It is impossible to capture in numbers the subtle forms of Japanese protection. It is marked by government suggestion rather than overt measures, encouraging rather than ordering Japanese firms to buy Japanese. Concealed administrative barriers are preferred to blunt quotas. Health and safety standards for products are used to keep out competing imports.

carry. In 1983, one estimate held that 27 percent of all third world manufactured exports—excluding oil—were textiles; 29 percent of developing country sales to the rich were textiles.[46]

About 80 percent of the world's textile trade is now conducted through the blocked corridors of the Multifibre arrangement. No uniform deal exists, however. Each rich importing nation works out its separate limits with every exporter. GATT's principle of nondiscrimination, no favored access to markets, has been scrapped.

The trade is marked with other peculiar features, notably bad faith. The United States and the Common Market originally promised that their quotas would allow exports to grow 6 percent a year.[47] That has been junked, and deals are now made chiefly to hold the line. The developing countries, particularly Hong Kong and Singapore, have been quick to find loopholes. Limited to a fixed number of pieces, they have turned to producing costlier shirts and sweaters. So their sales increase even if their volume is static, and consumers are deprived of inexpensive goods. The quotas, of course, are valuable to holders in exporting nations. A brisk trade has grown up in Hong Kong and Taiwan, where permits to sell to the United States are exchanged for cash. In the 1980s, export permits for a dozen sweaters sold for $11.30 and for jeans, $8. Local businessmen reap a windfall that would otherwise have been enjoyed by American and European consumers.[48]

The conventional defense holds that export limits are needed to protect an uncompetitive domestic industry. But thanks to investment in new machines, Western mills can more than hold their own in some lines. The rich on balance export man-made knitted fabrics and manufactured carpets. The quotas, then, merely enable them to drive up prices.

The other great industrial market, Japan, has frequently taken another, more flexible route. It has paid Japanese firms to scrap uncompetitive spindles and encouraged companies to join those it can't defeat. Firms have been encouraged to make deals with third world rivals, either to invest outright in developing countries or hire third world subcontractors for textile products. In contrast, the Western arrangement is an immovable barrier, holding resources in inefficient lines and increasing living costs for citizens generally.

Steel, with its costly capital investment, is likely to be produced by only a few firms in a country or region. They will be strongly tempted to suppress competition at home and from abroad. Skills on the plant floor are relatively unsophisticated, so steel is a strong candidate for an early industry in a large developing country. The combination inevitably spurs barriers to trade. By the mid 1970s, the United States and Europe were rapidly deploying devices unsanctioned by GATT to relieve domestic mills. Washington first induced Japan to sign an Orderly Marketing Agreement, curbing imports in five categories of specialty steels.[49] But South Korea had become an exporter, and Brazil was not far behind. The Carter administration next invented the "trigger price," forcing foreigners to sell their steel above a minimum price or suffer automatic duties that would lift their exports to levels at which the United States could compete. The Common Market, originally designed as a coal and steel cartel between French and Germans, employed minimum prices to discourage competition from Bulgaria, Canada, Czechoslovakia, Japan, South Korea, Poland, and Spain. The Community invited Eastern Europe, Japan, South Korea, Brazil, and South Africa to fix physical limits as well as prices on their exports.[50] The great carve-up of the world's steel trade had begun.

Since then there has been a rapid proliferation of techniques unrecognized by GATT rules to preserve the less efficient mills of the traditional producers. Brazil, the world's eleventh largest steel maker in 1984, was repeatedly accused by the United States of subsidizing its output or selling it below some just price.[51] This brought down antidumping or countervailing duties on Brazil's exports. The result was a bonanza for the technologically rigid American industry. U.S. Steel (now USX) raised its prices so high it could break even operating only 60 percent of its plant.[52] The new barriers were raised against old producers too. Europeans accepted "voluntary" curbs on their sales to the United States. By 1985, Washington was well on its way toward achieving a 50 percent cut in the foreign share of the American steel market, from about 30 percent to 20 percent.[53] The Europeans and Japan were each allowed about 5 percent. The rest was divided among South Korea, now the world's fifteenth producer, Brazil, Spain, South Africa, Mexico, Australia, Canada, Argentina, and Finland. India, the sixteenth producer, would have to find markets in Europe. Bethlehem Steel, the third largest American producer, forecast that these new barriers would enable the industry to raise its prices a comfortable 5 percent.[54]

The long slump of 1980–82 helped build higher walls against the new third world steel makers.[55] The squeeze in Western markets was damaging what had been a promising development. Together, Brazil, Chile, Venezuela, Mexico, and South Korea had spent $4.8 billion investing in steel mills in 1979. By 1983, the Western slump and the cutoff in commercial bank loans reduced this to $2 billion. The Reagan administration's devotion to comparative disadvantage took on almost evangelical overtones. Lionel Olmer, the under secretary for commerce, urged Japan and other suppliers against providing equipment for a new and efficient mill proposed in South Korea. In contrast to summit generalities in favor of trade and development, Olmer called for an "international consensus on not financing such additional steel capacity."[56] Washington, moreover, devised another tool to spur nations reluctant to limit their steel exports. The United States compiled an "unfair trade" practices list embracing nearly every foreign steel producer. The list contained an implicit warning: Accept a quota or pay penalty duties.

Manipulated trade has spread to autos and other industries. Japan, Canada, West Germany, and the Benelux countries all agreed to limit car exports to the United States.[57] Britain made similar arrangements to curb Japan. (In the United States, the Japanese limits were lifted in 1985 at the urging of General Motors, which had learned the Japanese technique of allying with a foreign competitor and now wanted to import its Japanese cars. But Tokyo was given to understand that United States tolerance for Japanese cars still had a ceiling, even if unstated.)[58] Television sets and tubes, videotape recorders and other consumer electronics, a fast-growing industry not only for Japan but Singapore, Brazil, South Korea, Argentina, Mexico, and India, have all been brought under managed trade. Export markets are now shaped by treaty, force, and threat; price competition is a phrase for textbooks and speeches.

The new barriers are infectious. If the Common Market limits imports of Japanese autos, it has every reason to curb forklift trucks, motorcycles, and other vehicles, and does so. If Britain and France license tableware from Korea, glassware becomes an irresistible target. When "voluntary" agreements to cut back imports work too slowly, Western nations employ penalty tariffs, antidumping and countervailing duties. In 1982 alone, UNCTAD counted 400 penalty tariffs.[59] The American targets included Brazil, South Korea, Taiwan, Mexico, the Philippines, Singapore, and Trinidad and Tobago.

The Reagan administration has invented the notion of the "level playing field" to justify its penalties against imports, contending that Washington only erects barriers against unfair foreign competitors. The two principal unfair practices are "dumping," the sale of a good below its cost of production or at a price under the charge in the producer's home market, and "government subsidies" that lower an exporter's costs. For consumers in an importing nation, a dumped or subsidized foreign product is a gift. Consumers gain from low-priced goods. But this provides little comfort to the competing domestic manufacturer who loses sales. GATT recognizes this. The basic agreement permits the levying of duties against dumped goods and urges negotiation over subsidies that damage competing firms of importing nations. The new protectionism, however, distorts GATT's rules, imposing far more sweeping penalties than the code provides, ignoring the injury test. In a less anarchic world, trading nations would seek a detailed code to govern subsidies, abide by the one already adopted for dumping, and create the level playing field within the GATT.

Not all exporters are unhappy with manipulated trade. Those with quotas are assured sales, and the door is barred to newcomers. Some nations adjust to the system better than others. Mexico and Singapore try to sell products through American or European multinationals, acquiring a domestic character to elude the curbs. Hong Kong attempts to get into a market ahead of third world competitors, before the bars come down. It has done so with radios, watches, plastic bags, and toys.

But none of this has much to do with comparative advantage; it places a premium on administrative and political skills, devaluing least cost and efficiency. It replaces the price system with government fiat in international marketplaces. Under manipulated trade, all nations are unequal, and their market share is a matter of political caprice. Indeed, the physical limits themselves breach a GATT prohibition. The code permits only tariffs as a barrier, a device that is public and can be overcome by an efficient producer.

It is impossible to calculate how much the ingenious and pervasive devices to protect Western industry from competition have hampered the development of third world countries. The raw statistics, moreover, tell of an explosive growth—not a setback—in the manufactured exports of a score of third world nations. The unanswered question is how much more they would have grown and which other nations would have joined their ranks in an open and expansive environment.

GATT examined forty-six developing countries who account for most of the third world's output, apart from oil. Between 1966 and 1981, their manufactured exports multiplied twenty times, from $3.8 billion to $78.7 billion. Although inflation accounted for perhaps two thirds of this expansion, the result is still remarkable. Their share of world manufacturing exports rose from 6 percent to 11 percent, nearly double. At the same time, the traditional reliance of the forty-six on a handful of commodity exports was shrinking. Raw materials exports expanded six times, from $14.9 billion to $92.2 billion; their share of world exports was unchanged at 12 percent.*[60] The World Bank, using a larger sample, calculated that manufactured exports from the third world surpassed raw materials in 1981, $135 billion to $127 billion, not counting oil.[61]

To be sure, a relatively small group of third world nations dominate the trade. The Newly Industrializing Countries of Hong Kong, Taiwan, Singapore, South Korea, Mexico, Brazil, and India account for a large share. But Malaysia, Thailand, and others are expanding their output so rapidly they form a category of their own, second tier Newly Industrializing Countries. Clearly, all these nations would have sold even more, grown faster, and been better able to pay off the huge debts several amassed if manipulated trade had not arisen.

Curiously, third world nations have been remarkably subdued about the new protectionism. The Group of 77 issues routine statements deploring the barriers, UNCTAD churns out statistics to demonstrate their iniquitous effects, but the focus has been elsewhere, on commodities, on aid, on the behavior of multinationals. In part, this is because the debt crisis absorbed the energies of leading third world nations, although the link between ability to repay and the narrowing of Western markets is direct. In part, it is because so many in the third world are still not significant exporters of manufactures. Perhaps the principal reason is that third world nations protect their own markets so zealously. Tariffs sometimes reach several hundred percent. Licenses for imports determine what comes in without even the guaranteed market provided by a quota. These practices are justified because developing countries run, as they must, balance of payments deficits and because they want to protect their new industries from competition. Too much stress on Western protection might encourage the West to intensify its pressure on developing countries to open their markets. A reasonable argument can be made that young countries—the United States in the nineteenth century for example—should build up infant firms behind a high tariff wall. But the other developing world techniques, particularly licensing, are an invitation to inefficiency and corruption.

Habit dies hard, however, and the 77 have sustained their demand for tariff preferences, cut-rate duties on their exports to the rich. Once again, the third world has mistaken a tree for the forest. The virtual disappearance of tariffs in GATT trade negotiations has all but erased the value of preferences. If a rich nation's duty on a product falls to 4 percent, granting a developing country a zero tariff is of little help. The OECD, the West's club, claimed that preferences have "clearly made a contribution" to opening the markets of the rich, but then it is OECD members who grant the preferences.[62] To support its claim, OECD figured that exports enjoying preferences expanded 27 percent a year between 1976 and 1980 in the markets of the rich[63]; all third world exports, however, grew nearly as fast, 20 percent.

The new protectionist wave is sweeping away preferences. The West contends that third world countries with rapidly growing manufacturing industries should "graduate" from preference status and pay the same duties as the rich. So the United States stripped preferences from ninety-four Mexican products in 1980 and 1981. By 1984, Washington was taking away zero tariffs from South Korean fishing reels, Brazilian bully beef, and Mexican waterbeds. Indian goat leather and Taiwanese rulers lost their preferences two years later. If this is peculiar behavior for the world's most powerful economy, it reflects the spirit of the times.[64] By 1985, preferences, never a strong tool of trade, were rapidly breaking in the hands of their users. Another element of the New Order was heading for extinction.

The cost to consumers, the inflationary consequences of the protectionist web is incalculable. Apart from secrecy, not even GATT has been able to keep track of the mushrooming arrangements to curb imports. However, studies of individual products in some countries at least suggest the price that is being paid. The World Bank, for example, calculated that the barriers against Asian and Latin shoes, sugar, meat, and television sets cost American consumers an extra $4 billion in the years 1975 and 1977 alone.[65] Australians lost about 1.1 billion Australian dollars in 1980 to protect clothing, shoes, and drapery.[66] A 1979 study by the Food and Agriculture Organization estimated that the Japanese pay more than $10 billion to shelter their rice growers; the Common Market's combination of farm subsidies and protection increased prices for wheat, sugar, and dairy products by no less than $27 billion in 1978.[67] American builders, auto makers, and other steel consumers could buy hot rolled coils 40 percent cheaper if barriers were dropped against South Korea, nearly 30 percent cheaper if quotas ended against Japan.[68] If there had been no quotas, American consumers would have saved an estimated $2,000 on each Japanese car in 1984. Since Japan was limited to 1.85 million cars, a crude measure of the total added cost is $3.7

billion.*[69] But the actual cost is far greater. With no quotas, Japan would have supplied far more of the market, and cars assembled in India and elsewhere in the third world would have further driven down prices.

A 1981 report found that textile curbs in Britain added 70 pence to £1.50 on every pair of blue jeans, 65 pence to 80 pence for each blouse, and £1.70 on each knitted sweater.[70] These scattered samples make clear that trade barriers are an expensive luxury for the rich, adding tens of billions of dollars to prices. Impelled by the second round of oil price increases, the West turned to disinflation in 1979, drastically cutting back on demand and employment to reduce inflation. Scrapping the new protection would have been a far less painful alternative.

A major victim of the new protection is the GATT itself and its system of rules built up over twenty-five years to achieve open trading. As it happened, the third world's preferences helped tear GATT's fabric. Preferences are a form of discrimination, no matter how benign, on behalf of the poor. The point should not be exaggerated. Preferences may have contributed to a rule-breaking spirit, but the new protection is propelled by deeper forces. The World Bank put it gently: "The recent record shows . . . a shift towards forms of 'escape' that, although not inconsistent with GATT, tend to go against [its] principles."[71] The Bank, however, looked only at penalty tariffs and ignored the quota restraints and marketing agreements.

UNCTAD was blunter. Its officials reported to the sixth meeting at Belgrade in 1983 that the new protection in the West "can only function effectively in an atmosphere of general disrespect for the rules. . . . The resort to managed trade frustrates the attempt to allocate resources according to comparative advantage and thus halts the process of development, which is expected to occur through the effective operation of the GATT system."[72] As a prime exponent of managed trade in almost every sphere, UNCTAD is an odd admirer of Ricardo, but this does not diminish the force of the words. One UNCTAD trade specialist, Colin Greenhill, has said that GATT "has broken down, not collapsed, but there is certainly a crisis in the system."[73] Down the road in Geneva, GATT's chief economist, Jan Tumlir, was gloomier. He said: "GATT is becoming extinct. That's how it looks. Deals on universal negotiations. That's played out."[74]

The prospect of halting, let alone reversing the growth of manipulated trade—governments rather than markets determine who and what shall exchange—is grim. If heavy unemployment and weak growth broke down the old system, it is unclear that a return to high employment and steady 4 percent growth would reverse matters. The new protectionism, Tumlir and his colleagues have written, is "unstable, expansive and ultimately uncontrollable."[75] The GATT secretariat observed that the modest Western recovery in the 1980s failed to stem the tide. This experience, GATT wrote, "gives grounds for serious doubts that the protectionist pressures can be expected to decline as economic recovery progresses."[76]

UNCTAD was stinging. Its secretariat said, "A world where one group of countries is faced with severe problems of unemployment and underutilized productive capacity due to the lack of demand for their products, while their largest group of potential customers are denied the means of increasing their income and purchasing power, cannot be described as a world of economic efficiency under any standards."[77]

A study for Chatham House, the private London center for studies of foreign policy, said, "To be realistic, it must be recognized that the world is moving in a protectionist direction and that the Newly Industrializing Countries will be singled out for relatively harsh treatment because of their diplomatic weakness."[78] The official West, speaking through the OECD, has concluded: "One cannot be confident that the present deviations from the principles of free trade are only temporary. It cannot be excluded that there are also more fundamental forces at work."[79]

The pessimism is explicable. There are powerful forces, social and economic, driving rich, industrial nations toward ever-expanding protection. Managers and workers become attached to their jobs, not only for the income it brings but for deep-seated psychological reasons. Job and community are bound together and not easily abandoned. Habitual work is comforting; the new is unknown and perilous.

Nevertheless, millions of Americans voluntarily change jobs and homes every year. Change is the one constant in economic life. Despite the elaborate network of trade barriers, the more costly firms and industries tend to shrink, cheaper imports somehow penetrate. The Luddites who resist technological change have lost out everywhere. There is no reason to think that a declining Western industry can freeze time permanently with an Orderly Marketing Agreement or a Voluntary Export Restraint. If imports do not destroy it, some domestic entrepreneur will find a substitute product that will. The question then is not whether protectionism will grow indefinitely but rather how to find the least painful way back to the open trade of the first twenty-five postwar years. Sensible answers can enhance both the well-being of the North and the newly thrusting industries of the South.

Evidently, owners, managers, and workers in less efficient industries should move to more profitable sectors. This, however, is banal advice unless growing sectors exist. A necessary—but not sufficient—condition for overcoming the powerful tide of protection is a return to the high growth, high employment economy of the 1950s and 1960s. This problem will be examined in the last chapter.

Meanwhile, and even during a period of high growth, two critical changes could make the transition smoother. One aims at transparency, at making clear the cost of every piece of protection sanctioned by a government. A quota to drive up a price is a hidden tax, a form of monopoly patent granted by the state. Every such grant should be made public, ending the secrecy of "voluntary" restraints or "orderly marketing." Moreover, a United States government agency, a Japanese bureau, and the European Commission should estimate the consequences of each device for consumer prices. If a quota limits shoes, autos, or cold rolled steel, an analysis should be made and published, computing the cost. These studies might alter the political balance. Citizens as consumers could then better measure the cost of fellow citizens acting as producer-lobbyists.

No state patent to protect an industry or a firm should be an unrequited grant. The recipients should be obliged to draw up a plan explaining how they intend to correct the conditions that made them victims of import competition. The plan should pledge investment in new machinery to increase efficiency or start new product lines. A declining company or industry should map out an orderly program to shut down capacity and reduce the work force. With union approval, the plan might describe how workers will reduce costs, either through the abandonment of restrictive work practices or through wage cuts. The government used this technique when it rescued the Chrysler Corporation from bankruptcy. It is a useful model to follow. Finally, every protective patent should run for a specified and limited period, as some do now. Three to five years is a reasonable time for change. Transparency, cost, and payment should govern all present and future arrangements to tax consumers without their consent.

In a world of imperfect markets, it would be harsh and wasteful to discard unwanted workers, managers, or owners who cannot meet foreign competition. They are at least as worthy of special consideration as a capital gain or a depleting oil well. The second crucial reform is a program—money—to encourage the movement of these people from dying to growing industries. This is no more wasteful and less expensive than the concealed subsidies given private firms through managed trade.

Workers laid off because of foreign competition should be retrained, preferably by industry but at government expense, for new tasks in expanding areas of the economy. Government counselors should advise workers where jobs can be found that would match their old or new skills. Workers should receive pay supplements to bring them near their accustomed living standard until they found new jobs. Those too old for retraining could receive early pensions, again enlarged by a government benefit. The program should provide allowances to help workers move and compensate them for the possible loss of value in their homes.

Managers and owners in companies hurt by imports should also benefit. Government-guaranteed loans could help firms invest in plant or machinery to improve old lines or develop new ones. The program should pay for management consultants or research and development that might lead to a new or improved product. If there is no hope of converting a plant to more productive use, an outright grant should compensate owners for their destroyed capital.

Such a program would clearly cost billions, and the possibilities for abuse are obvious. But the price would be a fraction of the burden of protection. It cannot be argued that this is an increase of government intervention in private markets; intervention is far greater now under the system of patent grants.

None of these are new ideas in the United States, although taken together they go well beyond anything yet attempted. The Kennedy administration, to smooth the way for its round of tariff cuts in the 1960s, enacted a Trade Adjustment Act to compensate workers laid off as a result of a trade concession.[80] But this fixed so narrow a basis for eligibility that not a single worker was helped for seven years. Then, a slight liberalization released a marginal sum, less than $15 million a year. In 1975, the law was substantially loosened. Imports now only had to "contribute importantly" to unemployment, and checks were written liberally. In the peak year of 1980, 532,000 workers received $1.6 billion. Autos and steel, with sophisticated union officials, collected the bulk of the funds, and there was little adjustment to trade. Of the 532,000, only 20,000 or less than 4 percent applied for help in seeking a new job, retraining, or moving allowances. Most simply went back to their old tasks. Some of the more enterprising were paid during temporary layoffs for auto model changeovers. The program was welfare run riot. Congress should have required workers to accept retraining and seek jobs in another industry as a condition of aid. The Reagan administration has all but shut down trade adjustment assistance, providing only modest loans and grants for small firms seeking new ventures.

The dismal experience of programs that were either too tight or too loose, however, should not condemn a sound idea. In a high employment climate, properly administered subsidies to shift owners and workers from declining to thriving industries would diminish the demands for protection, help curb inflation and expand Western economies. These are no mean achievements and a more pragmatic politics will exploit the opportunity to realize them.

Practical politics, it may be argued, renders visionary any prospect of reducing United States trade barriers when $100 billion trade deficits are a commonplace of economic life. This, however, reflects a misunderstanding of the causal links. The trade deficit is largely the result of an overvalued dollar created by foreign investors' demand for dollars. In the contemporary world, capital flows, as Geoffrey Bell has observed, drive trade; trade is no longer the principal lure for capital. The daily flow of capital across national borders is more than $100 billion, ten or fifteen times the export of goods and services. It is this inrush of marks, francs, and pounds—and above all, dollars returning home from Europe and Latin America—that drove the dollar to dizzying heights, until 1985, making American exports dear and cheapening foreign imports.[81]

If trade had been decisive, the dollar would have fallen. The American deficit means that world traders have an abundance of dollars, and the currencies of other nations are in short supply. But traders' transactions are overwhelmed by the banks, insurance companies, and the treasuries of large corporations. Their demand for dollars—strictly speaking, high yielding dollar investments—far outweighed the currency needs of traders in goods and services. The dollar demand had much to do with the banks' flight from third world loans, the repatriation of their capital. It had more to do with the monetary restraint of the central bank, the Federal Reserve. Easier money and lower interest rates would have driven capital back to Europe and Japan, lowered the dollar's value against other currencies, cheapened American exports and made imports costlier. The American trade balance would then right itself and become a trade surplus.

Just this was beginning to happen in 1985. Fearing a slump, the Federal Reserve eased its control of the money supply, interest rates fell, and the dollar declined against other currencies. But the central bank's preoccupation with inflation, a threat better met by other institutional arrangements, placed severe limits on its willingness to continue the process. The U.S. Treasury Secretary and other Western finance ministers then took matters in their own hands and pushed the dollar down sharply. The crucial point is this: Protection is not a necessary accompaniment of a trade deficit, particularly a deficit flowing in considerable measure from the operations of the central bank. The IMF regularly warns the third world against overvalued exchange rates; it is a pity that Washington did not ponder this good advice sooner.

If the protectionist tide is not turned, the South might be expected to seek a fresh course in trade. One approach, cited repeatedly in third world documents, urges "self-reliance." This suggests that developing countries should somehow delink their economies from the North and concentrate on trade among themselves. However, this South-South solution appears more romantic than practical. It would mean a massive shift in markets. In 1982, two thirds of the developing world's exports went North; less than a third of the South's trade was within the bloc.[82] There is no doubt of the potential third world demand for food, clothing, consumer products, and capital goods. But translating potential into effective demand requires cash. Poor consumers conspicuously lack it. Sixteen of the larger third world nations began giving tariff preferences to each other in 1971; they stimulated little extra trade.[83] These nations are competitive rather than complementary, and each fiercely protects its own firms. Heavy demand from the new oil-rich aroused expectations of enlarged trade within the South. But the changed prices and fortunes of the oil exporters have dampened this hope. Finally, the road to modernization, to develop skills and industries, lies through the trade routes to the North, at least in the foreseeable future. The South-South solution is a chimera.

In one forum or another, the North has repeatedly told the South that its future depends on the existing order of money and trade, that a new global system is neither desirable nor practical. Industrial countries, particularly the United States, have frequently urged developing countries to thrive within the system, to join GATT and observe its rules. This injunction is mocked by the West's expanding breaches of GATT's code, by the new protectionism that strikes with special force at the young industries of the third world. In trade, it is the North that has wrenched the system out of joint in a futile bid to preserve less efficient industries. The more ingenious manufacturers in Taiwan, Brazil, South Korea, India, and elsewhere are likely to find ways around or through the barriers, or discover markets that have not yet been pinched. But much third world industry and agriculture is frustrated, and Northern consumers bear heavy costs.

Apart from the material gains and losses, the preservation of Northern smokestacks diminishes Northern life. For a Korean or a Bengali, work in a steel mill is a leap forward from the misery of peasant labor to a world that offers literacy, skill, leisure, the elements of development. For a Western worker, a steel mill is a hot, noisy, dirty workplace that offers only high pay. If the North gives up its smokestacks and concentrates on the new growth areas, the veteran steelworker—supported by adjustment pay—can retire in dignity. His son, properly retrained, can look forward to a richer, cleaner, more satisfying work life. If comparative advantage is allowed full scope, if the barriers are rolled back, North and South will gain. Both qualitatively and quantitatively, the world will enjoy a richer life.

Chapter 7

Easing the Debt Crisis

Less than three years after Silva Herzog sent out his distress calls from Mexico, Western financial authorities assured the world that the debt crisis was over. The World Bank congratulated lenders, debtors, and officials on a mostly splendid performance. "The international community's confidence in its ability to manage financial problems has been hard won," the Bank said, "but it is not misplaced."[1] A catastrophe had been averted, and the crisis was downgraded to a "serious but manageable problem."[2] Indeed, the Bank even put the word "crisis" in quotes, signifying disapproval of the term.

Others were equally enthusiastic. Otmar Emminger, the former head of Germany's cautious central bank, hailed the "dramatic turnaround in the payments situation."[3] William R. Rhodes of Citibank, leader of the commercial bankers rearranging third world loans, claimed that, "We have made considerable progress, and I believe we should continue to do so."[4] Rhodes, however, cast a thin shadow over the sunny appraisals. He warned that "dire prophecy . . . had given way to excessive optimism."[5] Nevertheless, the prevailing note was optimism, at least in public.

After all, by mid-1985 no third world borrower had repudiated its debt (although Bolivia, Zaire, Sudan, and Nicaragua were hopelessly behind with their interest payments). Above all, Mexico and Brazil, the two biggest borrowers, had accepted much of the belt-tightening imposed by the IMF and produced dazzling trade surpluses, at least for one year. Each had exported \$13 billion more than it imported in 1984, halted the slide in its economy, and enjoyed some modest growth. This performance had encouraged the bankers to stretch out Mexico's debt to the end of the century and to prepare a similar scheme for Brazil.[6] Argentina had flouted the IMF's free market prescription but drastically reduced its raging inflation with price and wage controls. So the Fund grudgingly gave its blessing to President Alfonsin's measures; practical results overrode ideological preconceptions.

Total third world debt to the commercial banks was still climbing—from $428 billion in 1983 to an estimated $508 billion in 1985—as banks were compelled to make new loans to save old ones.[7] But the borrowers, thanks largely to curbs on their imports and a United States recovery with an overvalued dollar that sucked in goods from abroad, had sharply reduced the deficits in their foreign accounts. These deficits had been slashed from $108 billion in 1981 to $53 billion in 1983; by 1984, they had fallen to $40 billion and the World Bank expected roughly the same amount of red ink the next year. Mexico, the financial community's role model (at least until prices began rising steeply in 1985, the trade surplus fell, and the peso began sinking) had even reduced its deficit without forcing further declines in the living standards of its people.[8]

In the view of the authorities, all should now go smoothly. The banks would continue to collect interest, $45 billion in 1983, provided only that a few things happened.[9] The United States must continue its recovery and bring a laggard Western Europe in its wake. The growth must be rapid enough to absorb a growing stream of goods and services from the South. These increased exports, moreover, must not inspire new barriers to seal off markets like those erected against Mexican and Brazilian steel. The Federal Reserve must not force interest rates higher because so many loans to the largest borrowers carry a floating rate. Even better, interest rates should come down. Every one percentage point drop saves Argentina about $450 million, Brazil $800 million, and Mexico $750 million.[10] Oil prices should neither rise (that would hurt importers like Brazil and Argentina) nor fall (which would cost exporting Mexico and Venezuela foreign exchange). Borrowers must not abandon the path of financial rectitude, resort to inflationary budget deficits or credit excesses, fix overvalued exchange rates that draw in imports and make exports dearer, or waste their substance on subsidies for consumer goods or state agencies. In this setting, debtors could expect to meet their bankers' bills and become creditworthy again. The banks, who had profited so handsomely from past loans, would no longer limit themselves to providing money for old debt but would extend genuine new loans to promote development. Creditworthiness and the provision of new loans was held out as the South's carrot. Its nutritive value would ultimately depend on steady growth in the North.

This is an attractive but dubious scenario. The United States and the major European countries have consciously abandoned the fiscal tools that brought high employment and high growth in the 1950s and 1960s. Taxes are raised and lowered, government spending is enlarged or reduced with little conscious effort to expand or shrink demand. If the United States recovery from the deep slump of the early 1980s falters, the Reagan administration has renounced fiscal instruments, taxes and spending, to revive it. In Europe, major nations like Britain and West Germany have demonstrated a similar aversion to countercyclical fiscal techniques. This self-denial condemned the United States and the six other leading industrial economies to grow only 2.2 percent a year in the first half of the 1980s; this was less than half the 5.7 percent of the 1960s and even below the level of 3.6 percent in the oil-shocked 1970s.[11] It leaves central banks and monetary policy as the last mechanism to guide economic activity.

As a class, central bankers tend to fear expansion more than contraction, price increases more than unemployment. The Federal Reserve even tightened credit and pushed up interest rates in the 1980s slump just as it did in the depths of the Great Depression. If economic recovery in the middle 1980s generates inflationary pressure (or if the United States economy stagnates but a declining dollar strips away the price restraint of import competition), the Federal Reserve is likely to renew its assault on prices. That means higher, not lower interest charges for the debtors. Among the creditors, growth will again abort, and the markets on which the borrowers rely will shrink.

In the best of circumstances, these markets are uncertain because of the swelling tide of protectionism. As newly industrializing nations in the South enlarge their exports, in accord with the benign scenario, they can expect to run up against cries of "unfair trade" and will be invited to place "voluntary" or "orderly" curbs on their sales. A major change in sentiment, prolonged Western prosperity, and substantial aid to workers and plants idled by import competition is needed if the South is to export on the scale required to pay its debt.

The future course of oil prices is, of course, unknown. It is almost certain, however, that they will not remain fixed. Inevitably, there will be third world winners and losers whose ability to service their debt will fluctuate with the movements in oil. The stunning and unforeseen plunge in prices in 1985 and 1986 underscored the absurdity of predicting stability.

The optimists' narrative then rests on flimsy hopes and forecasts about the West's performance. The behavior of the South —its willingness to pursue austerity and pay interest—depends on the promise of new loans. This is equally doubtful. Some credits will be forthcoming. Banks surely can be expected to postpone the payment of principal, indefinitely if need be. The stretched-out debt will, it is assumed, continue earning interest, preserving bank assets and profits. In some cases, banks will even lend a portion of the interest coming due; this keeps the asset "performing" and spares the banks from reporting losses. None of this, however, enables a debtor to enlarge its claims on foreign resources, on the goods and services that can spur growth. This is lending for old loans, the exchange of a new promise to replace a broken one.

Beyond this, the volume of new lending is likely to be scarce. Banks will accommodate their better corporate customers and finance the export of their goods to the South, particularly if the loan carries a guarantee from a government credit agency like the U.S. Export-Import Bank. The commercial banks are also eager to lend to nations with little or no debt, India and China in particular. But the big borrowers of the past cannot expect much new money, no matter how glittering their trade statistics.

In private, bankers readily acknowledge that they seek to reduce their "exposure," the volume of loans to big third world debtors. A leading British banker, with large credits to Mexico, Brazil, Venezuela, and Argentina, expects to make no new Latin loans for ten years. "We are trying to get our exposure in Latin America down," he said.[12] He and his counterparts in New York are clear: You reduce, not expand loans to debtors who threatened your solvency.

There are other views. Rhodes of Citibank and Emminger of West Germany predicted that Mexico would receive a voluntary loan—untied to past debt—sometime in 1985. But the Mexicans complained that their good behavior had failed to earn the funds they expected. Silva Herzog, the Finance Minister, warned ominously that payments owed foreign banks "cannot take precedence over the needs of the people."[13] Indeed, those less well-behaved than Mexico cannot expect even token loans. Bank shareholders will not look kindly on executives who expand credit to problem nations.

The banks' retreat from the third world began before the crisis became widely known. Between 1981 and 1983, private lending to Mexico, Argentina, Brazil, Venezuela, and Chile fell more than $30 billion or 51 percent.[14] Harold Lever, economic adviser in British Labour governments, has dismissed as "vague hopes" the promise of voluntary lending.[15] The carrot to induce the unbroken payment of interest on old debt is a fragile stalk.

The briefly glowing trade surpluses of Mexico and Brazil blinded the optimists to the harsh fact that lenders and debtors are caught in a mutual trap. The big borrowers must continue selling abroad more than they buy to pay interest. But this course could also condemn the debtors to economic stagnation. A developing country grows by bringing in more resources than it sends out, by taking in more raw materials, tools, machines for investment and output than it exports. A Mexico can grow only if its trade surplus is more than matched by an inflow of claims on the resources of others, by fresh loans. But its prospect of gaining a significant volume of new loans is thwarted by the banks' strategy to reduce "exposure." The problem is sharpened by heavy interest charges. These are claims on the resources of Mexico and Brazil and drain away output just as exports do. A continued drain would soon force a third world economy into decline, further reducing living standards, creating an intolerable plight for political leaders and their people.

The Mexican and Brazilian export surpluses, then, are likely to be a temporary phenomenon. Apart from the fact that the sales may inflame Western protectionism, these shipments can only be maintained by new loans which are unlikely to be forthcoming. Without the loans, the surge in exports takes resources from poorer countries and transfers them to the rich.

In sum, there is strong reason to doubt each assumption behind the belief that the debt crisis had ended. Western growth is uncertain as long as abstinence from fiscal tools prevails. The abdication of economic policy to central banks makes even higher interest rates a possibility. Banks are unlikely to make large new loans to large old debtors. Deprived of fresh capital and laboring under interest burdens, the third world drive for ever-expanding exports must steer between the rock of protection and the ditch of a domestic resource drain. Borrowers and lenders then are locked together in an unsteady marathon dance. Here North and South have a clear joint interest in sustaining each other.

If the big debtors cannot grow, cannot assure rising living standards for their people, irresistible domestic political pressures will force them to scrap their good intentions. "We have made a terrible adjustment already," said Dilson Funaro, Brazil's finance minister. Rio would no longer accept IMF austerity. "Another recession is out of the question," Funaro said. "So, any new agreement with the IMF will have to ensure that we'll be able to grow."[16] The multibillion dollar sums Brazil and others must pay out yearly for debt acquired so easily in the 1970s is a heavy brake on this growth. So some debtors will simply stop paying the charges on loans of infinite maturity.

The trigger for such an episode is usually pulled in an unlikely place. Bolivia, for example, might simply announce that it can no longer maintain the futile pretense of paying debt and will resume only when it is able. A Peru might then be tempted to follow. Indeed, Peru startled the bankers in 1985 with a modest step in this direction. Lima said it would limit its interest payments to 10 percent of its exports, regardless of whether this fell short of what was owed.[17] Threats to seize Bolivian or Peruvian property in the United States will frighten no one; United States holdings in both countries are far larger. Even a ban on short-term financing for imports will avail little; barter deals and new suppliers will be found. Soon a major debtor, perhaps Argentina, under the pressure of huge demonstrations, will join Bolivia and Peru. Indonesia could be drawn in. Others, even the model debtors, may feel compelled to stop payments that failed to induce new loans.

Mexico, staggered by the slump in oil prices, suggested in 1986 that it might suspend interest payments. This frightened Western financiers and their governments, since it threatened to wipe out a fifth or more of the capital of major banks.[18] They promptly put together another package of loans so Mexico could keep on paying. This time, the World Bank joined in with the IMF, using public funds for what was essentially a bailout of private banks. A halt in interest by one nation would induce others to follow. Then, the long-feared debtors' cartel could emerge, a common front demanding the extinction of some debt and easier terms for the rest.

That would destroy the profits and capital of the biggest American and British banks. The Federal Reserve and the Bank of England would print enough money to keep them afloat. But the ensuing financial panic, the terrifying uncertainty and paralysis everywhere in loans and investment could bring about a slump unseen since 1929.[19]

Conservative public policy then must reconcile seemingly contradictory objectives, reducing handicaps to the growth of debtors, preserving the solvency of banks. Several commentators have proposed some once-and-for all solutions to this dilemma. They are, of course, largely unwelcome to monetary authorities and commercial bankers convinced that everything is working for the best. Nevertheless, the proposals may gain luster when events wear optimism thin. The most sweeping would substitute public credit for private loans, shifting the risk of default from the banks to the taxpayers. The public debt swapped for third world loans would carry less interest and longer maturities, forcing the banks to bear some of the burden. In one version, Felix Rohatyn of Lazard Frères proposed that an international agency, backed by Western governments, issue bonds to the banks in exchange for their third world paper. This debt would then be stretched out to twenty-five or thirty years at a 6 percent rate of interest, about twice the length and less than half the charge on Mexico's rescheduled loans. The banks' new bonds would carry similar terms, sharply cutting the nominal value of bank assets and their income. Rohatyn, however, would ease the pain for his fellow bankers by compelling taxpayers to absorb some of this cost.[20] Peter Kenen would also establish a new international agency. It would give the banks ninety cents for every dollar of third world debt, thereby erasing about 20 percent of the capital of the major banks. The new agency, like Rohatyn's would then lengthen its newly acquired third world debt and reduce interest costs with its ten cent saving on the dollar.[21]

These and similar proposals meet a stock set of objections from authorities and bankers. Each country's problem is unique, and each debtor should be treated as a separate case. There is no need for bankers to take any loss. "Banks see no need . . . of writing down the value of assets that they expect will be serviced in full," the World Bank said primly. In fact, United States, German, and British banks have already written down some of their third world debt, but how much and for which countries remains a secret between the banks and their regulators. Writing down a debt means valuing a loan at less than the amount on its face. Some United States banks have sold portions of their loans at a discount, at less than one hundred cents on the dollar. Peru's debt reportedly sold for as little as 32 percent of its face value, Brazil's for 75 percent, and Mexico's for 78 percent.[23] None of this, however, means relinquishing any claim on the debtor (although some debtors have shrewdly bought back their own loans at the discounted rate). His loan may be carried at seventy-five cents on the dollar but the bank still seeks one hundred cents worth of interest.

Western taxpayers will not accept any plan, the orthodox contend, that uses government credit to bail the banks out of their folly. The plans would encourage borrowers to act loosely and depart from the austere path marked out by the IMF. They would discourage the voluntary loans the banks will someday provide. They are unfair to a Mexico which is straining every resource to meet its obligations in full.

Since new loans are doubtful, and there is every reason to believe that Mexico would welcome a scheme to cut its interest costs by $3 billion a year, most of the standard objections do not appear overwhelming. The problem of using public credit cannot be dismissed so easily. But if government guarantees are needed to avert a collapse of the banking system, taxpayers might be persuaded to support a bailout that imposed a heavy cost on bank shareholders.*

Other plans deal with the problem of new loans, typically by insuring them against default. Lever proposed an international credit insurance agency, with the IMF monitoring the insured loans.[24] Henry C. Wallich of the Federal Reserve Board urged an insurance fund financed by a tax on new loans. Since at first the fund would be too small to cover risks, governments would have to contribute, at least temporarily.[25] A combination of inertia, complacency, and perhaps skepticism toward any new loans has prevented the insurance plans from making any progress.

It is evident that no grand design, no overarching plan will be put in place until the crisis again becomes acute. One sign of growing concern was thought to have been raised by the new U.S. Treasury Secretary James A. Baker. Late in 1985 he proposed that commercial banks expand their third world loans by $20 billion over three years with additional lending of $9 billion from the World Bank and the Inter-American Development Bank.[26] But there may have been less here than meets the eye. Baker's proposal would enlarge commercial loans by a mere 2.5 percent a year; the banks did not rush to meet even this modest

*An imaginative scheme has been proposed by Allan H. Meltzer of Carnegie-Mellon. He wants banks to swap their paper for shares in the nationalized companies of debtors, a Brazilian steel mill or a Mexican oil company. The banks would become stockholders instead of creditors. But there are serious problems with this. Banks might end up with illiquid assets of uncertain worth since there is no market for Brazilian or Mexican utility shares. The debtors would regard the handover of national assets to foreign banks as political suicide. However, some Latin nations have toyed with a variant, offering shares in their listed, private concerns for the debt paper. See "A Way to Defuse the World Debt Problem," *Fortune*, November 28, 1983, p. 137.

target since he offered them no guarantees. His $20 billion, moreover, could be read as a low ceiling rather than a floor, a warning against too much new lending rather than an invitation for an open purse. So the debtors' plight was unrelieved. The World Bank, hostile to grand schemes that could threaten its credit rating, must have been pleased with Baker's central thrust, a call to deal with each borrower separately. As the Bank liked to say, "The case by case approach has been vindicated as has the reluctance to fix things before they are evidently broken. Policy-makers have avoided systemic solutions to problems that are highly country specific. . . ."[27] In plainer terms, Western authorities and Western banks much prefer dealing with a Mexico or a Bolivia singly rather than seeking one solution for all. The politics are irresistible; the authorities, notably the IMF and the Federal Reserve, mobilize the bankers in a common front; they then deal with separate countries. A common solution could create the grouping or cartel of debtors that all lenders fear would extract fresh concessions.

At a minimum, however, some new regulation is needed to quell the enthusiasm of banks, to make less likely a recurrence of the loose lending of the 1970s. Despite the present reluctance to lend to old borrowers, memories are short, and it is not hard to imagine another banking binge with the fast-growing, relatively debt-free nations of Asia. A competitive scramble for banking "presence" in China, India, Thailand, and Singapore could launch another round of folly. The banks should be preserved from their own imprudence by limiting their ability to lend, requiring a bigger capital base for loans, narrowing their exposure to any one borrower, and demanding larger reserves against shaky loans. The trouble is that these standards are set by officials who, like regulators everywhere, tend to adopt the views of those they regulate. A Federal Reserve official has privately said that the central bank relies largely on the judgment of the banks it examines to determine the soundness of any loan. The head of Ohio's state insurance fund boasted of the safety of the state's thrift banks three months before one collapsed and the others were temporarily closed.[28]

The Federal Reserve has belatedly recognized the problem and increased the required ratio of capital to assets by 25 percent, compelling its regulated banks either to raise more capital or reduce their loans.[29] But this still leaves the ratio at only 5.5 percent. Banks can still lend nearly $20 for every dollar of stockholders' investment. One former Federal Reserve chairman has said his greatest regret was not insisting on a more conservative standard. Chairman Volcker has now embraced a 9 percent minimum.[30] A ten to one ratio, which banks resist, would induce more prudent lending. A higher ratio of capital to assets, however, might have a perverse effect. With their ability to lend limited, banks might be tempted to make riskier loans to gain higher yields and profits. The answer is larger reserves against shakier loans. Banks do not like this because a loan loss reserve reduces the funds available for lending and profits. But bank judgment in these matters need no longer be regarded as the last word. Congress, not bank regulators, set a new standard for foreign loans in 1983. Banks are now required to set aside special reserves against debt whose value had been impaired.[31] This was defined as a sovereign loan with interest payments six months overdue and no prospect of an agreement with the IMF. Special reserves were then ordered, ranging from 10 to 75 percent of the debt, for Bolivia, the Sudan, Poland, Nicaragua, and Zaire. In contrast, loan loss reserves for all United States banks are a mere 1.28 percent.[32] Larger reserves against losses should be maintained for loans to foreign countries whose plight may not be so desperate as Zaire but who are still uncertain debtors. This would balance the lack of selectivity in raising capital-asset ratios.

The banks are forbidden to make more than 10 percent of their loans to one borrower, to spread the risk. It is simple to evade this requirement abroad, counting as single and separate borrowers the government of Mexico, the Mexican nationalized oil company, nationalized utilities, and more. These loans should obviously be lumped together, counted as one borrower, since one entity, the Mexican government, stands behind all of them. Consolidating loans for the different borrowers of a single sovereign would give the 10 percent rule some force.

Tighter regulation is no guarantee against recklessness or fraud. It is a modest step to help induce the prudence that is supposed to characterize lending. In one area, however, less regulation is desirable. This is the notorious conditionality of the IMF, the terms the Fund sets for its loans. They are too numerous, too intrusive, and finally too destabilizing. The riots in Brazil and the Dominican Republic, the 1985 coup in the Sudan are recent episodes in a long history of untoward events created by Fund policies. These policies tend to reflect the economic bias of central banks, a view that inflation is the cardinal sin and monetary restraint can cure it, that expansion is perilous and contraction is a precondition of health.

The Fund has been widely praised, and rightly so, for stitching together the network of banks and package of credits that eased the early stages of the debt crisis. The Fund's seal of approval for debtor policies enabled the banks to do what the larger ones wanted anyway, lend their shaky sovereign customers enough money to keep paying interest and stretch out the repayment of principal that nobody wants or expects to get back.

The Fund rations a pool of scarce currencies and properly insists on attaching conditions to its loans to assure repayment. It is the number and kind of conditions, however, that are in question, not conditionality itself. Whether or not the Fund is repaid depends on a nation's balance of payments, whether it will acquire more from its sale of goods and services abroad and the credits and investment it receives than it spends abroad on goods, services, repatriated profits, and investment. The Fund lends its scarce currencies to enable a nation to pay for a balance of payments deficit. The Fund then should concern itself exclusively with the borrower's progress in curing the deficit; any economic targets fixed by the Fund should relate intimately to the borrower's international payments.

The Fund does follow some self-denying rules, but they are of a very curious sort. It does not tell a third world debtor to stop spending for imported weapons, although they increase a payments deficit. Nor does the IMF tell a borrowing South Africa that it will become more productive and less indebted by ending apartheid, a system of subsidies for dominant whites provided by helot black labor.

The Fund does not hesitate, however, to demand that its third world customers cut their subsidies for food, fuel, and other welfare measures affecting large numbers of people. Apart from the peculiar bias, this takes the IMF into an area beyond its competence or its concern. The Fund should grant or withhold its loans depending on whether balance of payments targets are reached. Borrower governments should decide the route to those targets; they have to live—or die—with the consequences.

The level of the balance of payments is closely linked to the exchange rate. If Argentina has an artificially high rate, it will suck in imports and cut exports; the deficit in its foreign balance will widen. The IMF therefore properly insists that its borrowers adopt a value for their currencies that offers some prospect of achieving the target balance in foreign accounts. Beyond that, the Fund should not go. But it does, fixing levels for credit expansion, domestic budget deficits, wages, the deficits in state agencies, demanding an end to cheap utility rates. These are essentially political decisions that should be left to the political authorities of the sovereign states. (Although sometimes politicians welcome the Fund's edicts; an unpopular but necessary restraint can then be blamed on the IMF.)

The thrust of the IMF's conditions are equally arbitrary. The Fund rarely urges an expansion in economic activity, no matter how great the borrower's unused resources or the ability of world demand to accommodate more goods. Instead, the Fund almost invariably urges deflation, curbing demand.

How a borrower spends what it has, how it reaches the payments target set by the Fund ought to be the decision of the borrowing nation. It pays directly if things go wrong. It loses successive slices of a Fund loan when its payments are not put in order. If a borrower wants to hold down the price of rice or gas, that choice is no more eccentric and costs less foreign exchange than importing a squadron of jet fighters. There is no reason in economics or politics why the Fund should find the first course repugnant and the second acceptable.

The Fund argues that the policies it sets are necessary to cure the deficit in the balance of payments, that its targets won't be reached unless everything else is done. Loose credit and wage increases will bring on inflation, making exports expensive and imports cheap. But if the IMF insists on an appropriate and varying exchange rate, the problem cures itself. As domestic prices rise, the currency's foreign value will fall. Exports become competitive and imports dear. The targets once again come in sight.

Even within the Fund, there are officials who believe it sets too many conditions, although they would go beyond the balance of payments and exchange rate targets proposed here. One veteran official noted that Yugoslavia had to agree to twelve conditions for a loan; five, he thought, would have been enough.[33] Fund aides retort that they are not seeking short-term remedies to a nation's payments deficit but long-term solutions that cure flaws in the very structure of the borrower's economy. Even assuming that the Fund has the wisdom to identify these structural flaws —doubtful in view of the IMF's monetary and monetarist preoccupations—the IMF is the wrong agency to cure them. It is in the business of making medium-term loans, three to five years, and is entitled only to seek remedies for that limited length of time.

The reforms the Fund seeks are those of financial authorities, eager to slash government spending, hoping to restrain credit and prices. Wallich of the Federal Reserve Board argues that Fund conditions strengthen the finance ministries and central banks of borrowers against development ministers and other, more free-handed types. "You have to support the good guys against the expansionists," Wallich has said.[34] It is not clear, however, that on all occasions finance ministers and central bankers enjoy a monopoly of economic wisdom. After three years of dealing with the crisis, the Fund's record was described as "catastrophic" by Rudiger Dornbusch of MIT.[35] That could be overstatement. But it was clear that balky Argentina had checked its inflation, at least temporarily, by ignoring the Fund's advice. Brazil, once almost as docile as Mexico, then chose to ignore the IMF and succeeded in winning a deep slice in its interest charges. The Fund should avoid deep immersion in domestic policy issues and limit its terms to mapping a schedule for payments balance tied to realistic exchange rates.

There is a seeming contradiction between urging a rule of restraint on the IMF and encouraging IDA loans linked to politically sensitive conditions. Both institutions and loans are different, however. The Fund is essentially a production-limiting agency; the Bank's bureaucratic impulse is toward expansion. Moreover, borrowers pay interest on IMF loans and must repay in a few years. The loans have much of the character of a commercial transaction. The IDA loan is really a gift, repayable in fifty years with no interest charge. The attack on subsidized food prices in many third world cities lies through a land reform that will be politically painful and take many years. A gift of Western resources, provided it is large enough, can properly be tied to an acceptance of this task. But to insist on the immediate elimination of food subsidies in return for an interest-bearing loan over three years reflects a remarkable disdain for political realities. It is sometimes said that the IMF has overthrown more governments than Marx and Lenin combined. The quip contains a concealed plea for restraint, for limiting the IMF to its proper task of lending to overcome a payments deficit.

Neither of these sets of proposals—tighter regulation against a new rash of imprudent loans and curbing the IMF's interference with domestic political decisions—touches the problems raised by the third world's swollen debt. Neither prevents this burden from threatening the West's banking structure or choking growth in the South. Because the optimists' scenario is unconvincing, a fresh approach is needed, something more than treating each country with emergency ministrations by the IMF, development banks, and commercial banks.

The most modest measure would protect third world borrowers from another surge in interest rates. By 1984, the level was high enough for Tancredo Neves, president of Brazil, to describe the charges as "cruel."[36] His country paid the banks $10.2 billion in interest alone in 1985, Mexico $11.2 billion, and Argentina $4.8 billion.[37] This cost could be reduced by putting a ceiling on interest charges and lending the borrowers the difference. The IMF, which now covers export shortfalls for the third world, is the logical agency to make these loans. Since most of the Fund's money comes from Western governments, their credit in effect would substitute for that of the private banks. A new Interest Facility might fix a ceiling of perhaps 10 percent. If rates reached

14 percent (they topped that in 1981), the debtor country could draw on the IMF for half the difference, two percentage points; the other half must be loaned by its commercial bankers. They would have every reason to do so because a failure to collect interest strikes at profits. The IMF should not lend the entire interest differential; that would spare the banks from any burden while assuring them of all their payments. In effect, the banks would capitalize a portion of the interest due them, adding it on to the outstanding loan.

If interest charges fell below the ceiling, say to 6 percent, the borrowing nation would be required to pay off its debt with the extra four percentage points, first to the Fund Facility and second to the banks.

It has been argued that the banks will never let their third world clients become delinquent and will always lend them the interest they need to protect bank earnings. Perhaps. But Argentina and others have been unable to meet interest charges on time. A Fund Interest Facility would assure the banks of a steady interest stream and preserve the borrowers from an explosion in rates.

The debt has grown so large, however, that even an interest ceiling could subject the borrowers to a heavy charge. The interest might eat up so much of the earnings from exports that a borrower would lack exchange to buy the foreign machines and materials to keep its domestic plants running. Prolonged Western stagnation or slump or new barriers against imports could reverse the gains in Southern exports. It is doubtful that the debtors will endure further declines in living standards even to meet a reasonable interest ceiling. In 1983, Argentina gave up 57 percent of its earnings from exports to pay its interest bills; Brazil surrendered 40 percent and Mexico 32 percent. These are not sustainable levels.

A better arrangement would limit the service on debt to a fixed share of exports, perhaps the 20 percent that experience has shown is bearable. This would insure that four fifths of everything sold abroad could be used for imports. In years when exports shrank, for whatever reason, the drain would be limited. In boom years, the third world could make up the missed interest payments and perhaps even reduce the principal modestly.[38] This is a scheme based on ability to pay. It would spare the South from further slashing the material standards of its citizens.

So radical a departure from banking practice will confront outraged opposition from the lenders. Together, Mexico, Brazil, and Argentina paid 40 percent of their exports for interest in 1984. If this had been cut to 20 percent, profits of the eight largest United States banks would have fallen as much as 67 percent and no less than 22 percent according to one estimate.[39] An uncertain flow of interest will require changes in accounting to value assets and report profits. Banks are familiar and comfortable only with a fixed interest stream. It is almost inconceivable that the banks will voluntarily agree to such an arrangement. Like the new loan loss requirements for the shakiest debtors, the arrangement must be mandated by legislation.

Ability to pay presents other problems. Britain, Germany, and Japan must join the United States in a common front. Otherwise, the banks of any country outside the arrangement may collect their interest in full; that would eat up the funds provided by a 20-percent-of-exports limit, leaving nothing for banks abiding by it. Borrowers will be tempted to understate their exports to keep payments down, using false invoices or engaging in barter deals. The GATT might be called on to monitor debtor trade. Critics of ability to pay contend that it will weaken the incentive to export, since 20 percent automatically goes to the banks. But the largest debtors are already paying more than this level with no diminished will to export, so that argument falls. Within the IMF, officials worry that a limit might weaken the willingness to satisfy the Fund's terms for drawing. But these terms ought to be reduced drastically anyway. The Fund will still have the same carrot and stick, a loan or its withdrawal, approval or disapproval depending on the debtor's success in putting its payments in order and fixing a proper exchange rate.

Finally, it is argued that ability to pay, with its variable flow of interest payments, will frighten banks from making genuinely new loans to the large debtors. This contention, however, rests on the unlikely prospect that new loans will soon be forthcoming. There are believers—Mexico was one—who may think they are earning their passage back to creditworthiness and fear ability to pay will make them unworthy. The scheme need not be compulsory; any nation that expects to win fresh loans soon from frightened banks should be allowed to continue on its own course. The rest can be expected to welcome a tie between payments and exports.

As it happened, Mexico became the first big debtor to seek repayments tied to economic capacity. The Mexicans, whose principal export is oil, proposed tying interest and principal to the price of crude: the higher it rose, the more the Mexicans could and would repay banks; the lower the price, the smaller the repayments. Bankers, of course, were outraged at so sensible a proposal because it left their earnings uncertain. "Biggest absurdity we've ever heard of," one European banker declared.[40] Mexico did get a foot in the door at the IMF. That austere agency persuaded the banks to lend Mexico an extra $1.7 billion if its economy declined.[41]

Perhaps the most serious objection lies in the likelihood that the scheme would strengthen existing third world regimes and diminish any will to make fundamental reforms. This is not easily answered. Limiting interest payments to 20 percent of exports is a conservative proposal. But endangering regimes by compelling them to tighten further the belts of those with the smallest stomachs is not the best road to reform. More than likely, before things reach such a pass, these governments will simply refuse to pay the bills. Peru virtually adopted this course, announcing without agreement that it would limit its 1985–86 payments to 10 percent of exports, or less than 3 percent of its debt. If Peru's example is followed, an enforced rearrangement of the debt will ensue in a climate of crisis and panic. One way or another, ability to pay will govern the stream of interest. Marking out ground rules in advance provides for a more orderly, less dangerous route than improvisation under stress.

Preserving a large fraction of exports to pay for imports treats one problem. Another is stimulating new loans, funds needed to avert a dangerous hemorrhage of resources and money the banks cannot be expected to provide on their own. An insurance scheme along the lines of those proposed by Wallich and Lever would solve this problem. An international agency—the World Bank or a union of national export credit agencies—should create a fund to guarantee against default new bank loans to old third world debtors. The guarantee should cover only a part of the loan, perhaps half, to discourage reckless lending. Governments would finance the fund initially; in time, premiums charged to the lenders would replace the government credits. This cost would no doubt be passed on to the borrowers, a price they would pay for new claims on the resources of the West. The international agency would monitor the loans in an effort to assure they were used for productive projects and could reject dubious ventures. If the official optimists are right, the insurance agency will die from lack of demand because banks will make loans unaided. If, as seems more probable, they are wrong, the pool of premiums could overcome the timidity of commercial banks and restore at a more realistic level new lending to the third world.

Three devices have been proposed to relieve the stress caused by the debt excess of the 1970s: a ceiling on interest charges to protect against a surge in rates; reserving a fixed share of exports for imports by linking debt service and ability to pay; a guarantee for new loans that otherwise are unlikely to be made. These techniques are not simply designed to ease an otherwise difficult life for the debtors; they are also safeguards for the West against a serial default that could touch off a financial crisis with widespread repercussions on jobs and output.

A major problem remains and it is not easily solved, the endless character of the existing debt. Not even the most credulous banker or government official expects borrowers to pay back more than token amounts of the principal they owe. Eugene Rothberg, treasurer of the World Bank, has said flatly: "The principal is not going to get repaid."[42] This means that the banks will simply extend the loans as they come due, postponing payment indefinitely. The banks are delighted to do this just as long as that all-important interest is paid. Their asset is then sound and earning profits. In effect, the debt is converted into a form of consol, a sovereign obligation of infinite maturity, performing, yielding a return. Canada and Australia have had debt outstanding for more than one hundred years, the bankers observe.[43] The trouble is that neither Mexico nor the Philippines—to say nothing of Zaire or Bolivia—enjoy the economic, political, and cultural stability of Canada or Australia.

An infinite stretchout is politically insecure. Will Brazilian and Mexican politicians or their people pay indefinitely $10 or $12 billion a year in interest on old debt arranged in the years of easy lending? It is not hard to imagine some future populist demand to throw off the load and that demand could be irresistible. The conventional view holds that the punishment, a cutoff of further loans, would be so painful that no responsible government will follow this course. But if new loans are limited or unforthcoming, this is not much of a threat (although it would have more weight with a new loan insurance scheme in place).

A clean solution would provide an orderly rundown of the debt, reducing the principal by say 5 percent annually over twenty years. The weakest debtors are almost certain to win something like this. That would deflate the populist demands. The trouble is that universal debt forgiveness would wipe out the largest banks in the United States and Britain. They have loaned the big debtors more than their capital. Unless they could raise fresh money from stockholders—unthinkable if they are writing off huge assets—the banks would become wards of the Federal Reserve and the Bank of England. This is precisely the financial shock that all attempts to deal with the crisis seek to avoid. The clean solution, no matter how attractive, is unworkable. Forgiving the debt of large debtors, even gradual forgiveness, threatens the existence of the banks.

Economic forces could in time shrink the problem. If Western inflation averages 4 percent a year, a level near that of the mid-1980s, the real value of the debt will diminish by nearly half in ten years. If Mexico, Brazil, Argentina, and the others enjoy the best of all possible worlds and grow at a brisk, unbroken pace, the debt becomes a declining share of their enlarged output. But if neither happens and the domestic pressure to shed the burden becomes intolerable, the West will be faced with two choices: another set of ad hoc, case-by-case emergency renegotiations in an atmosphere of crisis; or a move to take the banks out of the business, exchanging their third world debt for some longer-term, lower-yielding instrument issued by an international agency. Neither is a happy choice. Both would strip banks of profits and chill prospects of even insured new loans. The second, swap route would demand a vast outpouring of public credit and a cry to nationalize the banks. The key to a less dramatic outcome then lies in the West, in its ability to create conditions for its own growth and that of third world economies.

Chapter 8

Rich North, Richer South

A prosperous economy is the single most powerful contribution that the rich North can offer the poorer South. Revival of the sustained, largely inflation-free growth that the industrial world enjoyed in the first quarter century after the War is crucial for the material well-being of the third world. All other remedies, the nostrums urged by the South and the measures proposed in this study, pale in significance compared to steadily expanding output in the North. This has a curious flavor, even a taste of trickle-down prosperity, but in a world where the bulk of third world trade is with advanced economies, it is an inescapable fact. Steady, rising demand in the North will answer directly many of the South's plaints.

Strong Northern growth—4 to 5 percent each year—will strengthen the prices of coffee, copper, sisal, cocoa, and the other raw materials on which so many third world nations depend; apart from accidents of nature, it is slump in the North that drives these prices and their export earnings down. In the same way, Southern exports of manufactured goods thrive when the North thrives, slump when the North slumps. Even worse, recession or meager growth in the North swells unemployment and intensifies fears of lost jobs and sales, strengthening the demand for protection against competing foreign goods, closing outlets for the South's new industry. The huge debt amassed by some of the third world in the 1970s now consumes, through interest payments, Southern goods and services that would otherwise earn foreign exchange to pay for enhanced Southern well-being. Northern prosperity will enable the debtors to expand their exports and shrink the relative interest burden. Above all, a prosperous North rid of inflation will cut the absolute debt burden. Stable prices in the industrial world encourage central banks to bring down interest rates, reducing the charges on all debt tied to the rise and fall of the price of money.

The proposals so far presented are chiefly safeguards, protecting South and North rather than stimulating Southern growth. They would protect commodity earnings against a precipitous fall, prevent a surge in interest rates from swallowing foreign exchange, preserve exports from creditors' charges. The recommendation to end national aid programs is also a shield, designed to protect the third world's poor from exploitation by a ruling elite and reduce temptation for the rich to engage in dangerous adventure. Tying international assistance to fundamental reform is different. It would enlarge Southern growth. Inevitably, however, this proposal will meet stiff resistance from those in the South who prefer things as they are, have a vested stake in the existing ownership of land, in price disincentives to farmers, in a tax system that spares the best off. Inflation-free growth in the North is different from all of these. It meets the critical test of costless assistance, requires no nation to yield anything for the uncertain prospect of benefiting another. It is an unsuitable subject for futile global wrangling. It can be accomplished by the policies of separate industrial nations, particularly the United States, without empty declarations.

Expansion in the North not only promises to spur third world economies by enlarging the demand for their raw materials and finished goods. More rapid growth in the South could then make less painful the changes in land tenure, foreign and domestic pricing, and other internal reforms that now languish. Rising prosperity feeds on itself and can help dissolve the vast array of social and economic barriers to growth.

The almost unbroken growth and mild inflation experienced by the United States and Europe after World War II was no accident but the result of deliberate policy. The Great Depression and Keynes had confounded the orthodoxy of an earlier era. Both taught that unemployment and slump were stable, not ephemeral phenomena that could be overcome if only wages were cut enough. The war reinforced Keynes's lesson. Government demand for goods and services could fill the gap left by inadequate private investment and spending. Appropriately designed, tax spending and monetary policies could tame business cycles. After the war, when a recession struck—and until 1974 they were brief and shallow—a tax cut or a spending increase combined with easier credit would revive economies. If prices rose, they were checked by draining demand from the economy, by reduced spending, a tax increase, and tighter money.

But a series of shocks discredited countercyclical policy. The war in Vietnam generated a huge government demand for goods and services in the United States that was not offset by cuts in other government outlays or a tax increase. The excess demand spilled over into prices. They accelerated again under the impact of quadrupled oil costs. Government efforts to overcome slumps with fiscal instruments—taxes and spending—pushed up prices at ever-increasing rates. Much of the West, particularly the United States and Britain, endured both inflation and stagnating output.

By the early 1980s, the West had largely abandoned the techniques that had brought a quarter century of prosperity. In the United States, by far the most important nation economically, in Britain and West Germany, conservative governments rejected the very idea that fiscal policy should guide an economy. Instead, they abdicated in favor of their central banks, singlemindedly combating inflation through tight money. The squeeze on credit threw millions out of work and idled plants, suppressing demands for higher wages and prices. In the United States, tight money, with its accompaniment of high interest rates, led to an overvalued dollar and a large trade deficit. The inflow of competing foreign goods further held back domestic prices. But instead of steering the economy, fiscal policy was used by the Reagan administration to transfer income from the less well off to the better off. The newest economics plainly reduced the rate of inflation but at an enormous cost in unemployed men and plant. The lamed American economy was producing over $500 billion a year less than it could.[1] The misery, the degradation of the millions vainly seeking work—for they alone are counted as unemployed in the United States—is immeasurable.

The willed means and ends were harshest in the United States and Britain. But other Western industrial countries were equally reluctant to employ familiar techniques to keep their economies growing; they too accepted high unemployment and stagnation from fear of price increases and depreciated currencies. The consequences for the South were baleful. Markets were lost, interest charges remained high, and commodity prices were depressed. A partial United States recovery beginning in 1983 gave some relief, but the Western economy generally suffered meager growth through the first half of the decade.

This unsatisfactory state of affairs is not likely to be tolerated by electorates for very long. The abandonment of fiscal policy is an episode, the sour fruit of the 1970s when tax and spending stimuli worked only at the price of higher inflation. At some point, Western voters will reject the waste and misery of policies that hold down prices by idling men and plants, particularly since inflation has persisted even if at a reduced rate. Once again, voters will insist on increased living standards, on a growing economy. The central problem for the West (the South now becomes an interested bystander) is reconciling this goal with a stable price level, reviving fiscal and monetary techniques to guide growing economies without igniting inflation.

The solution lies in the nature of price and wage decision making in the modern world. In an industrial economy, wages and prices rise in both boom and slump, climbing faster near full employment, more slowly but still climbing even in a recession. This is not what classical economics predicts. In the orthodox canon, prices and wages tend to rise and fall with the rise and fall of demand, assuming that the central bank neither floods nor drains the economy of money. All markets are competitive. No one producer or supplier of labor is large enough to affect either the price or output of any product or factor of production. All are price takers rather than price makers. In the classical model, the price mechanism guides all resources to their most efficient use. Each seeking his own gain is led by an invisible hand, in Adam Smith's celebrated phrase, to promote the welfare of all.

The modern world, however, is marked by conspicuously visible actors. The candy store owner in a city with scores of candy stores is a classical actor with no power over the price or the number of newspapers he will offer for sale. But IBM, General Motors, General Electric, Du Pont, Exxon, *The New York Times, Time* magazine, and the rest of the Fortune 500 and more are very differently placed. They have considerable discretion over the price of their products and how much they will produce and sell. Even in their weakened state, trade unions, the United Auto Workers, the International Association of Machinists, the United Steelworkers, and several dozen others enjoy an influence over wages denied to a lone worker. In Europe, large corporations and unions wield similar power. Markets in the West, then, are characterized by monopolistic or imperfect competition where prices are administered. The large corporations that dominate them are not free of all competition. None are perfect monopolies, and all must take account of the handful of firms who follow their lead, of substitute products, of foreign competition. Nevertheless, and over a wide range, the large corporations and big unions exercise pricing power. They can and do shrug off a stringent money policy that chokes off demand. Some even price perversely, increasing their markups to recover lost profits when demand falls.

The large corporations and unions build into modern economies an engine for higher prices and wages that inhibits all governments. Governments are reluctant to stimulate sagging economies with monetary and fiscal policy for fear that inflation will worsen. They know that corporations and unions will exploit an increased demand to raise their prices. The end result is slump, cautious recovery and stagnation, wasted resources and perpetual inflation, even if at a reduced pace. "The dynamics of inflation," wrote Arthur Okun, "are imbedded in the process of wage and price determination and cannot be eliminated solely by fiscal and monetary measures without incurring great losses of output and employment."[2]

To unfreeze fiscal policies, to use monetary policy to stimulate as well as repress, the power of the large corporations and unions must be tempered. The direct method is through government controls, fixing maximum price and wage increases. In the stress of war, governments employ this approach, rationing scarce goods. At least in the United States, government price fixing is unacceptable in peacetime. A raging inflation might make controls palatable for a brief period, but their life almost certainly must be short. More importantly, price controls destroy the virtues of markets, even imperfect ones. Price fixing distorts the distribution of resources, prevents their most efficient use. Prices are a set of signals, directing labor, materials, and investment where they are most wanted, in greatest demand; price signals send resources away from firms and industries where demand is falling. Despite the distortions created by the power of corporations and unions, the price system, the system of markets, is the best technique known for achieving the optimum deployment of resources, for encouraging investment in the more promising industries and discouraging it in the less promising, for stimulating technological advance, for promoting maximum growth.

How then is this circle squared? How can we retain the flexibility, efficiency and freedom of the price and market system and curb the price-making power of unions and corporations?*

The answer has a drab name, incomes policy. This is a technique of voluntary restraint on the appetites of corporations and unions. It can be strengthened by government penalties or rewards. Incomes policy is a familiar phrase in Europe where it has been employed since the 1960s. It has an esoteric ring in American ears, although the Kennedy guidelines of 1962 are one variant.

The Europeans—West Germans, Austrians, Scandinavians, and, with some local variations, the British—relied on consensus to make the policy work. Governments sought to achieve an understanding between unions and business over appropriate wage and price behavior to avoid inflation and free authorities to promote high employment and growth. In the heyday of incomes

*In theory, textbook markets could be re-created by the unrelenting exercise of antitrust to break up large corporations and outlaw unions. But in practice this is hopelessly utopian. The major economic institutions of the Western world cannot be legislated out of existence. The open trade policy urged in Chapter 6 would also compel some corporate and union actors to behave as if they confronted classical markets. But in some industries, even global markets can be controlled and organized by a handful of large multinational firms. This is beginning to happen in autos and computers; the spread of international concentration is likely to prove irresistible.

policy, the Germans solemnly referred to labor and business as "social partners."

Although the shape of incomes policy varied from country to country and from time to time, the form often followed these lines: A group of experts—private, government, from the central bank, or the unions and business—constructs a model of the economy's prospects for the year ahead. The experts describe the consequences of different levels of wage increases for employment, unemployment, and inflation. Business is assured that government fiscal and monetary policies will underwrite a growing level of demand provided that the price level is held. Unions are equally assured of an increasing number of jobs if wage increases are moderate. Union officials negotiate with business a wage contract covering organized labor or a key industry that sets the pace for the rest of the labor force. Both business and labor representatives come from centralized federations that enjoy enough power or influence to insure that individual unions and firms will adhere to the bargain. Firms remain free to set their own prices but risk losing bank loans or suffer some other penalty if they increase traditional margins over costs. Since Europeans export a greater share of their output than Americans, the fear of foreign competition acts as a further measure of restraint.

In the 1960s and 1970s, variations on this abstract model were deployed with mixed success, particularly on the Continent. (Britain swung back and forth between mandatory wage and price controls and voluntary wage limits set by the government after consulting federations of unions and employers.) How much incomes policies contributed to the prosperity of the period is still debated. But whether the technique was a ritual or a prime force, the fact is that Europeans generally enjoyed high employment, moderate inflation, and steady growth.

The star performer was West Germany, where incomes policy —economic scenario, consultation, and key bargain—was highly developed. From 1960 to 1977, when disgruntled unions left the arrangement, the West Germans enjoyed the lowest misery index—the combination of unemployment and inflation rates—of every industrial nation in every year except 1972.

By the early 1980s, few formal incomes policies were still in force in Europe. Now conservative governments embraced the monetarism in vogue in the United States, relying on credit curbs and idled workers to tame unions and prices. The postwar goals of high employment and steady growth were scrapped. Political tolerance of long dole queues appears far greater than had been imagined. Unions pushed up wages for their members, indifferent to the consequences for employment. Employers relished their freedom from the restraints of incomes policy. Jobless rates of 10 percent and more were common. Output stagnated.

Incomes policies had succumbed to the twin pressures of inflation and deflation touched off by the oil shocks, to the end of government pledges to sustain demand and employment, to the inevitable irritation with curbs on decision making, no matter how voluntary.

But just as there is a reason to believe that monetarism* is a passing phase in the United States, so too in Europe it is likely that political demands to employ the jobless, to revive economic growth will call forth a different approach. Then incomes policy can return. The logic of corporate and union power dictates as much.

In a searching study of Europe's attempts to achieve voluntary price and wage restraint, Robert J. Flanagan, David W. Soskice and Lloyd Ulman wrote: "Incomes policy could be regarded as a policy of the second best [the best being the unattainable world of purely competitive markets, the textbook model]; in a world inhabited by large-scale government, institutional restraint is necessary to produce results that would issue from the com-

*Apart from its contractionist bias, monetarism confounds its central bank practitioners. Its ancestor is an Irving Fisher equation, a tautology that asserts the price level depends on the volume of money multiplied by its velocity, the speed with which it is transferred from hand to hand. In an age that constantly invents new financial instruments, it is exceedingly difficult to describe the money supply. Hence, a growing list of definitions are used, a bewildering variety of targets are set by policy makers. They are represented by the symbols M_1, M_2, M_3 . . . M_n. Just as bad, the authorities are baffled by changes in velocity, by changes in the public propensity to hold or spend cash. Velocity can only be measured after the fact; it is difficult to predict or influence. Those who rely on monetary policy then are pinning their hopes to one variable that cannot be defined and a second that is beyond control.

pletely unregulated behavior of income-maximizing and rationally foresighted workers and firms under atomistically competitive conditions." Despite its current eclipse, "incomes policy is likely to survive as an important component of overall macroeconomic policy."[3]

If the European problem—reconciling growth with corporate and union power—plagues the United States, then an American incomes policy is a necessary condition for renewing a high employment, inflation-free economy. Adapting an incomes policy to the peculiar structure of the United States economy should be the single greatest domestic challenge confronting policy makers in the last half of the 1980s.

The European model cannot be imported intact. The Continent depended on highly centralized business and labor federations, capable of striking a bargain and disciplining their members. They have no counterparts in the United States. The National Association of Manufacturers or even the prestigious Business Roundtable have no influence on the price or wage making of their corporate members. They exist to make demands on government, not receive its proposals. In the same way, the AFL-CIO at its strongest cannot guide the negotiating package of small locals, let alone an international union. Autonomy is a ruling principle of the federation.

The United States economy is distinguished by price and wage organization within a market, not across markets. This fragmentation compels an American government to play a much more visible role than European authorities in any incomes policy. And it has. The first American incomes policy—never labeled as such—was the Kennedy administration's wage and price guidelines. Announced without consulting union and business leaders (a critical mistake since consensus is needed for a successful policy), the guidelines were based on the yearly gains in productivity. This is the increase in the output of workers that flows from improved machinery, better management, and more intensive use of labor. In general, unions were urged to limit their pay increases to the rise in productivity; then labor costs for each ton of steel, each automobile, each electrical machine would hold constant and prices need not rise. No law was passed to enforce the guidelines. Instead, Kennedy used the considerable prestige of his office to point a stern finger at those who departed from them, succeeding notably in steel.

The guidelines, introduced when unemployment was nearly 6 percent and price increases barely 1 percent, went hand in hand with a remarkable period of well-being. Between 1961 and 1965, consumer prices rose an average of only 1.4 percent a year and unemployment was brought down to 4 percent. With price pressures reduced, Kennedy was free to employ fiscal policy to expand jobs. He did, proposing a tax cut that was enacted after his death.[4]

Did Kennedy's finger-pointing or jawboning really affect prices? There was evidently considerable support for restraining corporations and unions. Both feared public opprobrium. The guidelines and the presidential lectures must be credited with some of the success by all except those who believe oligopoly is an illusion and competitive markets rule everywhere.

This first United States incomes policy was a casualty of the Vietnam War. The guidelines were swamped by an excessive and unrestrained demand for war goods and services, a demand sustained by easy money and the absence of tax or spending restraint by the government. Prices began accelerating in 1966, and presidential injunctions could no longer hold the tide. The outcome was instructive. An incomes policy can only reinforce but cannot replace sober fiscal and monetary decisions.

An attempt to revive guidelines was undertaken by Jimmy Carter. But inflation was now so strong, his standard for pay increases was overwhelmed among other things by automatic cost-of-living gains. The Carter administration, moreover, attempted to set norms for strict, numerical corporate price and profit margins, an untried and complex measure in a period of sharply rising costs. Although the program was initially greeted with strong support from most corporate leaders, its price and profit guides were rapidly undermined.

Since inflation rose from 9 percent to 11.4 percent in the two years of Carter guidelines, his own aides had to acknowledge that "the program would have to be called a dismal failure."[5] The new Reagan team dismissed incomes policy entirely. Its first Economic Report asserted that "neither guideposts nor price controls . . . have succeeded in stopping inflation."[6] This conveniently overlooked the Kennedy episode to say nothing of successful controls in World Wars I and II and at the end of Vietnam.

It is unlikely that the Kennedy experience can be repeated. A special set of economic conditions, low inflation and substantial unemployment, a president who caught popular imagination, and the sheer novelty of the attempt made guidelines and jawboning something of a success. For the longer run, a new and more durable incomes policy must command support from unions, a support that is now far easier to win when unions are weak and several million of their members are idle. The promise of high employment for wage restraint could be an attractive offer. The policy must also enlist the major corporations, and this is a harder task. Employers relish a buyers' market for labor and have a vested interest in a slack supply. But if the large corporations are forced to endure a continuing cycle of slump, abortive recovery, and stagnation, the promise of steadily expanding demand and profits will appear inviting. Then corporate leaders, who typically prize predictability and stability, may accept price restraint. The very executives who provide Reagan with his strongest support initially hailed the Carter incomes policy. It is not inconceivable that a new one, properly designed, could enlist the corporate leaders again.

In the twentieth century, the United States has frequently turned to its tax system to promote desired economic ends—new business investment, exploration for oil, home building, pensions for the aged, and much more. The tax system, then, could be used to promote the desired wage and price behavior.

The principle of a tax-based incomes policy or TIP is simple: Tax penalties or credits are given to firms or workers whose price or wage behavior exceeds or falls short of some standard. The penalties are like fines imposed on polluters. They would internalize the costs of inflation, compelling firms and unions to pay for acts that harm the community.

TIP leaves corporations and unions free to make decisions but penalizes those that harm or rewards those that further the public interest in a stable price level. It allows considerable scope for market forces, for something near the optimum distribution of resources promised by competitive markets; but it inhibits through taxes the wrongful exercise of market power.

TIP need not cover all firms, only the largest with market power, the 2,000 biggest corporations who account for nearly half the economy's output. The government would set a wage standard, perhaps the yearly gain in productivity plus half the current inflation rate. By the mid-1980s, this standard would have been about 4 percent. Large firms that gave average hourly pay increases of more than 4 percent would pay a penalty tax on their incomes.

Economists who believe that major corporations set prices at an unvarying markup over costs would leave things there. But this is unreal. It is unlikely that unions would accept an arrangement penalizing wage increases and leaving prices or profits untouched. Moreover, there is no reason to believe that large corporations, particularly aggressive American concerns, passively fix prices as a multiple of wages. Ambitious new executives make their mark by widening margins, increasing profits for each unit of sale. A politically plausible TIP, a TIP adapted to business reality, must govern prices or margins.

TIP, however, is no panacea and raises several disturbing problems. A TIP on average wages could discourage efficiency, penalizing a firm that hired one high-priced professional to replace several lower paid craftsmen. A company with expanding demand might have to pay more than the standard to attract needed workers; it could do so, but only by accepting a tax penalty. Finally, at least part of any wage TIP could be passed on to consumers through higher prices.

A TIP on prices comes perilously close to price control. It might discourage new investment and the flow of other resources to firms with increasing demand. A TIP on profits or margins would weaken incentives to cut costs, discourage innovation, and repel new investment in an expanding industry. A properly drawn measure must provide tax credits to offset unintended penalties. Finally, a TIP on margins presents complex problems for corporations producing thousands of constantly changing products whose quality frequently changes, for better or worse.

Fixing a standard for hourly wage costs or a single product is relatively simple; determining whether the standard has been met or breached for many different products could lead to a bureaucratic nightmare.

Okun once wrote that he favored a TIP, "not because that policy is beautiful but because it is a lot less ugly than alternative policy strategies."[7] If the United States and the other industrial economies are to employ their resources of men and plant fully, some instrument must be designed to inhibit the power of corporations and unions. Incomes policy, despite its difficulties and uneven past, is the most promising technique to achieve these goals. In the United States, where large corporations and unions cannot speak with a single voice, a workable incomes policy can be created by basing it on the tax system.

Here is a paradox. An inquiry into third world demands has ended in a proposal for coping with inflation to regain growth in the United States and the North generally. Such matters are rarely discussed, and then at the margin, in the U.N., UNCTAD, or any North-South forum. This only underlines how sterile so much of that talk has been. Everything of concern to governments in the South, the burden of debt, the level of commodity prices, the nature of foreign investment, prospects for trade, even the volume of capital, depends above all on a prosperous North.

A case has been made to expand and liberalize an IMF fund to assure the third world a steadier flow of export earnings from its raw materials. But the best assurance lies in steadily growing Northern demand. This will support prices against precipitous falls; it will enlarge the volume of raw materials purchased.

The South insists that raw materials prices invariably fall against those of imported manufactured goods, that its terms of trade are doomed to worsen. Although neither theory nor experience support this claim, it will be further undermined by a prosperous North that is also free of inflation. Then the prices that the South pays for its imports should remain more or less stable. At least one blade of the terms of trade scissors will have been blunted. Indeed, expanding Northern demand for third world commodities should increase their price, turning the Prebisch dilemma upside down.

Southern manufactured goods must similarly benefit from sustained growth in the North. Markets for television sets, shoes, autos, and more would expand. Political pressure to seal off industrial markets against Southern competitors would shrink. In a world of full employment, Northern managers and workers displaced by imports could find new jobs more easily, even without the special assistance proposed in this book. The South's search for preferences, for advantaged entry has boomeranged. It has opened the door for elaborate and widespread discrimination against all foreign goods. A far better strategy for the South is to demand that Northern nations live by their words, adhere to GATT rules, and maximize open trade. Sustained Northern prosperity will then afford large and growing markets for Southern goods.

The South's unending cry for aid has forged another double-edged sword. These funds carry heavy political, military, and commercial obligations. Northern donors do not give away billions from an excess of altruism but to achieve foreign policy objectives. From the recipient's standpoint, the money may do more harm than good for all but the governing elite group, and its dignity, its independence is weakened by its client status. The funds persuade rulers to put off needed reforms for growth, rarely reach the large mass of impoverished, and insure the underuse of human and physical resources that characterize so many nations in the South. Trade is better than aid, and industrial prosperity is the key to exchange.

A prosperous North will probably generate an excess of savings, beyond that most profitably employed at home. This capital will seek outlets in the third world, will flow again as it did in the 1970s—although perhaps less recklessly—to fill the gap left by the shortage of third world savings. A businesslike arrangement with a Northern bank should be far more preferable than the unequal relationship imposed by aid. There are countries too poor to expect commercial loans in the next decade and beyond. They can be served by a World Bank with expanded lending power. Those who cannot afford the Bank's terms become eligible for IDA aid; but then they should undertake politically painful reform.

Finally, the great debts amassed in the 1970s become far more bearable in a world of industrial prosperity. Its inflation-free character should induce the most obdurate of central banks to keep interest rates down. That will cut sharply the cost of servicing all the debt tied to floating rates. The enlarged markets envisioned for Southern goods, moreover, should serve as an engine of growth for some in the third world. Their debt then becomes an ever-decreasing fraction of total output. Placing a ceiling on interest charges is a useful, short-term safeguard against repudiation; Northern prosperity is a far more powerful instrument to slash the debt burden and protect the banking structure of the industrial world.

There is no forum where the South can effectively urge sound policy on the North; if there were, the North would not pay much attention. All the attempts at global bargaining—except for the Law of the Sea—have foundered because they were so one-sided. The scenario has been simple: The South makes unrequited demands on the North; the North offers an occasional, marginal concession but generally rejects the demands with varying degrees of politeness. There is no reason to think this pattern will change unless and until the South has something to offer in return. Third world nations thought they had found something in the price of oil, but this proved empty because the oil producers would not bargain away their power and, in time, their power vanished, thanks to substitution and new discoveries. Debt could yet turn out to be the oil of the 1980s. If the North, obsessed with inflation, continues to stagger between slump and abortive recovery, the debt load could become intolerable for large third world nations. They might then combine to impose terms on their creditors, on the commercial banks, fixing lower interest charges, wiping out portions of their debt, even seeking guaranteed prices for their commodities and direct aid. This debtors' collective might be potent. It could threaten to repudiate its debt with fearful consequences for the leading United States and British banks. But apart from a confrontation under the threat of catastrophe, a grim meeting in which both sides have something to give and get under duress, it is hard to imagine any North-South negotiation that does not end in empty rhetoric by the South bouncing harmlessly against a stone wall from the North. The threat to the West's financial structure, the need to avoid a North-South clash of wills, is still another reason for seeking growth in the North. For then debt as a problem dissolves.

A steady expansion of Northern economies requires the full use of all resources, manpower, and plant. A stretched economy with high employment and expanding demand will call forth new investment in machinery, in plant, in innovative technology. These are the critical ingredients for raising the efficiency or productivity of workers and increasing the rate of growth. But inflation will frustrate the full employment of men and plant unless new approaches are taken to restrain the pricing power of corporations and unions. This is the compelling logic behind incomes policy.

A prosperous North cannot in itself assure improved material well-being for the poor of the third world. Southern elites, rooted cultural attitudes, caste and power relations will decide whether the life of the impoverished is bettered. The prospects for the worst off can improve, however, if third world economies grow. No matter how the South maldistributes its added wealth, a richer third world nation can more easily accommodate fundamental reform than a stagnating society. Whether the South grows depends in great measure on the North, on the ability of industrial economies to renew the sustainable economic advance of the first postwar generation. All the futile schemes to extract free claims on Northern resources, all the vain attempts to fix the unfixable or open the unopenable shrink in significance beside the vital necessity of prosperity in the North.

Notes

Chapter 1: The Great Debt Trauma

1. Mexican bailout, 1982—Joseph Kraft, *The Mexican Rescue* (New York: The Group of Thirty, 1984), pp. 2–16. For a follow-up, see *The Economist,* September 15, 1984, pp. 85–86.

2. Oil crisis impact on third world—William R. Cline, *International Debt and the Stability of the World Economy* (Washington, D.C.: Institute for International Economics, 1983), p. 21. See also *World Economic Outlook,* IMF Occasional Paper No. 27 (Washington, D.C.: 1984), p. 43. Compare to total foreign aid received, \$30.3 billion—OECD, *Development Cooperation* (Paris: 1981), p. 77

3. Inflationary restraint, 1974—*Economic Report of the President 1975,* p. 19.

4. Inflation, 1973–78—*OECD Economic Outlook* (Paris: July 1980), p. 140.

5. Growth of third world lending by commercial banks—letter to the author from External Relations Department, International Monetary Fund, dated April, 18, 1985.

6. "A country does not go bankrupt"—Walter Wriston, "Banking Against Disaster," *New York Times,* September 14, 1982, p. 27.

7. Nineteenth century sovereign defaults—Robert Solomon, "The United States as a Debtor in the 19th Century," *International Economic Letter,* January 18, 1983, pp. 1–3.

8. Bank profits in Brazil—author's interview with Thomas Hanley, chief bank stock analyst, Salomon Brothers, November 10, 1985:

1982 Citicorp earnings of which:		\$746 million
from Brazil	\$149	
from Argentina	30	
from Mexico	25	
	\$204 million (or 27.3% of total earnings)	

See also *The Economist,* May 5, 1984, pp. 89–90.

9. Wealthiest third world nations get bank loans—*World Bank Annual Report 1985,* pp. 178–80.

10. Commercial banks' portion of total LDC debt—*New York Times,* December 6, 1985, p. D2.

11. Clausen congratulates bankers—A. W. Clausen, *Remarks to the International Monetary Conference* (Vancouver: World Bank, May 25, 1982), pp. 1–4.

12. Growth of debt service ratios—Darrell Delamaide, *Debt Shock: The Full Story of the World Credit Crisis* (Garden City, N. Y.: Doubleday, 1984), p. 99. See also Cline, op. cit., p. 17. For a country-by-country summary, see *Wall Street Journal,* June 22, 1984, p. 38.

13. Growth of public works projects—*World Bank Development Report 1984* (New York: Oxford University Press, 1984), p. 27. On Argentina, see *The Economist,* April 7, 1984, p. 11.

14. Excessive Latin borrowing: "Lack of supply constraints"—Thomas O. Enders and Richard P. Mattione, *Latin America: The Crisis of Debt and Growth* (Washington, D.C.: Brookings Institute, 1984), p. 7.

15. Abuses by Argentina's state petroleum company—*New York Times,* May 12, 1984, p. 35.

16. Capital flight—on Mexico and Argentina, see *The Economist,* June 23, 1984, p. 73; on Zaire, see Delamaide, op. cit., p. 59. For an analysis of capital flight in Latin America, see Enders and Mattione, op. cit., pp. 1–30.

17. 1982–85 capital flight—Morgan Guaranty Trust Co., *World Financial Markets,* February 1986.

18. BIS defense of third world loans—Bank of International Settlements, *53rd Annual Report* (Basel, Switzerland: June 1983), p. 130.

19. Watson's support of third world loans—Paul M. Watson, *Debt and the Developing Countries* (Washington, D.C.: Overseas Development Council, 1978), p. 49.

20. Burns's praise of banks' behavior—Watson, op. cit., pp. 35–36.

21. Rise of third world lending—John Williamson, "The Outlook for Development Finance After the Debt Crisis," in Khadija Haq, ed. *Crisis of the 80's* (Washington, D.C.: North South Roundtable, 1984), p. 82.

22. Rise of oil prices—*World Economic Outlook,* IMF Occasional Paper No. 21, p. 144. For a broader survey, *OECD Economic Outlook,* 1980, pp. 114–124.

23. United States anti-inflation policy, 1979–80—*Economic Report of the President, 1981,* p. 46.

24. Slowdown in inflation—in the United States, *Economic Report of the President, 1984,* p. 283. In the OECD, *OECD Economic Outlook* (Paris: July 1983), p. 167.

25. Rise in Federal Funds rate and Libor—IMF, *International Financial Statistics* (Washington, D.C.: June 1984), pp. 62–63.

26. OECD on high interest rates—*OECD Economic Outlook* (Paris: July 1982), p. 19.

27. Reagan on high interest rates—*Economic Report of the President, 1982*, p. 47.

28. Unemployment in the OECD—*OECD Economic Outlook, 1982*, p. 153.

29. Unemployment in the United States—U.S. Bureau of Labor Statistics, *Monthly Labor Review*, May 1983, p. 63.

30. OECD questions tight money—*OECD Economic Outlook, 1982*, p. 9.

31. Effects of interest rate changes on debt payments—*The Economist*, May 25, 1985, pp. 67–68. See also *The Economist*, May 26, 1984, pp. 88–93 and April 14, 1984, p. 77.

32. Fall in sugar prices—World Bank, *World Development Report 1983* (New York: Oxford University Press, July 1983), p. 11.

33. Estimated costs of the deflation policy—Cline, op. cit, p. 25.

34. Banks' exposure to third world debt—*The American Banker*, March 17, 1983, p. 1. See also Benjamin J. Cohen, "International Debt and Linkage Strategies," *International Organization*, Autumn 1985, p. 717.

35. 1974 Basel communiqué—G. G. Johnson with Richard K. Abrams, *Aspects of the Safety Net*, IMF Occasional Paper No. 17 (Washington, D.C., March 1983), p. 25.

36. Brazilian bailout—M. S. Mendelsohn, "New Hope for Solution to Brazilian Debt," *The American Banker*, October 31, 1983, p. 1.

37. IMF shares—IMF, *International Monetary Fund Directory* (Washington, D.C., March 18, 1985), pp. 1–8.

38. Drop-off in bank lending to the LDCs—IMF, *World Economic Outlook 1984* (Washington, D.C.), p. 10.

39. Debt won't be paid—for Galveas, *New York Times*, July 30, 1984, p. D1; for Guenther, *Wall Street Journal*, June 22, 1984, p. 39; for Roosa, see Robert V. Roosa, "The International Financial System in Crisis," Ernst Sturc Memorial Lecture, Washington, D.C., November 2, 1983, p. 1.

40. Argentine bailout, 1984—*New York Times*, May 26, 1984, p. 35. See also *The Economist*, April 7, 1984, p. 11. For Manufacturers Hanover's profit cut, see *New York Times*, July 13, 1984, p. D1.

41. Praise for bailout—Wilfried Guth, "International Debt Crisis: The Next Phase," *The Banker*, July 1983, p. 25.

42. Rise in unemployment and decline in income in third world—*Santiago Statement on World Monetary, Financial, and Human Resource Development Issues* (Santiago, Chile: The North South Roundtable and the Economic Commission for Latin America, February 27–29, 1984), p. 1.

43. Decline in Latin GNP/person—Richard S. Weinert, "Coping with LDC Debt," *Journal of International Affairs,* Summer 1984, p. 10. See also *Wall Street Journal,* June 22, 1984, p. 35.

44. 1985 Drop in Latin GNP/person—*The Economist,* April 12, 1986, p. 78.

45. Brookings study: "resentment and fustration exploding . . ."—Enders and Mattione, op. cit., p. 56.

46. IMF riots and strikes—in the Dominican Republic, *New York Times,* May 26, 1984. p. 1; in Peru, *Wall Street Journal,* April 20, 1984, p. 1; in Sudan, *Washington Post,* March 28, 1985, p. 23, and *New York Times,* April 7, 1985, p. 1.

47. Latin inflation rates—Letter to author from IMF, April 18, 1985.

48. BIS self-congratulation—BIS *53rd Annual Report* (1983), p. 6.

49. IMF self-congratulation—Jacques de Larosière, "The IMF and the Developing Countries," a speech at the University of Neuchâtel, Switzerland, published in IMF, *External Debt in Perspective* (Washington, D.C.: September 1983), p. 38.

50. A banker's skepticism on debt repayment—Barton Biggs, managing director of Morgan Stanley, quoted in Delamaide, op. cit., p. 228–29.

51. Reduced fees for Mexico and Brazil—Weinert, op. cit., p. 9.

52. Brazil's 1985 growth—*New York Times,* January 6, 1986, p. D8.

53. Brazil agreement—*The Economist,* March 8, 1986.

54. BIS advocacy of incomes policy—BIS, *51st Annual Report* (1981), p. 23.

55. Call for global economic conference—Seventh Conference of Heads of State or Governments of Non-Aligned Countries, *Final Documents* (hereafter, Seventh Conference, *Documents*) (New Delhi, India: March 1983), pp. 96 and 102.

Chapter 2: The Rising South

1. Economics in the U.N. charter—*Charter of the United Nations and Statute of the International Court of Justice* (New York: United Nations, undated), Chapter 1, Article 1, page 3.

2. Lie commission on internal third world reform—*Measures for the Economic Development of Under Developed Countries* (New York: United Nations Department of Economic Affairs, May 1951), p. 13.

3. Proposal for an international development agency—ibid., pp. 84–85.

4. Political test for aid—ibid., p. 87.

5. LDC document: "massive transfers"—Seventh Conference, *Documents,* p. 108.

6. Syria warns "full scale war" from inequality—*Official Records of the*

U.N. General Assembly (hereafter, *Official Records, U.N.*), 10th Sess., 2nd Comm., October 17, 1955, p. 47.

7. Chile favors U.N. agency—*Official Records, U.N.*, 4th Sess., 2nd Comm., 1949, p. 61.

8. Chile complains about loss of terms of trade—*Official Records, U.N.*, 5th Sess., 2nd Comm., 1950–51, p. 33.

9. Commodity price fluctuations—*International Financial Statistics* (Washington, D.C.: IMF, January 1985), pp. 74–75.

10. Comparison of commodity and manufactured good price fluctuations—F. Gerard Adams and Jere R. Behrman, *Commodity Exports and Economic Development* (Lexington, Mass.: Lexington Books, 1982), p. 18.

11. Tito on the political price for foreign aid—*Official Records,* U.N., 15th Sess., Plenary Meetings, June 7, 1960, p. 53.

12. Shares in the World Bank—*The World Bank Annual Report 1984*, Washington, D.C., pp. 176–78.

13. Aid cut off to Allende's Chile from June 1970 to June 1974—*Statement of Loans, 12/31/80,* International Bank for Reconstruction and Development.

14. Complaints about aid priorities—for Colombia, *Official Records, U.N.*, 3rd Sess., 2nd Comm., October 13, 1948, p. 60; for Pakistan, *Official Records, U.N.*, 3rd Sess., 2nd Comm., November 13, 1948, p. 280; for Brazil, *Official Records, U.N.*, 12th Sess., 2nd Comm., December 12, 1957, p. 291.

15. United States proposals—Resolution 1240 (XIII), adopted October 14, 1958, *Resolutions Adopted by the General Assembly during the 13th Session*, Vol. I, pp. 11–14.

16. Ceylon: "Thankful for small mercies"—*Official Records, U.N.*, 13th Sess., Plenary Meetings, September 30, 1958, p. 236.

17. Eugene Black: "The IDA was really an idea to offset the urge for Sunfed"—James H. Weaver, *The International Development Association: A New Approach to Foreign Aid* (New York: Frederick A. Praeger, 1965), p. 28. See also Edward S. Mason and Robert E. Asher, *The World Bank Since Bretton Woods* (Washington, D.C.: Brookings Institute, 1973), p. 386.

18. Herter: poverty leads to tyranny—*Official Records, U.N.*, 14th Sess., Plenary Meetings, September 17, 1959, p. 14.

19. IDA's impact on schools, housing, health—Mason and Asher, op. cit., p. 381. See also World Bank, *IDA in Retrospect* (New York: Oxford University Press, 1982), pp. 32–46.

20. Eased payment schedule for India—Mason and Asher, op. cit., p. 224–25.

21. Cuts in IDA funding—*Facts on File, 1982,* p. 283.

22. McCloy: the third world is a battleground—*Hearings before Subcommittee of the House Committee on Banking and Currency, concerning the In-*

ternational Development Act, 86th Cong., 2nd Sess. (March 15–17, 1960). p. 43.

23. Hoffman: "shrinking free world"—*Hearings Before a Subcommittee of the Senate Committee on Banking and Currency*, 85th Cong., 2nd Sess., March 18–20, 1958, p. 70. See also Paul G. Hoffman, "Blueprint for Foreign Aid," *New York Times Magazine*, February 17, 1957, p. 38.

24. 1960 U.N. membership (100 total members with four not classified) —*United Nations Chronicle*, Vol. XXI, no. 8 (1984).

25. Cairo declaration: third world progresses despite colonialism—"Cairo Declaration of Developing Countries," *Official Records, U.N.*, 17th Sess., Annexes, Vol. I, Annex 12. Cairo Conference held July 9–18, 1962.

26. Moscow's call for global economic conference—Diego Cordovez, "The Making of Unctad," *Journal of World Trade Law*, vol. 1 (May–June 1967), p. 255–256. For an interpretation of Soviet trade negotiation policy, see Charles Anthony Schwartz, "UNCTAD: Soviet Policy in the North-South Conflict," unpublished Ph.D. thesis, University of Michigan, Ann Arbor, 1973, pp. 28–50.

27. Gardner: "an economic Munich for the West"—conversation with the author, 1964.

28. Brandt: "The Group of 77 represents the solidarity of the developing nations . . . a common stand."—Willy Brandt et al., *North-South: A Program for Survival* (Cambridge, Mass.: MIT Press, 1980), p. 262.

29. State Department: third world a cohesive caucus despite disagreements—Carol Geldart and Peter Lyon, "The Group of 77: A Perspective View," in *International Affairs*, London, Winter 1980–81, p. 79.

30. Corea on third world parochialism—"North-South Dialogue," an interview with Gamani Corea, *Third World Quarterly* (London), October 1981, pp. 606–07.

31. Industrial countries having 70 percent of international trade—in 1964, developed countries had $118.2 billion in exports out of global exports of $173 billion, or 68.1%. UNCTAD, *Handbook of International Trade and Development Statistics* (New York: United Nations, 1979), p. 2. See also Fouad Ajami, *The Global Populists: Third World Nations and World Order* (Princeton, N. J.: Princeton University, 1974), p. 6.

32. Creation of IMF's Compensatory Finance Facility—Louis M. Goreux, *Compensatory Facility Financing*, Pamphlet No. 34 (Washington, D.C.: IMF, 1980), p. 37.

33. Prebisch Report on ever-deteriorating terms of trade—"Towards a New Trade Policy for Development," report by the Secretary General of UNCTAD, United Nations, 1964, p. 16.

34. Prebisch Report on South's demand for North's goods—ibid., p. 3.

35. Prebisch Report on unbalanced labor markets—ibid., p. 15.

36. Prebisch Report on fall in buying power of South's commodity exports—ibid., p. 18.

37. Prebisch Report on need for income transfer—ibid., p. 16.

38. Prebisch Report on end to trade barriers and preferential tariffs —ibid., p. 29.

39. Prebisch Report on aid as a compensation for past discrimination —op. cit., p. 120.

40. Prebisch Report: "Much remains to be done . . ."—ibid., p. 89.

41. Prebisch Report: "One's house must be put in order . . ."—ibid., p. 117.

42. Prebisch Report and the British Board of Trade's price table—A. S. Friedeberg, *The U.N. Conference on Trade and Development of 1964* (Rotterdam: Rotterdam University Press, 1970), p. 39.

43. UNCTAD's report on the terms of trade question—"Expert Group on Indexation," April 28–May 1, 1975, p. 1 (an unpublished report).

44. Friedeberg's criticism of Prebisch's theory—Friedeberg, op. cit., p. 40.

45. 1983 declaration on commodity prices: "steady deterioration"—Seventh Conference, *Documents,* p. 67.

46. 1981 ministerial meeting: "improve the purchasing power"—*New Delhi Declaration, Economic Part,* Ministerial Conference of Non-Aligned Countries, New Delhi, India, February 9–12, 1981, p. 66.

47. 1980 Group of 77: "protection of purchasing power"—Report of the Committee of the Whole, Established Under General Assembly Resolution 32/174, *Official Records, U.N.,* 11th Special Sess., Supplement No. 1, p. 8.

48. Dependency theory—Theotonio Dos Santos, "The Structure of Dependence," in K. T. Fann and Donald C. Hodges, eds., *Readings in U.S. Imperialism* (Boston: Porter Sargent Publishers, 1971), pp. 226–27.

49. Ease of control on foreign corporations—*Transnational Corporations in World Development: Third Survey* (New York, United Nations Centre on Transnational Corporations, 1983), p. 56. For more recent evidence, see *New York Times,* May 11, 1985, p. 1, or *The Economist,* February 9, 1985, pp. 61–62. For discussion of Japanese "dummy corporations" in the third world, see Franklin B. Weinstein, "Underdevelopment and Efforts to Control Multinational Corporations" in Fann and Hodges, op. cit., pp. 339–442.

50. U.N.: "increased flexibility and pragmatism"—*Transnational Corporations,* p. 61.

51. List of enemies of the third world—Seventh Conference, *Documents,* p. 83.

52. Voting patterns at the 1st UNCTAD conference—Harry G. John-

son, *Economic Policies Toward Less Developed Countries* (Washington, D.C.: Brookings Institute, 1967), p. 252.

53. United States disapproval of UNCTAD provisions—Speech by John Scali, *Official Records, U.N.*, 6th Special Sess., Plenary Meetings, May 1, 1974, p. 7.

54. United States analysis of allies' disloyalty in U.N. votes—*Report to Congress on Voting Practices in the United Nations,* U.S. Department of State, February 24, 1984, Table 2.

55. Soviets' disavowal of third world poverty—*Official Records, U.N.*, 7th Special Sess., September 3, 1975, p. 8.

Chapter 3: The New Order

1. IMF introduces Extended Fund Facility—Graham Bird, *The International Monetary System and the Less Developed Countries* (London: Macmillan, 1978), pp. 149–53.

2. Preferences increase third world exports—Craig R. McPhee, "Evaluation of the Implementation, Maintenance, and Improvement of the Generalized System of Preferences," *Official Records, U.N.,* 12th Sess., Special Comm. on Preferences, item 3, p. 1.

3. 1960's growth rates—*1982 Statistical Yearbook* (New York: United Nations, 1985), p. 8. See also Jagdish Bhagwati, "Introduction," in Jagdish Bhagwati, ed., *The New International Economic Order: The North–South Debate* (Cambridge, Mass.: MIT Press, 1977), p. 5.

4. Algiers on imperialism—Fourth Conference of Heads of State or Governments of Non-Aligned Countries, *Fundamental Texts* (hereafter, *Algiers Charter*) (Algiers: September 1973), p. 215.

5. Algiers on oil—"Economic Declaration of the Fourth Summit Conference of Non-Aligned Countries," in Moss and Winston, vol. 1, p. 418.

6. Algiers on cartels—General Assembly Resolution 3201, adopted May 1, 1974, p. 222.

7. Benites on NIEO conference: "a milestone"—*Official Records, U.N.*, 6th Special Sess., Plenary Meeting, April 9, 1974, pp. 2–3.

8. Boumédiènne foresees more cartels—*Official Records, U.N.*, 6th Special Sess., Plenary Meetings, April 10, 1974, p. 4.

9. Tunisia: "still shaking the old economic order"—*Official Records, U.N.*, 6th Sess., Plenary Meetings, April 11, 1974, p. 6.

10. Guinea's optimism on bauxite cartel—*Official Records, U.N.*, 6th Sess., Plenary Meetings, April 11, 1974, p. 6.

11. Oil crisis impact on third world—for Zambia, *Official Records, U.N.*, 6th Sess., Plenary Meetings, April 11, 1974, p. 22; for Ghana, *Official Records, U.N.*, 6th Sess., Plenary Meetings, April 12, 1974, p. 6; for

Sridath Ramphal, *Official Records, U.N.*, 6th Sess., Plenary Meetings, April 15, 1974, p. 8.

12. Yamani disavows OPEC's responsibility—*Official Records, U.N.*, 6th Sess., Plenary Meetings, April 16, 1974, p. 9.

13. Levy: "Lopsided shifts . . . in power"—Ajami, op. cit., p. 12.

14. "Raw material producers . . . come of age"—Jahangin Amuzegar, "The North–South Dialogue," *Foreign Affairs*, April 1976, p. 551.

15. Bergsten: "Significant change in the old order"—Panel discussion in Bhagwati, op. cit., p. 352.

16. Escalation of commodity conflict—C. Fred Bergsten, "The U.S. Must Now Deal with Other Cartels," *New York Times*, June 1, 1975, Section 4, Page 4.

17. "A new international economic order"—Karl P. Sauvant, "From Economic to Socio-Cultural Emancipation: The Historical Context of the New International Economic Order and the New International Socio-Cultural Order," *Third World Quarterly*, January 1981, p. 57.

18. Aid—*Official Records, U.N.*, 7th Special Sess., Resolution 3362, adopted September 16, 1975 (hereafter, *Resolution 3362*), Article II, Sections 1 and 2.

19. Trade—*Algiers Charter*, p. 219 and p. 230.

20. Commodities—*Official Records, U.N.*, 5th Special Session, Resolution 3202, adopted May 1, 1974, Article I, Section 3 (hereafter, *Resolution 3202*); *Resolution 3362*, Article I, Sections 3a, 3b, and 3c.

21. International Monetary Fund, World Bank—*Resolution 3202*, Article II, Section 1d; *Resolution 3362*, Article II, Section 16; *Algiers Charter*, pp. 219–20 and 231.

22. Compensatory finance—*Resolution 3202*, Article I, Section 3, Part ix; *Resolution 3362*, Article I, Section 3d.

23. Link—*Resolution 3202*, Article II, Section 1f; *Resolution 3362*, Article II, Section 3; *Algiers Charter*, pp. 231–32.

24. Debt—*Resolution 3202*, Article II, Sections 2f and 2g; *Resolution 3362*, Article II, Section 8; *Algiers Charter*, p. 232.

25. Technology—*Resolution 3202*, Article IV; *Resolution 3362*, Article III, Section 3; *Algiers Charter*, pp. 228 and 232–33.

26. Cartels—*Official Records, U.N.*, 29th Session, 2nd Committee, Resolution 33281, *The Charter of Economic Rights and Duties of States*, adopted December 12, 1974 (hereafter, *Resolution 3281*), Chapter II, Article 5; *Algiers Charter*, pp. 222 and 228.

27. Private foreign investment I—*Resolution 3202*, Article V; *Algiers Charter*, pp. 221–22 and 235–36.

28. Private foreign investment II—*Resolution 3202*, Article II, Section 2e.

29. Shipping—*Resolution 3202*, Article I, Section 4; *Algiers Charter*, p. 233.

30. Landlocked and least developed nations—*Resolution 3202,* Article II, Section 2i, and Article X; *Resolution 3362,* Article II, Section 12; *Algiers Charter,* p. 220.

31. Treaties—*Algiers Charter,* p. 222.

32. Drought—*Resolution 3202,* Article I, Section 2c.

33. Food—*Resolution 3202,* Article I, Section 2g; *Algiers Charter,* pp. 220–21.

34. Duties—*Resolution 3202,* Article I, Section 3, Part vi.

35. Synthetics—*Resolution 3202,* Article I, Section 3, Part xii.

36. Southern currency reserves—*Resolution 3202,* Article II, Section 1c.

37. Industry—*Resolution 3202,* Article III; *Resolution 3362,* Article IV, Section 2.

38. World Bank, International Development Association—*Resolution 3362,* Article II, Section 5.

39. Sunfed—*Resolution 3362,* Article II, Section 11.

40. Reserves—*Resolution 3362,* Article II, Section 15.

41. Brain drain—*Resolution 3362,* Article III, Section 10.

42. 1974 conference on sovereign equality and interdependence—*Resolution 3281,* Introduction.

43. "The international economic system will not be changed"—Karl P. Sauvant, "The Poor Countries and the Rich—A Few Steps Forward," *Dissent,* vol. 5, no. 1 (Winter 1978), p. 47.

44. Cost of the oil price rise to third world—Roger Hansen, *Beyond the North-South Stalemate,* (New York: McGraw-Hill, 1979), pp. 104–105. For OPEC's aid preference for Muslim countries, see Askari and Cummings, op. cit., p. 47.

45. Oil complaints of the third world—for India: *Official Records, U.N.,* 7th Special Sess., September 2, 1975, p. 15; for Zaire, *Official Records, U.N.,* 7th Special Sess. September 4, 1975, p. 13. for Costa Rica, *Official Records, U.N.,* 7th Special Sess., September 5, 1975, p. 2.

46. Kissinger: "serious blow to stability"—staff report on the Conference on International Economic Cooperation, held in Paris, December 16–19, 1975, House Committee on International Relations, February 9, 1976, p. 13.

47. Failure of International Bauxite Association—George C. Abbott, "United States: Who Pays the Piper?" in Helge Ole Bergesen, Hans Henrik Holm, and Robert D. McKinlay, *The Recalcitrant Rich* (New York: St. Martin's Press, 1982), p. 207–208.

48. List of requirements for a successful cartel—Carmine Nappi, *Commodity Market Controls: A Historical Review* (Lexington, Mass.: Lexington Books, 1979), p. 185.

49. OPEC built by oil companies—Fred Hirsch, "Is There a New International Economic Order?," *International Organization,* vol. 30, no. 3 (Summer 1976), p. 524.

50. Decline in oil prices—for a summary of the peak price years, see *New York Times,* January 21, 1985, p. D1; for Saudi output increase decision, see *Wall Street Journal,* September, 24, 1985, p. 2; for the collapse of OPEC's $28/barrel price level, see *New York Times,* December 9, 1985. p. 1.

51. Oil mergers—*Facts on File,* 1984, p. 166.

52. King Fahd: "Never the guardian of anyone"—*Wall Street Journal,* September 24, 1985, p. 2.

53. Bush mission to Saudi Arabia—*New York Times,* April 2, 1986, p. 1.

54. Mitterand announces oil relief plan—press conference, Cancun, Mexico, October, 1981.

55. McNamara plan for oil development—Pedro-Pablo, Kuczynski, "Action Steps After Cancun," *Foreign Affairs,* vol. 60, no. 5 (Summer 1982), pp. 1033–36.

56. World Bank estimates 15 percent of world's oil in non-OPEC LDC's—Maurice Strong, "The Energy Issue and Cancun," *Cancun: A Candid Evaluation* (New York: North South Roundtable and The Society for International Development, undated), p. 56.

57. Garvin argues against World Bank's oil program—letter to W. Michael Blumenthal, U.S. Secretary of the Treasury, January 15, 1979.

Chapter 4: Law at Sea

1. Truman proclaims U.S. sovereignty (1945)—quoted in Leslie M. McCrae, "Customary International Law and the United Nations' 'Law of the Sea Treaty,' " *California Western International Law Journal,* Spring 1983, p. 214.

2. Ickes' concern for petroleum reserves—Ann L. Hollick, *U.S. Foreign Policy and the Law of the Sea* (Princeton, N. J.: Princeton University Press, 1981), p. 44.

3. Mexico seizes American shrimpers—Hollick, *Law of the Sea,* p. 69.

4. Proclamations of 200-mile limits—Kaldone G. Nweihad, "Assessment of the Extension of State Jurisdiction in Terms of the Living Resources of the Sea," in John King Gamble, ed., *Law of the Sea: Neglected Issues* (Hawaii: Law of the Sea Institute, 1979), p. 26.

5. Wounding of an American sailor—Hollick, *Law of the Sea,* p. 89.

6. Seizure of twenty tuna boats—ibid., p. 87.

7. Iceland-British "Cod War"—Robert E. Osgood, "U.S. Security In-

terests in the Law of the Sea," in Roger C. Amacher and Richard James Sweeney, eds., *Law of the Sea: U.S. Interests and Alternatives* (Washington, D.C.: American Enterprise Institute, 1976), p. 12.

8. Attacks on foreign fishermen—William Wertenbaker, "The Law of the Sea," *The New Yorker,* August 1, 1983, p. 46.

9. Recognition of the twelve-mile limit—Elliot L. Richardson, "Power, Mobility, and the Law of the Sea," *Foreign Affairs,* Spring 1980, p. 904.

10. Choke points or straits—Commodore O. P. Sharma, "Navigation Through International Straits," in Ram Prakash Anand, ed., *Law of the Sea: Caracas and Beyond* (New Delhi: Radiant Publishers, 1978), pp. 114–15.

11. "Innocent passage" defined—Ram Prakash Anand, "Introduction," in Anand, *Caracas and Beyond,* p. 14.

12. "Manifest capacity"—Richardson, op. cit., p. 907.

13. Nixon: "fundamental security interest"—quoted in Sharma, op. cit., p. 114. For the original, see *Department of State Bulletin,* February 9, 1972, p. 409.

14. United States mission to Bangladesh (1972)—Osgood, op. cit., p. 25.

15. United States resupply to Israel (1973)—ibid., pp. 24–25.

16. United States-Soviet joint strategy (1967–69)—Ann L. Hollick, "United States Ocean Politics," *San Diego Law Review,* May 1973, p. 471. See also, Hollick, *Law of the Sea,* p. 175.

17. Pardo: "common heritage of man"—Jones, op. cit., p. 17.

18. Compromise over "maximum sustainable yield"—*United Nations Convention on the Law of the Sea,* Articles 61 and 62. (New York: United Nations, 1983)

19. Seven rich nations get lion's share—B. S. Chimni, "Law of the Sea: Winners and Losers," *Economic and Political Weekly* (Bombay, India), June 12, 1982, p. 990.

20. Fleet passage permitted in exclusive economic zones—Mohamed El-Baradei and Chloe Gavin, *Crowded Agendas, Crowded Rooms* (New York: Unitar, 1981), pp. 4–5.

21. Indonesia gains archipelagic rights over 2.2m square miles of territory—R. P. Barson, "The Law of the Sea," *Journal of World Trade Law,* vol. 17, no. 63 (June 1983), p. 200. For a comparison to similar United States gains, see Ann L. Hollick, "The Third United Nations Conference on Law of the Sea," in Amacher and Sweeney, op. cit., p. 128.

22. Fleet passage permitted within archipelagic rights—Thomas A. Clingan, Jr., "Freedom of Navigation in a Post-UNCLOS III Environment," *Law and Contemporary Problems,* vol. 46, no. 2 (1983), p. 119.

23. Sixty-nine nations hold twelve-mile or greater claims (1973)—S. Houston Lay, Robin Churchill, and Myron Nordquist, *New Directions in*

the Law of the Sea (Dobbs Ferry, N. Y.: Oceana Publications, 1973), pp. 835–54.

24. Libyan–United States conflict (August 1981)—*Facts on File,* 1982, p. 178. See also Wertenbaker, op. cit., p. 46.

25. Estimate of value of offshore oil—Anand, "Introduction," in Anand, *Caracas and Beyond,* op. cit., p. 11.

26. Oil companies favor national sovereignty—H. Gary Knight, "Special Domestic Interests and the United States Ocean Policy," in Robert G. Wirsing, ed., *International Relations and the Future of Ocean Space* (Columbia, S.C.: University of South Carolina Press, 1974), p. 28.

27. Few states have coastal margins—Ram Prakash Anand, "Limits of National Jurisdiction in the Sea-Bed," *India Quarterly,* April–June 1973, p. 93.

28. Oil is "most powerful private interest"—Hollick, "United States Ocean Politics," p. 471.

29. Exploration of the Northern Pacific—David B. Johnson and Dennis E. Logue, "U.S. Economic Interests in Law of the Sea Issues," in Amacher and Sweeney, op. cit., p. 40.

30. Mining potential of the sea—for 1.6 trillion tons figure, see George A. Doumani, *Ocean Wealth: Policy and Potential* (New Rochelle, N. Y.: Spartan Books, 1973), p. 11; for percentages of mineral content, see Johnson and Logue, op. cit. p. 39.

31. Domestic ore supplies to last twenty-five years—Jonathan I. Charney, "Law of the Sea: Breaking the Deadlock," *Foreign Affairs,* vol. 55, no. 3 (April 1977), p. 620. For the original study, see *Mineral Resources Perspectives,* U.S. Geological Survey Professional Paper No. 940, 1975, Table II, p. 6.

32. "The foundations of a new economic order"—Elizabeth Mann Borgese, "Law of the Sea: The Next Phase," *Third World Quarterly* (London), October 1982, p. 709.

33. Earlier United States Administrations favored Law of the Sea—for Nixon administration, see Hollick, "United States Ocean Politics," p. 481; for Carter administration, author's interview with Roy Lee, United Nations legal staff, July 15, 1985.

34. "Detailed regulation . . . is staggering"—Thomas A. Clingan, Jr., "Legal Problems Relating to the Extraction of Resources of the Deep Sea Bed Other Than Magnesium Nodules," in Gamble, op cit., p. 83.

35. Kissinger proposal on mining—Ram Prakash Anand, "Winds of Change in Law of the Sea," Anand, *Caracas and Beyond,* p. 57.

36. Law of the Sea and commodity prices—Andres Aguilar, "How will the Future Deep Seabed Regime Be Organized," in Gamble, op cit., p. 50.

37. United Nations Convention on the Law of the Sea, Article 151 (New York: 1983).

38. Producers constrain their own production—Richard G. Darman, "The Law of the Sea: Rethinking U.S. Interests," *Foreign Affairs,* January 1978, p. 393.

39. "Unregulated prices and production spell disaster"—V. K. S. Varman, "Management of Resources of the International Sea-bed," in Anand, *Caracas and Beyond,* p. 271.

40. Canada's support for production curbs—Barry G. Buzan and Danford W. Middlemiss, "Canadian Foreign Policy and the Exploitation of the Seabed," in Barbara Johnson and Mark W. Zacher, eds., *Canadian Foreign Policy and the Law of the Sea* (Vancouver: University of British Columbia Press, 1977), p. 31.

41. Discovery of polymetallic sulfides—on a Pacific island, see Chimni, op. cit., p. 990; for the Red Sea, see David A. Ross, "Resources of the Deep Sea Other than Manganese Nodules," in Gamble, op. cit., p. 65.

42. "Fair and reasonable prices" for mining technology—*United Nations Law of the Sea Treaty,* Article 144, 2a.

43. Availability of mining technology—for a Department of the Interior study, see John S. Bailey, "The Future of the Exploitation of the Deep Seabed and Subsoil," *Law and Contemporary Problems* (Duke University Law School), vol. 46, no. 2 (Spring 1983), p. 74. See also Marne A. Dubs, "Comment on Bailey," p. 92. For a GAO study, see testimony by Elliot L. Richardson. *Hearings before the House Merchant Marine Subcommittee,* 97th Cong., 2nd Sess. (July 20, 1982), p. 220.

44. Reagan's opposition to mining provisions—*Hearings before the House Committee on Foreign Relations,* 97th Cong., 2nd Sess. (April 30, 1982). See also Tullio Treves, "The Adoption of the Law of the Sea Convention: Prospects for Seabed Mining," *Maritime Policy* (London), January 1983, p. 4.

45. "Pioneer investors" provision—Treves, op. cit., p. 10.

46. Vote on the Law of the Sea—Kurt Michael Shusterich, *Resource Management and the Oceans: The Political Economy of Deep Seabed Mining* (Boulder, Colo.: Westview Press, 1982), p. 17.

47. United States concern for "liberation movements" in treaty—statement of President Reagan, July 9, 1982, quoted in *Hearings Before the House Merchant Marine Subcommittee* (July 20, 1982), p. 173.

48. United States objections to the treaty—James L. Malone, "The United States and the Law of the Sea after Unclos III," in *Law and Contemporary Problems,* vol. 46, no. 2 (Spring, 1983), p. 30.

49. Customary law argument (Reagan)—testimony of James L. Malone, *Hearings Before the House Foreign Relations Committee,* 97th Cong., 2nd Sess. (August 12, 1982), p. 102.

50. McCrae: "custom requires duration"—McCrae, op. cit., p. 202.

51. Elements of customary law—George A. B. Pierce, "Selective Adoption of the New Law of the Sea: The United States Proclaims Its Exclusive Economic Zone," *Virginia Journal of International Law,* Summer 1983, p. 589.

52. American Law Institute's codification of customary law—Thomas A. Clingan, Jr., "Freedom of Navigation," p. 107.

53. Irish patrol sinks Spanish trawler—*New York Times,* October 21, 1984, p. 17.

54. Darman urges force (1978)—Darman, op. cit., p. 377.

55. Western nations sign separate pacts—*Oceans Policy News,* August 1984, pp. 2–4.

56. Cost of mine site investment—testimony of Elliot L. Richardson, *Hearings Before the House Committee on Foreign Relations,* 97th Cong., 2nd Sess. (August 12,1984), pp. 90–91. See also an interview with Marne A. Dubs, *E & M Journal,* September 1981, p. 133.

57. GAO: no development with Law of the Sea—Jesper Grolin, "The Future of the Law of the Sea: Consequences of a Non-Treaty or a Non-Universal Situation," *Ocean Development and International Law,* vol. 13, No. 1 (1983), p. 22.

58. Kennecott official: development with a United States guarantee—see testimony of Marne A. Dubs, *Hearings Before the Subcommittee on Oceanography and the House Committee on Merchant Marine and Fisheries,* 97th Cong., 1st Sess. (October 22, 1981), p. 13.

59. Landlocked nations betrayed by fellow developing nations—Ibrahim J. Wani, "An Evaluation of the Conference on Law of the Sea from the Perspective of the Landlocked States," *Virginia Journal of International Law,* Summer 1982, p. 629.

60. "Devoid of meaning"—ibid., pp. 642–43.

61. "Completely forsakes the common interests"—ibid. p. 657.

62. "Humiliating dependence"—ibid., p. 658.

63. Law of the Sea and pollution—Allan E. Boyle, "Marine Pollution Under the Law of the Sea Convention," *The American Journal of International Law,* vol. 79, no. 2 (April 1985), pp. 353–54. See also Robert McManus, "Environmental Provisions in the Revised Single Negotiating Text," in Edward Miles and John King Gamble, eds., *Law of the Sea: Conference Outcomes and Patterns of Implementation* (Proceedings) (Cambridge, Mass.: Ballinger Publications, 1977), p. 276.

64. Lack of environmental concern—James L. Johnston, "Geneva Update," in Amacher and Sweeney, op. cit., p. 187.

65. No pollution controls for the third world—Allan Kinton, "Developing Country View of Environmental Issues," in Miles and Gamble, op. cit., p. 281.

66. Two-hundred-mile zone most important scientifically—testimony of David Ross, *Hearings Before the House Merchant Marine Subcommittee* (July 20, 1982), p. 242.

67. Military share of marine research (50 percent)—Hollick, *Law of the Sea,* p. 183.

68. Oceanographic community unhappy—testimony of John Knauss, *House Subcommittee on Domestic Internal Science Planning, Analysis, and Cooperation,* 95th Cong., 1st Sess., p. 5.

69. Treaty offers uniform treatment—testimony of David Ross, *Hearings Before the House Merchant Marine Subcommittee* (July 20, 1982), p. 243.

70. Koh: "Treaty is likely to widen the gap"—quoted in Lewis W. Alexander, "The 'Disadvantaged' States and the Law of the Sea," *Marine Policy* (Sussex, England), July 1981, p. 242.

71. "High level of friction in the oceans"—Hollick, *Law of the Sea,* p. 389.

72. "Principles of equity not visible"—Arvid Pardo, "Comment," in Miles and Gamble, op. cit. p. 411.

73. Increase in inequalities—ibid., pp. 411–12.

74. "Maintain some semblance of a global law of the sea"—Arvid Pardo, "Before and After," in *Law and Contemporary Problems,* vol. 46, no. 2 (Spring 1983), p. 101.

75. "Costs of isolation"—Leigh S. Ratiner, "The Law of the Sea: A Crossroad for American Policy," *Foreign Affairs,* Summer 1982, p. 1021.

Chapter 5: Aid for Whom?

1. Agriculture as a percent of output—World Bank, *Accelerated Development in Sub-Saharan Africa* (Washington, D.C.: 1983), p. 45.

2. Aid quintuples (1973–81)—OECD, *Development Cooperation, 1983 Review* (Paris: Development Assistance Committee, 1983), p. 136.

3. African Farm Aid—World Bank, *Accelerated Development,* p. 47.

4. Stagnant food production—ibid., p. 143.

5. Population outpaces food production—ibid. p. 43.

6. Nyerere on danger of cooperatives—*Washington Post* (National Weekly Edition), December 3, 1984, p. 16.

7. Zambian mismanagement (1965–80)—OECD, *Development Cooperation, 1983,* p. 20.

8. "Indigenous colonialism"—ibid., p. 26.

9. U.S. surplus grain (6.1m tons in 1983, 5.6m in 1982)—U.S. International Development Cooperation Agency, *Congressional Presentation, Fiscal Year 1985,* p. 14.

10. Change in eating habits—World Bank, *Accelerated Development,* p. 48.

11. "External assistance can weaken the resolve"—World Bank, *Towards Sustained Development in Sub-Saharan Africa* (Washington, D.C.: 1984), p. 45.

12. "Strategic considerations . . . outweigh"—World Bank, *Towards Sustained Development*, p. 4.

13. "Inflexibility of foreign donors"—*Toward Sustained Development*, p. 38.

14. India's farm growth—United Nations, *Statistical Yearbook 1982*, (New York: 1985), p. 504.

15. "Starving military officer"—Independent Commission on International Humanitarian Issues, *Famine: A Man-Made Disaster?* (London: Pan Books, 1985), p. 63.

16. World Bank: "tax poor farmers"—Paul Streeten, et al., *First Things First: Meeting Basic Human Needs in Developing Countries* (New York: Oxford University Press, 1981), p. 128.

17. Donors and recipients of aid in 1983—OECD *Development Cooperation*, 1984; for Western total amount, see p. 64; for number of recipients, see pp. 74–75; for United States' amount, see p. 82.

18. Truman: bold new program—Judith Hart, *Aid and Liberation* (London: Victor Gollancz, 1973), p. 22. See also *New York Times*, January 21, 1949, p. 4.

19. Marshall program—Hadley Arkes, *Bureaucracy, the Marshall Plan, and the National Interest* (Princeton, N.J.: Princeton University Press, 1972), p. 363.

20. Congress: "strengthen the forces of freedom"—cited in Robert E. Asher, *How to Succeed in Foreign Aid Without Really Trying* (Washington, D.C.: Brookings Institute, 1964), p. 127.

21. "No greater danger to peace"—Lester B. Pearson, *The Crisis of Development* (New York: Praeger Publishers, 1970), p. 29.

22. "Catastrophic and immediate consequences"—Pearson, op. cit., p. 31.

23. "Large scale transfer of resources"—Willy Brandt, et al., op. cit. p. 36.

24. "Private sector initiative"—M. Peter McPherson, *Development Issues: U.S. Actions Affecting Developing Countries, 1983 Annual Report* (Washington, D.C.: Development Assistance Committee, 1983), p. 75.

25. Aid administrators: poverty is security concern—U.S. International Development Cooperation Agency, op. cit., p. 12.

26. Economic Support Fund: "promotes economic and political stability"—ibid., p. 43.

27. Diefenbaker: aid is "cheap insurance"—Robert Carty and Virginia Smith, *Perpetuating Poverty: The Political Economy of Canadian Foreign Aid* (Toronto: Between the Lines, 1981), p. 45.

28. Rusk: aid is an "unavoidable responsibility"—*Hearings Before the Senate Foreign Relations Committee on the Foreign Assistance Act of 1962,* 87th Cong., 2nd Sess. (April 5, 1962), p. 5.

29. Harriman: aid counters subversion and poverty—*Hearings Before the Senate Foreign Relations Committee on the Foreign Assistance Act of 1962,* 87th Cong., 2nd Sess. (April 13, 1962), p. 346.

30. McNamara: "foreign aid program is the best weapon"—quoted in Denis Goulet and Michael Hudson, *The Myth of Aid* (Maryknoll, N.Y.: Orbis Books, 1973), p. 98.

31. Fulbright: aid undermines peace—*Hearings Before the Senate Foreign Relations Committee on the Foreign Assistance Act of 1973,* 93rd Cong., 1st Sess. (February 22, 1973), pp. 55–56.

32. Nooter: "sweeping land reform"—ibid., p. 6.

33. Congress: "basic human needs"—Congressional Budget Office, *Assisting the Developing Countries* (Washington, D.C.: Government Printing Office, 1980), p. xiv.

34. United States aid breakdown by Development Assistance and Economic Support—U.S. International Development Cooperation Agency, op. cit., p. 75.

35. U.S. aid breakdown by country—Agency for International Development, *Congressional Presentation, Fiscal Year 1985,* pp. 648–50.

36. U.S. direct military aid—ibid., pp. 649–50.

37. British aid 62 percent to ex-colonies—Stephen H. Arnold, *Implementing Development Assistance: European Approaches to Basic Needs* (Boulder, Colo.: Westview Press, 1982), p. 159.

38. Soviet aid program—Karel Holbik, *The United States, the Soviet Union, and the Third World* (Hamburg: Verlag Weltarchiv, 1968), p. 78. For $3 billion per year figure, see OECD, *Development Cooperation 1984* (Paris: Development Assistance Committee, 1984), p. 64.

39. Fall in OPEC aid—OECD *Development Cooperation 1984,* loc. cit.

40. Baran: governments represent status quo—quoted in Peter Donaldson, *Worlds Apart* (London: British Broadcasting Corporation, 1971), p. 149.

41. "Aid increases the power"—Peter T. Bauer, *Equality, the Third World, and Economic Delusion* (London: Weidenfeld and Nicolson, 1981), p. 103.

42. "An insult to human dignity"—Robert S. McNamara, "Preface" to World Bank, *The Assault on World Poverty Problems of Rural Development, Education, and Health* (Baltimore: Johns Hopkins University Press, 1975), p. v.

43. ILO poverty study—cited in Keith Griffin, *International Inequality and National Poverty* (London: Macmillan, 1978), p. 123. Original study made by Keith Griffin and Azizur Rahman Kahn.

44. "Rich take benefits"—C. P. Bhambhri, "The Politics of Foreign Aid: A Case Study of India," *Foreign Affairs Reports,* December 1979, p. 215.

45. India's poor are doing better—Jagdish N. Bhagwati, "Is India's Economic Miracle at Hand?," *New York Times,* June 9, 1985, p. F3. For a definition of "pull-up," see Bhagwati, "Growth and Poverty," lecture at the Center for Advanced Study of International Development, Michigan State University, April 4, 1985. pp. 8–12.

46. World Bank: hunger in third world—Streeten, et al., op. cit., p. 155.

47. Ownership or security necessary—Wolf Ladejinsky, "Agrarian Reform in Asia," in Harvey G. Kebschul, ed., *Politics in Transitional Societies* (New York: Appleton Century Crofts, 1968), p. 339.

48. Reform affects power base—McNamara, op. cit., p. vi.

49. Tube wells in Bangladesh—Francis Moore Lappe, Joseph Collins, and David Kinley, *Aid as an Obstacle* (San Francisco: Institute for Food and Development, 1980), p. 57.

50. Change in United States program—AID, *Congressional Presentation 1985.* For Indonesia, p. 400, for Liberia, p. 330, for Senegal, p. 343.

51. World Bank: obstacles are political—Streeten et al., op. cit., p. 122 and p. 57.

52. Promises of success (Philippines, India, Indonesia)—ibid., p. 169ff.

53. Elites ignore extreme poverty—Charles R. Frank and Richard C. Webb, *Income Distribution and Growth in the Less Developed Countries* (Washington, D.C.: Brookings Institute, 1977), p. 13.

54. U.S. Aid helped LDC's—Robert E. Asher, *Development Assistance in the Seventies* (Washington, D.C.: Brookings Institute, 1970), p. 13.

55. Large projects in Brazil—Judith Tendler, *Inside Foreign Aid* (Baltimore: Johns Hopkins University Press, 1975), pp. 58–68.

56. Large projects in Indonesia—Lappe, Collins, and Kinley, op. cit., p. 61.

57. Large projects in Tanzania—*Washington Post* (National Weekly Edition), December 3, 1984, p. 17.

58. Pearson: aid and growth uncorrelated—quoted in John White, *The Politics of Foreign Aid* (London: The Bodley Head, 1974), p. 125.

59. Aid twice as important as savings or investment—Gustav F. Papanek, "Aid, Foreign Private Investment, Savings, and Growth in Less Developed Countries," *Journal of Political Economy,* January-February 1973, p. 122.

60. Papanek is wrong—Paul Mosely, "Aid, Savings, and Growth Revisited," *Oxford Bulletin of Economics and Statistics,* vol. 42, no. 2 (May 1980), p. 82.

61. U.N. study of conditions for growth—see the Lie Commission

report, *Measures for the Economic Development of Under Developed Countries* (New York: United Nations, 1951).

62. Literacy gains—in Cuba, see Streeten et al., op. cit., p. 116; in South Korea, Frederick M. Bunge, ed., *South Korea: A Country Study* (U.S. Department of the Army, 1982), pp. 92–93; in Somalia, Harold N. Nelson, ed., *Somalia: A Country Study* (U.S. Department of the Army, 1982), p. xiv.

63. Growth depends on cultural characteristics—Bauer, op. cit., p. 100.

64. Failure of Nyerere's Ujamaa in Tanzania—Michaela von Freyhold, *Ujamaa Villages in Tanzania* (London: Heinemann, 1979).

65. Alliance for Progress, $20 billion in ten years—Jerome Levinson and Juan de Onis, *The Alliance That Lost its Way* (Chicago: Quadrangle Books, 1970), p. 11.

66. Alliance rejects Chile's education plan—ibid., p. 207.

67. Alliance derails Brazilian land reform—ibid., p. 194.

68. Unequal land holdings in Brazil—*The Economist,* June 8, 1985, p. 40.

69. No land or educational reform—Levinson and de Onis, op. cit., p. 205.

70. World Bank helps United States foreign policy—U.S. Department of the Treasury, *United States Participation in the Multilateral Development Banks* (Washington, D.C.: Government Printing Office, 1982), p. 61.

71. "Rhetoric . . . has outdistanced results"—McNamara, op. cit., p. 93.

72. "Bank cannot force structural change"—ibid., p. 199.

73. "Played a minor role"—ibid., p. 288.

74. "Dominated by special interests"—ibid., p. 29.

75. Multilateral institutions must keep in line—I. G. Patel, "Aid Relationships for the Seventies," in Barbara Ward, J. D. Runnalls, and Leonore D'Anjou, eds., *The Widening Gap* (New York: Columbia University, 1971), p. 305.

76. Aid helps only the productive—White, op. cit., p. 58.

77. Only six African states adopt structural adjustment—World Bank, *Sub-Saharan Africa: Progress Report on Development Prospects and Programs* (Washington, D.C.: 1983), p. 21.

78. "Powerful political interests"—ibid., p. 21.

79. Food price rises in sixteen nations—OECD, 1984, p. 28.

80. Food prices rise in Egypt and the Sudan—OECD, *Development Cooperation, 1984,* p. 29.

81. Food prices rise in Zimbabwe—*The Economist,* January 12, 1985, p. 62.

82. Reform is tentative—World Bank, *Towards Sustained Development,* p. 37 and p. 2.

83. Development Assistance Committee: farm reform plans "are yet to be completed and implemented"—OECD, *Development Cooperation, 1984*, p. 34.

84. $1.1 billion African fund—*New York Times,* February 12, 1975.

85. Stern: cannot buy policy changes—interview with author, March 27, 1985

86. Bank turns to IMF-like loans—*The Economist,* May 5, 1986, p. 91.

87. Growth in Pakistani aid—White, op. cit., p. 71.

88. Malnourishment and food policy in Zaire—Guy Gran, *Development by People* (New York: Praeger, 1983), p. 37 and p. 62.

89. Zaire a "kleptocracy"—ibid., p. 131.

90. Aid or anarchy—address by Julius Nyerere, "Aid and Development: The Recipient's Point of View," New Zealand Institute of International Affairs, Wellington-Christchurch, New Zealand; March 18, 1974, p. 7.

91. Poverty doesn't breed revolution—Gunnar Myrdal, *The Challenge of World Poverty* (New York: Pantheon Books, 1970), p. 390–91.

92. United States AID mission to India twice the size of embassy—from John P. Lewis, former director of AID mission to India. 133 employees worked for AID and about sixty worked in the embassy.

93. "Administrative-academic complex"—Tibor Mende, *From Aid to Recolonialization* (New York: Pantheon Books, 1973), p. 130.

94. Botswana aid tied to locomotive purchase—*New York Times,* January 24, 1985, p. 1.

95. Aid diminishes hardship—Brandt, et al., op. cit., p. 226.

96. "Only permanent interests"—quoted in George Seldes, *Lord Palmerston in Great Quotations* (New York: Lyle Stuart, 1960), p. 545.

97. U.N. Development Fund, $800 million/year—author's interview with Zahir Jamal, director of information, U.N. Development Fund, January 10, 1986.

98. Oil loans data—letter to author from the Public Affairs Department at the World Bank, April 5, 1985

99. "Largest shareholder makes a lot of noise"—author's conversation with Robert Saunders, World Bank, March 28, 1985.

Chapter 6: The Uncertain Flow of Trade

1. LDC exports mostly commodities—UNCTAD, *Commodity Issues: A Review and Proposals for Further Action,* January 1983, p. 5.

2. Commodities percentages for specific countries—John Ravenhill, "What is to be done for Third World Commodity Exports," *International Organization,* Summer 1984, p. 537.

3. "Administered prices are anathema, unless . . ."—Robert L. Rothstein, *Global Bargaining: UNCTAD and the Quest for a New International Economic Order* (Princeton, N. J.: Princeton University Press, 1977), p. 78.

4. United States backs coffee pact to oppose Castro—Christopher P. Brown, *The Political and Social Economy of Commodity Control* (New York: Praeger Publishers, 1980), p. 28–29.

5. "Years of negotiation and mountains of paper"—L. N. Rangarajan, "Commodity Conflict Revisited: From Nairobi to Belgrade," *Third World Quarterly,* July 1983, p. 590.

6. Rangarajan: "commodity scene is bleak"—ibid., p. 608.

7. Commodity gyrations—IMF, *International Financial Statistics,* May 1985, pp. 74–77 and January 1984, pp. 70–73.

8. Kenya's tea strategy—author's interview with Lahdasa Hulegalle, UNCTAD, October 31, 1984. See also Brown, op. cit., p. 197.

9. Indira Gandhi's tea election strategy—*The Economist,* September 15, 1984, p. 77.

10. Chile's copper strategy—*The Economist,* December 12, 1984, p. 71–72.

11. Failure of iron ore pact—Carmine Nappi, *Commodity Market Controls* (Lexington, Mass.: Lexington Books, 1979), p. 148.

12. Operation of the tin agreement—for a view of the functioning tin market, see Bernard Engel, "The International Tin Agreement," in Geoffrey Goodwin and James Mayall, ed., *A New International Commodity Regime* (New York: St. Martin's Press, 1980), pp. 86–89.

13. Collapse of tin agreement—*The Economist,* November 2, 1985, pp. 17 and 85, and November 23, 1985, p. 88. See also *Wall Street Journal,* April 7, 1986, p. 23.

14. Collapse of cocoa agreement—Alan Spence, "The Receding Mirage of Commodity Price Stabilization Schemes," *The Banker,* October, 1980, p. 25. See also Ursula Wasserman, "Breakdown of the International Cocoa Agreement," *Journal of World Trade Law,* July–August 1980, pp. 360–61.

15. Collapse of coffee agreement—testimony of C. Fred Bergsten, *Hearings Before the House Committee on Banking, Finance, and Urban Affairs,* 95th Cong., 1st Sess. (June 8, 1977), p. 24.

16. Ivory Coast and "tourist coffee"—L. N. Rangarajan, *Commodity Conflict: The Political Economy of International Commodity Negotiations* (London: Croom Helm, 1978), pp. 247–48.

17. Morocco boycotts phosphate talks—Brown, op. cit., p. 60.

18. "To regulate price, you must regulate volume"—author's interview with Gamani Corea, October 16, 1984.

19. "No agreement has been able to exert . . . influence"—Brown, op. cit., p. 6.

20. UNCTAD Common Fund proposal—David L. McNichol, *Commodity Agreements and Price Stabilization* (Lexington, Mass.: Lexington Books, 1978), p. 87. See also Helen O'Neill, *A Common Interest in a Common Fund* (New York: United Nations, 1977), pp. 28–30

21. West cuts Common Fund—*The Economist,* February 8, 1986, p. 62.

22. Thirty-seven third world nations fail to ratify Common Fund proposal—UNCTAD, *Review of Progress in the Implementation of the Integrated Program for Commodities,* January 5, 1983, p. 10. For Norway's offer, author's interview with Agziz Megzari, Common Fund, October 31, 1984.

23. Common Fund leads to tin pact collapse—author's interview with Agziz Megzari. For a similar reaction among cocoa pact members, see Wasserman, op. cit., p. 361.

24. Commodity stability increases U.S. growth—Jere R. Behrman, "International Commodity Agreements: An Evaluation of the UNCTAD," in William R. Cline, ed., *Policy Alternatives for a New International Economic Order* (New York: Praeger Publishers, 1979), p. 101.

25. IMF Compensatory Financing Facility loans—*IMF Survey,* vol. 13 (September 1984), p. 1.

26. Compensatory Financing Facility quotas—*International Monetary Fund Directory* (Washington, D.C.: IMF, March, 1985).

27. IMF study of borrowers' shortfalls—author's correspondence with Nihad N. Kaibni, IMF, March 28, 1985.

28. Full compensation delays reforms—Louis M. Geroux, *Compensatory Facility Financing,* IMF Pamphlet Series No. 34 (Washington, D.C.: 1980), p. 41.

29. United States resists doubling IMF resources—*Facts on File,* 1982, pp. 677 and 925. See also *The New York Times,* September 9, 1982, Section 4, p. 25.

30. Eighty percent shortfall coverage would cost 1.6 billion SDRs—calculated from data sent by the IMF. In 1984, 815 million SDRs lent represented 40.5 percent coverage of the revenue shortfall.

31. Seven percent interest on IMF loans—author's interview with Nihad M. Kaibni, IMF, March 26, 1985.

32. Group of Seven: protectionism fosters unemployment—Sidney Golf, "The New Protectionism," in Irving Levinson and Jimmy W. Wheeler, eds., *Western Economies in Transition* (Boulder, Colo.: Westview Press, 1980), p. 343. See also *New York Times,* May 9, 1977, p. 12.

33. Group of Seven: "Open multilateral trading is essential"—*New York Times,* May 5, 1985, p. 16.

34. Average tariff rates—Paul Dymock and Donna Vogt, "Protectionist Pressures in the U.S. Congress," *Journal of World Trade Law,* November–December 1983, p. 510.

35. Rise in nontariff barriers—Sheila A. B. Page, "The Revival of Protectionism and its Consequences," *Journal of Common Market Studies,* September 1981, p. 30.

36. Rise of nontariff barriers—Jan Tumlir, "Economic Policy for a Stable World Order," *Cato Journal,* vol. 4, no. 1 (Spring/Summer 1984), p. 357.

37. Extent of nontariff barriers—World Bank, *World Development Report 1984* (New York: Oxford University Press, 1984), p. 18.

38. Trade limits for 96.6 percent of goods—UNCTAD Secretariat, *Protectionism, Trade Relations, and Structural Adjustment* (Belgrade, Yugoslavia: June 1983), p. 11.

39. Malmgren: barriers on "a heck of a lot of trade"—*New York Times,* August 5, 1984, Section 3, p. 1.

40. Smoot-Hawley affected 3,000 products—E. E. Schattsneider, *Politics, Pressure, and the Tariff* (New York: Prentice Hall, 1935), p. 25; 3,221 items were affected by Smoot-Hawley, and an item could cover a dozen individual products.

41. 1962 Cotton Agreement: "promote development of LDC's"—Preamble to Long-Term Cotton Agreement, *Hearings Before the House Agriculture Committee,* 87th Cong., 2d Sess. (March 22, 1962), p. 9. See also Vincent Cable "Protection of Manufactures," in *Protectionism: Threat to International Order,* Commonwealth Economic Papers, No. 17 (London: Commonwealth Secretariat, 1982), p. 196.

42. European limits on Japanese steel—Bahram Nowzad, *The Rise in Protectionism* (Washington, D.C.: IMF, 1978), p. 13–14.

43. Multifiber Agreement hits 123 products—*Financial Times,* October 29, 1984.

44. Sri Lanka's limits on textile exports—Vincent Cable, *An Evaluation of the Multifibre Arrangement and Negotiating Options* (London: Commonwealth Secretariat, 1981), p. 34.

45. United States uses Orderly Marketing against Korea and Taiwan —Cable, op. cit., p. 201.

46. Importance of textiles—Bhagirath L. Das, "The GATT Multi-Fibre Arrangement," *Journal of World Trade Law,* January–February 1983, p. 95.

47. United States, EEC promise textile import growth—Page, op. cit., p. 26.

48. Resale market for United States export permits—Brian Hindley, "Voluntary Export Restraints and Gatt's Main Escape Clause," *The World Economy* (Amsterdam, Netherlands), November 1980, p. 318.

49. United States, Japan sign steel agreement—Nowzad, op. cit., p. 11. Carter administration invents "trigger price" mechanism—Trent Jones,

"The Political Economy of Voluntary Export Agreements," *Kyklos*, vol. 37 (1984), p. 98.

50. EEC steel protectionism—Nowzad, op. cit., pp. 13–14.

51. United States accuses Brazil of dumping steel—*Financial Times*, November 5, 1984, p. 9.

52. U.S. Steel breaks even at 60 percent capacity—author's conversation with Virginia Saam, Stockholder Relations, U.S. Steel, January 10, 1985. See also U.S. Steel Corp., *Operating and Capital Expenditures Data*, November 8, 1985.

53. United States cuts steel imports—*Financial Times*, November 5, 1984, p. 9. See also *Wall Street Journal*, December 20, 1984, p. 27.

54. Bethlehem Steel raises prices 5 percent—*Financial Times*, November 5, 1984, p. 12.

55. 1980–82 slump cuts LDC steel investment—ibid., p. 9.

56. Olmer: "consensus on not financing"—*New York Times*, December 26, 1983, p. D1.

57. United States limits auto imports—*The Economist*, January 5, 1985, p. 55.

58. GM urges lifting auto import barriers—*Wall Street Journal*, March 4, 1985, p. 1. See also *New York Times*, December 3, 1984, Section 4, p. 2.

59. Four hundred penalty tariffs in 1982—UNCTAD Secretariat, "Protectionism and Structural Adjustment," February 13, 1984, p. 37.

60. LDC manufacture exports outpace raw materials—GATT, *Prospects for Increasing Trade Between Developed and Developing Countries* (Geneva, Switzerland: 1984), p. 24.

61. LDC exports now mostly manufactures—World Bank, *World Development Report 1984*, p. 28.

62. OECD: "clearly made a contribution"—OECD, *The Generalized System of Preferences: Review of the First Decade* (Paris: 1983), p. 55

63. OECD: preferences opened trade—OECD, *The Generalized System*, p. 47.

64. United States strips preferences—for Mexico, Dale Story, "Trade Politics in the Third World: A Case Study of the Mexican GATT Decision," *International Organization*, Autumn 1982, p. 793; for India, see *Wall Street Journal*, April 2, 1986, p. 25; for other nations, see *The Economist*, April 7, 1984, p. 26.

65. World Bank: costs of U.S. tariffs—UNCTAD Secretariat, *Protectionism*, p. 40ff.

66. Australia's losses from protectionism—ibid.

67. FAO study of costs of protectionism on food—cited in D. E. Morris, "Measures of Agricultural Protectionism in Major Markets," in *Protectionism: Threat*, p. 63.

68. Asia's cost advantage over United States in steel—*The Economist*, March 10, 1984, p. 80.

69. Cost of United States-Japan auto restraints—cited in *New York Times*, September 9, 1984, Section D, p. 1. Original study by Lawrence Krause.

70. Cost of British textile curbs—Cable, op. cit., p. 27.

71. "Shift towards forms of 'escape' "—World Bank, *World Development Report 1984*, p. 19.

72. "General disrespect for the rules"—UNCTAD Secretariat, *Protectionism*, p. 35.

73. "Crisis in the system"—author's interview with Colin Greenhill, October 29, 1984.

74. "GATT is becoming extinct"—author's interview with Jan Tumlir, October 28, 1984.

75. GATT: "unstable, expensive, and ultimately uncontrollable"—Richard Blackurt, Nicolas Marian, and Jan Tumlir, *Trade Liberalization, Protectionism and Independence* (Geneva: GATT, 1977), p. 52.

76. Doubts protectionism will decline—GATT, *Prospects for Increasing Trade*, p. 16.

77. "Cannot be described as a world of economic efficiency"—UNCTAD Secretariat, *Protectionism*, p. 41.

78. Chatham House: "moving in a protectionist direction"—Louis Turner, Colin I. Bradford, Jr., Lawrence G. Franko, Neil McMullen, and Stephen Woodcock, *Living with the Newly Industrializing Countries*, Chatham House Papers No. 7 (London: Royal Institute of International Affairs, 1980), p. 44.

79. OECD: "more fundamental forces at work"—OECD, *Positive Adjustment Policies: Managing Structural Change* (Paris: 1983), p. 110.

80. Trade Adjustment Act liberalization—Harold A. Bratt, "Issues in Worker Certification and Questions of Future Direction in the Trade Adjustment Assistance Program," *Law and Policy in International Business* (Georgetown University Law Center), vol. 14, no. 3, pp. 820–825.

81. Capital flows dominate trade flows—Geoffrey Bell, "The Dollar and Financing the U.S. Payments Deficit," unpublished paper, April 18, 1985.

82. Two thirds of LDC exports go to North—GATT, *Prospects for Increasing Trade*, p. 16.

83. Intra-LDC trade preferences have no effect—Alexander J. Years, *Trade and Development Policies* (New York: St. Martin's Press, 1981), p. 33. See also Oli Havrylshyn and Martin Wolf, "Recent Trends in Trade Among Developing Countries," *European Economic Review* (Amsterdam, Netherlands) May 1983, p. 357.

Chapter 7: Easing the Debt Crisis

1. "International community's confidence . . . has been hard won"—World Bank, *Coping with External Debt in the 1980's* (Washington, D.C.: March 1985), p. xxvi.

2. "Serious but manageable problem"—World Bank, *Coping with External*, p. vii.

3. "Dramatic turnaround"—Otmar Emminger, "The International Debt Problem and the Banks," remarks at a Bankers' Meeting in Luxembourg, October 31, 1984, p. 2.

4. "We have made considerable progress"—William R. Rhodes, speech at Pace University, New York City, March 13, 1985, p. 23.

5. "Dire prophesy . . . had given way to excessive optimism"—ibid., p. 1.

6. Mexico and Brazil hold surpluses—ibid., pp. 6 and 10. See also C. Fred Bergsten, William R. Cline, and John Williamson, *Bank Lending to Developing Countries* (Cambridge, Mass.: MIT Press, 1985), pp. 6–7.

7. LDC government debt rises—World Bank, *Coping with External*, p. ix. The figures used are the sum of two columns in the table.

8. LDC trade deficit falls—World Bank, *Coping with External*, pp. xxv–xxvi.

9. Banks continue to collect interest—World Bank, *Coping with External*, p. xi.

10. Fall in interest rates—Rhodes, op. cit., *University*, p. 17.

11. Growth in seven Western nations—Morgan Guaranty Trust Co., *World Financial Markets*, December 1985, p. 2.

12. British banker: "try to get our exposure . . . down"—author's interview with Jeremy Morse, chairman, Lloyd's Bank, November 12, 1984.

13. Herzog: "cannot take precedence over the needs of the people"—*The Economist*, November 30, 1985, p. 77.

14. Fall in private lending—World Bank, *Coping with External*, p. xv.

15. "Vague hopes" of lending promises—Harold Lever, "Drowning in Debt," *Time and Tide*, undated, p. 12.

16. Funaro: "another recession is out of the question"—*Wall Street Journal*, December 5, 1985, p. 8.

17. Peru announces repayment limits—*New York Times*, July 28, 1985, p. 1. See also *The Economist*, August 10, 1985, p. 64.

18. Mexican suspension—*Wall Street Journal*, June 10, 1986, p. 2.

19. Banks' exposure to loans—*New York Times*, June 11, 1986, p. D5.

20. Rohatyn's refinancing proposal—Felix G. Rohatyn, "A Plan for Stretching out Global Debt," *Business Week*, February 28, 1983, p. 15.

21. Kenen's refinancing proposal—Peter A. Kenen, "A Bailout Plan for the Banks," *New York Times,* March 6, 1983, p. F3.

22. "Banks see no need . . . of writing down"—World Bank, *Coping with External,* p. xx.

23. Loan portfolio discounted—*The Economist,* November 16, 1985, p. 96. For an update, see *The Economist,* April 12, 1986, p. 82.

24. Insured credit proposal—Harold Lever, "The International Debt Threat—A Concerted Way Out," *The Economist,* July 9, 1983, pp. 14–16.

25. Insurance fund proposal—Henry C. Wallich, *Insurance of Bank Lending to Developing Countries,* Group of Thirty Occasional Paper No. 15 (New York: Group of Thirty, 1984).

26. Baker's refinancing plan—Christine A. Bogdanowicz-Bindert, "World Debt: The United States Reconsiders," *Foreign Affairs,* Winter 1985/86, p. 268. See also *New York Times,* October 9, 1985, p. D1.

27. "Case by case approach . . . vindicated"—World Bank, *Coping with External,* p. xv.

28. Ohio regulator boasts of soundness before collapse—*Wall Street Journal,* March 29, 1985, p. 6.

29. Fed raises capital requirements—*Financial Times,* November 16, 1984, pp. 1 and 27.

30. Volcker backs capital requirement—*Wall Street Journal,* September 12, 1985, p. 3.

31. Congress passes special reserve requirement—*The Economist,* September 8, 1984, p. 86. See also Bergsten, Cline, and Williamson, op. cit., p. 29.

32. Current loan loss reserve at 1.2 percent—Wallich, op. cit., p. 4.

33. IMF official: too tough on Yugoslavia—author's interview with Jacques Polak, March 26, 1985.

34. "Support the good guys . . ."—author's interview with Henry C. Wallich, March 25, 1985.

35. IMF record "catastrophic"—author's conversation with Rudiger Dornbusch, July 15, 1986.

36. Neves: interest rates "cruel"—*New York Times,* February 2, 1985, p. 54.

37. Interest charges of major debtors—letter to author from World Bank Press and Information Office, March 21, 1986.

38. Interest as a portion of debtors' export earnings—Bergsten, Cline, and Williamson, op. cit., p. 163.

39. Potential loss of bank profits from interest limits—George Salem, bank analyst at Donaldson, Lufkin, Jenrette, quoted in *The Wall Street Journal,* August 2, 1985, p. 17.

40. Mexico's tied repayments—*Wall Street Journal,* Sept. 5, 1986, p. 23.

41. Mexico's IMF loan—*The Economist,* July 26, 1986, p. 73; *New York Times,* October 2, 1986, p. D1.

42. Rothberg: "principal is not going to be repaid"—*International Herald Tribune,* November 14, 1984, p. 1.

43. Canadian and Australian debts lasted 100 years—author's interview with Sir Kenneth Berrill, chairman, Vickers da Costa, November 15, 1984.

Chapter 8: Rich North, Richer South

1. Economy produces less than potential—Edward F. Denison, *Trends in American Economic Growth, 1929–1982* (Washington, D.C.: Brookings Institute, 1985), pp. 7–8.

2. Anti-inflation policies cost jobs—Arthur M. Okun, *Prices and Quantities* (Washington, D.C.: Brookings Institute, 1981), p. 234.

3. Incomes policy is second best—Robert J. Flanagan, David W. Soskice, and Lloyd Ulman, *Unionism, Economic Stabilization, and Incomes Policies: European Experience* (Washington, D.C.: Brookings Institute, 1983), p. 663.

4. Effects of the Kennedy tax cut—*Economic Report of the President 1965,* p. 109; and *Economic Report of the President 1966,* pp. 92 and 237.

5. Carter aide: "a dismal failure"—Council on Wage and Price Stability, *Evaluation of the Pay and Price Standards Program,* January 16, 1981, p. 43.

6. Reagan Administration: incomes policies were a failure—*Economic Report of the President 1982,* p. 49.

7. Incomes policies "a lot less ugly"—Arthur M. Okun, "A Reward Tip," in Joseph Pechman, ed., *Economics for Policymaking: Selected Essays of Arthur M. Okun* (Cambridge, Mass.: MIT Press, 1985), p. 67.

Index